Praise for

AMERICA FIRST

"*America First* is a clear-eyed, realistic assessment of the implications of Trumpian foreign policy across the globe. It amounts to, in short ...WINNING."

> —**LARRY SCHWEIKART**, author of *A Patriot's History of the United States* and co-author of *The Politically Incorrect Guide® to the American Revolution* and *How Trump Won: The Inside Story of a Revolution*

"Danny Toma, a widely traveled member of the U.S. Foreign Service, brings tremendous insight to the Trump administration's 'America First' foreign policy. Drawing on history and personal experience and breaking down the issues on a nation-by-nation basis, Toma shows that 'realistic pragmatism' in foreign diplomacy has a long and successful history in this nation. I highly recommend the book to all who are interested in world affairs."

> —**RONALD J. RYCHLAK**, Jamie L. Whitten Chair of Law and Government Professor at the University of Mississippi School of Law and co-author of *Disinformation* and *Looming Disaster*

"President Trump said that 'the fight for the West does not begin on the battlefield' but in 'our minds, our wills, and our souls.' In *America First*, Danny Toma details how this belief is being translated into a comprehensive foreign policy strategy designed to restore and sustain our national greatness."

> —**JAMES S. ROBBINS**, author of *Erasing America: Losing Our Future by Destroying Our Past*

"If you've ever wondered what an America First foreign policy would look like, this is the book for you. In this richly detailed tour de force, Danny Toma convincingly argues that America would be safer, and Americans far securer, if we only intervened in the affairs of other countries if our vital national interests are at stake. Drawing upon his decades of experience in the U.S. Foreign Service, he argues that America First does not mean America alone, but it does mean that we stop trying to impose the values of Hollywood and Manhattan on countries and peoples who have no interest in following the West into demographic and sexual suicide."

—**STEVEN W. MOSHER**, founding president of Population Research Institute and author of *Bully of Asia: Why China's Dream Is the New Threat to World Order*

AMERICA FIRST

AMERICA FIRST

UNDERSTANDING THE TRUMP DOCTRINE

DANNY TOMA

REGNERY PUBLISHING

A Division of Salem Media Group

Regnery® is a registered trademark of Salem Communications Holding Corporation

Cataloging-in-Publication data on file with the Library of Congress

ISBN 978-1-62157-774-4
ebook ISBN 978-1-62157-841-3

Published in the United States by
Regnery Publishing
A Division of Salem Media Group
300 New Jersey Ave NW
Washington, DC 20001
www.Regnery.com

Manufactured in the United States of America

10 9 8 7 6 5 4 3 2 1

Books are available in quantity for promotional or premium use. For information on discounts and terms, please visit our website: www.Regnery.com.

To Dana, Nicolae, Mimmo, Patrick, and Emily,
who have traveled the world with me.

CONTENTS

ONE

A NEW POLICY THAT IS NOT SO NEW AFTER ALL

With all the focus on how divided we are as a nation, the casual observer could be forgiven for thinking that there has been no consensus on policy in the United States. While that may be the case in many areas of our politics, foreign policy has been a notable exception. The Obama administration did push the envelope. But even when he took it to the point of having our embassies fly rainbow flags, Obama was simply expanding a precedent established by his immediate predecessors. While there may be disagreement over what exactly American values *are*, there has been a remarkable consensus in recent years that it is America's role to *impose* those values on the world—to dictate to other countries what is right and what is wrong, and woe be unto any nation that seeks to defy our will. Although it was a Democrat, Madeleine Albright, who famously said, "We are the indispensable nation. We stand tall and we see further than other countries into the future," that sentiment could have been

1

expressed by most recent Republican candidates for president, up to the 2016 election cycle.

With Donald Trump's election to the presidency, that consensus appears to have come apart. The media would have us believe that President Trump's call for a more restrained "America First" foreign policy is unprecedented and unworthy of our nation's chief executive. They have highlighted discontent among our foreign affairs professionals to argue that Trump is somehow outside the mainstream of American thinking. But is that actually the case? As Queen Gertrude said in *Hamlet*, "The lady doth protest too much, methinks."

The supposedly traditional view of America's role in the world is anything but traditional. And it has been used by our secularist elites on the Left to help uproot traditional values. What's more, their useful idiots on the Right, enamored with any display of American might, have gone along even when the results have been destructive of core conservative values. As noted atheist Christopher Hitchens crowed about foreign policy under our last Republican president, "George Bush may subjectively be a Christian, but he—and the U.S. armed forces—have objectively done more for secularism than the whole of the American agnostic community combined and doubled."[1]

In early 2016 the media and the rest of the bicoastal elites were convinced that the quiet revolution they had launched to transform our world into a leftist utopia was destined to prevail. The self-appointed, self-righteous, self-congratulatory cabal of "progressives" were finally on the very cusp of dismantling the foundations upon which our Republic was founded and establishing themselves as the arbiters of the new morality. That new morality—which is not really that new, but as old as the Serpent in the Garden—confuses liberty with libertinism and is far more concerned with Man (or should we say Person?) in the abstract than with living breathing human beings.

They were struggling against the weight of more than two hundred years of American history and values. But they controlled the major media outlets, and they believed the inalterable course of history had foreordained the victory; they did not see any other outcome. Twenty sixteen was to be Year One of their revolution. The shackles of common sense and traditional morality—they were devoted secularists, all of them; for even the supposedly religious among them, human progress was the only transcendent thing beyond their own urges that they really believed in—were to be thrown off, and those who "cling to guns or religion" forever sidelined.

A funny thing happened on the way to utopia. One candidate began talking more like an American than a globalist, and for the first time in a generation, millions of citizens who had been told that their values were somehow unworthy finally had a champion. They turned out in droves and elected a man who was anathema to the elites and the Left—not because he advocated something new and sinister, as the bicoastal elites would have us believe, but rather because he sought to steer the country back to its roots, back to those values that made our country the greatest one on the face of the Earth, a country where hard work and honest living could bring rewards, and where we can once again hope that our children would have an even better life than their parents. The government of that country would not put up unnecessary barriers to her citizens' success, but step aside and concentrate on keeping those citizens safe and secure—from foreign foes, and also from foes within our society who envy those who create wealth and well-being, who would rather destroy than to create.

The same people who suggested before the election that Donald Trump was dangerous to American democracy because he might not abide by the election results now took to the streets to call into question the very legitimacy of the American form of government. And it is no wonder that his election generated so much wailing and gnashing of teeth. The Trump victory meant that their revolution was in doubt.

To suggest that maybe, just maybe, our forefathers got more right than they got wrong was "deplorable." Commentators on both the Left and the Right reacted with horror when Donald Trump suggested that NATO was less than sacred and that it might be a good thing for the American and Russian presidents to get along with each other. They called Trump's remarks unprecedented and led their followers to believe that the new administration was on the verge of taking American foreign policy in a radically new direction, never attempted before and fraught with peril. Consider this breathless paragraph from the left-wing newsletter *Counterpunch:* "What makes the Trump era different is the lack of that underlying continuity. Trump might look like vanilla or chocolate or some kind of swirl, but in reality he's Semtex in a cone. After pretending for a year or more that he's a natural product of the system, even top members of the governing party have become deeply worried about the orange brick of plastic explosive that now occupies the Oval Office."[2] *The Atlantic* referred to Trump's "Radical Foreign

Policy" and suggested that while "unprecedented" is a word that should be used with caution, it certainly applied to the then–presidential candidate's views on foreign policy.[3] The list could go on and on, and I suspect that some of these commentators actually believed the words they wrote.

But in fact, the "America First" foreign policy Donald Trump campaigned on is simply the traditional American view of world affairs—the policy that made America great in the first place. As George Washington famously warned in his 1796 Farewell Address, "The jealousy of a free people ought to be constantly awake, since history and experience prove that foreign influence is one of the most baneful foes of republican government. But that jealousy, to be useful, must be impartial, else it becomes the instrument of the very influence to be avoided, instead of a defense against it. Excessive partiality for one foreign nation and excessive dislike of another cause those whom they actuate to see danger only on one side, and serve to veil and even second the arts of influence on the other." Or, as Thomas Jefferson put it, more succinctly, "Commerce with all nations, alliance with none, should be our motto."

From the Founders' generation into the twentieth century, American presidents took the very same attitude. As Andrew Jackson said in 1830, "Our country, by the blessing of God, is not in a situation to invite aggression, and it will be our fault if she ever becomes so. Sincerely desirous to cultivate the most liberal and friendly relations with all; ever ready to fulfill our engagements with scrupulous fidelity; limiting our demands upon others to mere justice; holding ourselves ever ready to do unto them as we would wish to be done by, and avoiding even the appearance of undue partiality to any nation, it appears to me impossible that a simple and sincere application of our principles to our foreign relations can fail to place them ultimately upon the footing on which it is our wish they should rest."

And in 1920, Warren G. Harding, even as he was underlining how much the United States had changed from the time of the Founders, reaffirmed the traditional American foreign policy principle of eschewing what Jefferson had called "entangling alliances": "My countrymen, the pioneers to whom I have alluded, these stalwart makers of America, could have no conception of our present day attainment. Hamilton, who conceived, and Washington, who sponsored, little dreamed of either a development or a solution like ours of today. But they were right in fundamentals. They knew what was faith, and preached security. One may doubt if either of them, if any of the founders, would wish America to hold aloof from the world. But there has come to us lately a new realization of the menace to our America in European entanglements which emphasizes the prudence of Washington, though he could little have dreamed the thought which is in my mind."

Somehow, America allowed herself to change course. Our first internationalist president, Woodrow Wilson, involved the United States in a European struggle (World War I), which was none of our concern, and which set the conditions for a greater evil (World War II), which we could not safely ignore. Then the menace of international Communism forced us to expand our global presence in the interest of self-preservation. And when that threat subsided, rather than returning to the foreign policy that had served America so well for so long, we "went abroad in search of monsters to destroy," something that John Quincy Adams had warned us against during his tenure as Secretary of State and that has put us on perpetual war footing for almost two decades now.

No longer fighting simply to protect our citizens, the United States arrogantly determined that centuries-old border disputes in parts of the world most Americans had never seen were somehow our problem. We saw the promotion of democratic values as a fundamental foreign policy concern, even when a sizeable proportion of our own population might not agree with some of the "values" we were exporting, such as homosexuality and abortion. Instead of a shining beacon on a hill inspiring the nations, we were in danger of becoming a Western version of the Soviet Union, exporting our new secularist revolution to the unenlightened masses by force. And when a real threat to our security—radical Islamic terrorism—arose, we were no longer able to identify what we were fighting for and became mired in fruitless "nation building."

Making America great again in foreign affairs means a return to a foreign policy based on our national interest, one in which America would be second to none in terms of defense but would only use her military might to protect clearly defined national interests. Rather than promoting abstract ideology, the United States would reserve our resources for the protection of

> **PUTTING AMERICA FIRST**
> ## John Quincy Adams Edition
>
> "America.... has abstained from interference in the concerns of others, even when conflict has been for principles to which she clings.... She is the well-wisher to the freedom and independence of all. She is the champion and vindicator only of her own."
>
> —**JOHN QUINCY ADAMS**, Independence Day speech, 1821

the lives and well-being of our own citizens. Our forefathers understood it, and President Trump seems to get it, too: countries are at their best when they seek to serve their citizens and at their worst when trying to tell others what to do. We need to devote our foreign policy to serving our own people.

Candidate George W. Bush got it right during one of his debates with Al Gore when he said, "I'm not so sure the role of the United States is to go around the world and say, 'This is the way it's got to be.'" Bush's good instincts were soon suppressed by his advisors, but even in a post-9/11 world (which in some respects is no more perilous a place than the world that existed before, and certainly less perilous than at many times in our history), there is every good reason to return to this principle, which is not isolationist but realist. We must look at the world, see where our interests lie, and never hold back from doing whatever it takes to protect those interests. We must also identify where our interests *don't* lie—and avoid all inducements to become entangled in areas that are none of our concern.

I should add a disclaimer here: while I spent over twenty years as a Foreign Service Officer with the United States Department of State, serving in consular assignments across Europe and in the Middle East, reporting on political and economic affairs in Italy, supervising security upgrades in Poland, working on reconstruction in southern Iraq during our war efforts there, and taking temporary jobs in places as diverse as China, Cuba, El Salvador, the Dominican Republic, Greece, and Moldova, the views laid out in this book are mine alone and do not represent the positions of the U.S. government. I would be happy for them to become the positions of the U.S. government, but, for now, it is just one retired American diplomat adding his two cents.

TWO

IT MAY BE INTERESTING. BUT IS IT IN THE NATIONAL INTEREST?

You have seen it a thousand times. During every international crisis in any country in any corner of the globe, a reporter will show up and shove a microphone into the face of an anonymous bystander. This person, clearly distraught, will ask—no, demand—what the United States is going to do about this particular atrocity or misfortune. There is an automatic assumption that America should, by virtue of our size and power, be involved to right the wrongs that occur on a daily basis in every part of the world.

But when we actually *are* involved—one has seen a similar set-up an equal number of times. On this occasion, the international crisis is one in which the United States already has taken a stand. Something has gone wrong, and a reporter has shown up (perhaps the same reporter as in the previous scenario) and shoved a microphone into the face of yet another anonymous bystander. This time, the person, also clearly distraught, will ask—no, demand—that the United States cease the unjust intervention and pull out of the country where this particular atrocity or misfortune has occurred. Here the assumption is that America, by virtue of its size and power, is too often involved in areas of the world where we have no business.

The average American can be excused for thinking that we can't win—we're damned if we do, and damned if we don't. Part of the blame can be attributed to the twenty-four-hour news cycle. Unless there is a major ongoing crisis (the kind that used to trigger a "Special Report" in the middle of the morning soap opera), there really is not enough news to fully occupy every waking minute of every day. So a story that could be adequately reported in five minutes will be drawn out with commentary and analysis, and in order to keep things "interesting" reporters will drum up controversy where it doesn't really exist. Every action, however benign, naturally has *someone* who opposes it, and, in the interest of "balance," we have to give this person his say (except where the action goes along with the ideology of the news producers themselves, and then opposition will either not be reported upon or be caricatured). Today's reporters, covering the story of Christ's feeding of the five thousand, would bring in critics to point to other people who were not fed and suggest that Jesus was actually being stingy, or maybe have a food critic pipe up to claim that the food provided was not that tasty.

We are a nation of reactors. Rather than logically looking at the world and seeing what we need to do and what we need to avoid—what our real and long-term interests as a nation are—we react emotionally to the latest crisis. Here we get involved, there we don't, and the result is confusion, because not everything catches our attention in the same way. Pictures of dead children move all of us, and it is only natural that we feel compelled to do *something*, even if that something actually leads to the deaths of many more children. In another part of the world, there may be other dead children, but we don't react because no one has bothered to take photos that move us. Enacting a foreign policy on the basis of how really, really sad we feel is a recipe for a foreign policy that serves no one's interests—except our short-term interest in feeling good about ourselves for the length of approximately one news cycle.

We need to clear up a common misconception about our "interests." They can seem like a cynical motive for our actions. But it is actually just a realistic yardstick. While it is true that the United States is the world's only remaining superpower, magic wands are not yet a part of our foreign policy arsenal. Just because we have more power and more resources (and, I would argue, bigger hearts) than other countries does not mean that we can solve every problem everywhere. In fact, even a shallow look at the history of our country will show that sometimes, with all the good intentions in the world, we screw things up by getting involved where we don't need to be. Most of us understand that huge, distant bureaucracies are usually not the best places to devise solutions for localized problems. Those more directly affected tend to be better judges of what measures work best. This idea has long been enshrined in political thought and is even a part of Catholic social teaching, in which it is known as the principle of "subsidiarity"—the rule that communities of a higher order should not interfere in the internal life of communities of a lower order, thereby depriving them of their rightful freedom.[1] It is really just a matter of common sense. Conservatives instinctively feel this when we rail against tone-deaf decisions by federal agencies that don't take into account local conditions in our own communities. For some odd reason, however, many of these same conservatives think that the federal agencies they consider incompetent to solve *our* problems are somehow filled with superior wisdom when it comes to making decisions for people on the other side of the globe.

Our foreign policy needs to be guided by our brains and not our hearts. That may sound callous, but it really isn't. In fact, while nations are different from individuals (more on that later), even as individuals we do (hopefully) use our intellect to guide our responses in our daily life when our emotions tell us to do something differently. A careful consideration of our interests moderates our immediate emotional reactions.

Let's look at two examples. Attacking someone who makes you angry or afraid is a natural response. It is usually not the best one. If someone cuts me off in traffic in a dangerous manner, I will definitely be angry, and might even be a little frightened, depending on how close I came to having a collision. I will likely, however, not seek to kill him. For one thing, that would be wrong—a massive overreaction on my part. That's where morality—which, as we shall see, does have a role in foreign policy as well as in our individual choices—comes into play. But for another thing, if I physically attacked the other driver I would likely end up in jail, and that would certainly not be in my interests, nor those of my family. So I will allow my brain to overrule my heart and let the incident go.

But that is not the only possible response. Let's change the circumstances a bit. Having served in some dangerous places overseas during my career as a diplomat, I can definitely see how I might react differently in a different place. Let's say I am driving across Carjackistan, and someone cuts me off in traffic in a dangerous way. Again, I will likely be angry, but because of where I am I will also feel a high degree of fear. That's an emotional reaction, to be sure, but my intellect is also recognizing that I am at risk. In this case, rather than simply letting the injury go I might respond violently—by, say, ramming the other driver's car to clear the area ("get off the X," as they say in security circles). This would not mean that I have let my heart overcome my brain. On the contrary, I have analyzed the situation and decided that a violent response is in my best interest because my life could be in danger. The stakes are so high that I am willing to face whatever consequences may arise from my decision.

Intervening overseas is always fraught with risks, and there is never a guarantee of success. The question we should always ask ourselves is not whether we can do it, but whether we should. And the way we decide whether or not we should is if it is in our national *interest*. As in the driver scenarios above, our actions will vary according to circumstances, time, and place, but they should be consistent in reflecting what we hold to be not just important, but vital.

This brings us to the question, what is our national interest? The French phrase for national interest is *raison d'etat*. It is, in some ways, a much better phrase than the English equivalent, because it gets to the heart of the matter. *Raison d'etat*, literally, "reason of state," puts the country first. Individuals can sometimes heroically neglect their own personal well-being for the sake of others. We give medals to soldiers who throw themselves on grenades to save their comrades, and that is as it should be. Individuals who only care about themselves are called selfish, and we look down upon that trait (or did so until recently, at least). But nations are different because they are not individuals, but rather groups of individuals led by people who make decisions on their behalf. We don't deem someone noble who goes against his own country's interests for the betterment of another country. We call that person a traitor. Just as a father has a primary responsibility to his own family rather than to another family, so too the leader of a nation must look out for his own first, and, only then help others.

The morality of an action may vary depending on whether an individual or a nation is involved in its execution. While some actions might be wrong both for the individual and the state (such as, for example, the deliberate taking of innocent life), others may not be so black and white. If, as an individual, I skip meals and take the money I would normally spend on food and donate it to help build some great national monument I feel is important, people might

PUTTING AMERICA FIRST
Calvin Coolidge
Edition

"Patriotism is easy to understand.... It means looking out for yourself by looking out for your country."
—**CALVIN COOLIDGE**, The Price of Freedom, 1924

call me a patriot. But if, as the leader of a nation, I starve my people to build large national monuments (like Saddam Hussein or Enver Hoxha, the Communist dictator of Albania), people will call me a megalomaniac. On the flip side, if a government decides to embark on a public works program that they feel contributes to the public good, they will often require members of the general population to help pay for that project, whether through tariffs (resulting in higher prices on certain goods) or direct taxes (resulting in, well, direct taxes). One can argue over the wisdom of the project, its cost, and even the method of finance, but few outside of anarcho-libertarian circles would argue that no government anywhere should ever compel its citizens to pay for anything. All kinds of public goods, from parks and monuments to police and the national defense, are legitimately funded by money the government extracts from the citizens. But if I, as an individual, decided that I knew how to provide for the common good in my neighborhood (by, say, ensuring that anyone who paid me a required amount came to no harm), that would be criminal extortion. Another example— the state deprives certain individuals of their very lives if those individuals have committed a crime that is considered heinous or greatly detrimental to the public's well-being. If I as an individual, however, decided to deprive a malefactor of his life when my own was not in danger, I would be prosecuted as a murderer, and rightly so. It is important to remember that actions performed by the state must necessarily be judged differently than those done by an individual. It's not that morality is irrelevant to foreign policy, or that interests apply *instead of* principles. It's that some moral principles apply differently to nations than to individuals, and that our national interests factor into that calculus.

Now that we have all the preliminaries out of the way, let's take a stab at defining our national interest. Merriam-Webster defines national interest thus: "the interest of a nation as a whole held to be an independent entity separate from the interests of subordinate areas or groups and also of other nations or supra-national groups." When the dictionary definition leaves you even more confused than you were before, it is no wonder that people have difficulty agreeing. But the first part of this definition is quite helpful: "the interest of a nation as a whole." In other words, those things that are vital to us as a nation. The devil is in the details, especially given the fact that there are now several competing narratives out there as to what America is all about. But there are still some things that we all can agree on—and others that we *should*.

PUTTING AMERICA FIRST
Jeff Sessions Edition

"My belief is that the nation-state remains the one entity that can function, the one entity that can demand sacrifice from its constituents in the national interest. People are not going to sacrifice for the EU, they're not going to sacrifice for the Trans-Pacific Union."

—SENATOR JEFF SESSIONS
(now President Trump's attorney general) during a debate on the Trans-Pacific Partnership, 2015

The Declaration of Independence calls certain rights "unalienable." They are given to us by God, and no government has the authority to take them away. The first of these rights is the right to life. Every human being, no matter how big or small, has the right to live and breathe. Of course, no right is absolute. As we have already seen, certain criminals are deemed to have forfeited their right to life on account of their heinous crimes. Someone may also forfeit that right by acting as an aggressor in a war. We can legitimately deprive an enemy soldier of his life to defend our own lives and those of our fellow citizens. But these are exceptions that prove the rule: the most fundamental of all rights is the right to life. It is extremely difficult to enjoy freedom of speech or religion or association in this world if one is dead. Since the right to life is the cornerstone of all other rights, then it stands to reason that one of the fundamental roles of government is to protect that most fundamental of rights. Even regimes that have violated that premise—Nazi Germany and Stalinist Russia, to name two—have taken great pains to couch their atrocities in terms that made them seem that they were perpetrated in order to protect the lives of others: the Jews had to be dealt with in order to protect the lives and well-being of the Aryans; the *kulaks* had to be starved to death to allow the proletarians to prosper. Incidentally, there are no better illustrations of the evil of the premise that "the ends justify the means."

If government's primary purpose, therefore, is to protect the lives of its citizens, then we would be safe in assuming that our primary national interest is the security of our people. The first question we should ask ourselves in dealing with any foreign policy issue is whether or not American lives are at risk. Sometimes, the answer is very easy. When foreign forces attack our country, we can assume that they seek our destruction. On December 6, 1941, there were a number of options as to how we could manage our relationship with the Empire of Japan. The next day, those options were off the table: the Japanese had attacked our fleet at Pearl Harbor. In light of that aggressive action, we faced only two choices: to submit or to resist. One could make the argument that resisting put American lives further at risk, but war is a special case. If a country submits to an aggressor, then it no longer has any say into what happens next. In an extreme circumstance, the country itself ceases to exist, and then it has no opportunity to protect the lives of its citizens, yielding that power to a foreign entity, which will not have the

---

PUTTING AMERICA FIRST
Donald Trump Edition

"The most basic duty of government is to defend the lives of its own citizens. Any government that fails to do so is a government unworthy to lead.... The American people will come first once again. My plan will begin with safety at home—which means safe neighborhoods, secure borders, and protection from terrorism."

—**DONALD TRUMP**, accepting the presidential nomination at the Republican Convention, July 21, 2016

---

best interests of Americans at heart. Resistance, therefore, even with the likelihood of the further loss of life, is the only option in this instance. This is not an "ends-justify-the-means" equation. We hope that none of our citizens may come to harm, even as we understand that likely some will. But we seek to punish the aggressor to keep him from inflicting even greater damage, as his attack has demonstrated he desires to do.

As an aside, when it is a foreign state actor that inflicts harm—not often the case in recent years—a declaration of war helps to clarify a nation's purpose. When the Japanese attacked Pearl Harbor, Franklin Roosevelt asked for and received a declaration of war from the U.S. Congress, which is, by the way, the constitutional order of things, if anyone cares about that anymore. While some might argue that a declaration of war is a mere piece of paper (sort of like a marriage certificate, I suppose), it is far more than that. It notifies not only the aggressor but the American people that we are in this conflict for the long haul. Unlike a "police action," that stops when it stops, leaving the situation ambiguous, a declared war only ends when one side or the other surrenders, or when both sides are so exhausted that they come to terms. In either case, the resulting treaty brings a certain degree of closure, and then we can move on. One of the problems with our recent military conflicts is that they seem to be interminable; they have no clean end point.

Another example of foreign aggression is, of course, the 9/11 attacks in 2001. The hijackers were not, strictly speaking, state actors, so there was no declaration of war, but it was clear which government—Afghanistan—was supporting them. We rightly invaded that country in order to protect our nation from further attack. Again, a lack of response on our part would have invited further loss of life on American soil. We can argue all day about whether or not flawed U.S. foreign policy contributed to our facing this particular set of circumstances, but on September 12, 2001, we did not have the luxury of engaging in that debate; we had to act to remove the immediate threat. We had to respond militarily to keep our nation secure. I will not get into the follow-through at this point (see chapter ten), but suffice it to say that a declaration of war against Afghanistan might have been a good thing. It could have focused our attention on accomplishing what we needed to do—rather than being distracted, as we soon were, with projects not germane to our national interest.

There may be times when quick military action, short of all-out war, is the best response. This is the case when an immediate threat arises that is localized and not likely to spill over into general warfare. It makes sense to act quickly to decapitate a snake that is about to strike, and never mind about seeking out all potentially dangerous snakes in the area. This is what the United States did in 1900 during the Boxer Rebellion in China. The Boxers, a group of non-state actors—admittedly, with at least moral support from the government of China—attacked the international diplomatic delegations in Beijing (Peking).

American and other Western diplomats were at risk of massacre, as were, incidentally, a number of Chinese Christians who had taken refuge from the Boxers in the diplomatic compound. We did not see general war with China as being in our national interest, even though there was ample evidence that the leaders of China were at least winking at the actions of the Boxers. Instead, we joined an eight-nation coalition that routed the Boxers and rescued our people. Of course, there was a risk that a greater conflict could have arisen, but we felt that the risk was worth taking in light of the near certainty that our people on the ground would face unspeakable atrocities if left unassisted.

Those are the easy cases. Our country is attacked, or our citizens are, and we respond to neutralize the threat. But most threats are not so clear-cut; the threat of violent harm is just that—a threat, but not yet a reality. In these cases it is the responsibility of our government to do all it can to see that the threat does not evolve into an actual attack. This does not always involve military action. In fact, on the principle that the first priority of a government is to protect the fundamental right to life of its citizens, military action should be the *last* option we consider. Supporting our troops does not mean rushing to put them in harm's way in every conceivable scenario. In addition, unwarranted military action may actually put Americans at greater risk of harm than if we tried to address the threat by nonlethal means. One example here would be Iran, which I will discuss at length in chapter ten. A very good argument could be made that Iranian nuclear weapons pose a threat to Americans, in combination with the Iranian government's not-so-subtle dislike of the United States. This would seem to support the case for a war that would take out not only any potential nuclear weapons, but also a hostile regime. But a relatively united country of eighty million people would probably not fold up like a house of cards, especially if the United States were seen as the aggressor. This is not to say that war should never be an option for addressing the Iranian threat, but that it should be considered only if we strongly believe we have no other option—that more Americans will die if we don't fight than if we do.

Most threats should be faced with our "soft power" resources. While because of my long experience as a Foreign Service Officer with the U.S. Department of State, I certainly have a bias, I strongly believe that effective diplomacy saves American lives. Winston Churchill, speaking at a White House luncheon in 1954, is quoted as saying that "it is better to jaw-jaw than to war-war" (British pronunciation makes it a much catchier phrase than it would be had an American said it). This is from the man credited with strengthening British resolve during the darkest hours of World War II. While "jawing" certainly has the appeal of not costing lives, it is superior to the use of military force—where the latter is not *necessary*—for another reason as well: it allows for greater flexibility and keeps more options open. Once the shooting starts, there is really only one way to go, and that is all out for military victory. Before the shooting starts, though, there are any manner of possibilities open, ranging from innumerable negotiation strategies to sanctions to yes, even war, should nothing else succeed. For America to effectively defend her primary national interest—the lives of Americans— our country must have not only a robust military but a diplomatic corps that is second to none.

A strong diplomatic corps serves our interests not only in the high-profile cases, where negotiations ward off impending conflict, but also by eliminating sources of tension in the first place, before they give rise to real threats. By maintaining relationships with governmental and nongovernmental actors, our diplomats serve as a first line of defense of American lives. In addition to noting and managing changes that could become serious threats, they also alert Americans to any potential dangers that may exist for those traveling overseas. The old proverb says, "To be forewarned is to be forearmed." Our diplomats protect American lives by providing us with information that we could not otherwise get.

The State Department is not very popular with many conservatives on account of a perceived liberal bias at Foggy Bottom (the area of Washington where the State Department is located). From personal experience, I would agree that most Foreign Service Officers have a definite left-of-center political orientation, but I believe that most of them follow orders and seek to implement U.S. policy regardless of their own personal views. The resignations of some senior State Department officials in the wake of the election of President Trump should be seen as a good thing. It means that those people who could not, in good conscience, support the president's agenda decided—or were convinced—to leave.

Trump's removal of his first Secretary of State, Rex Tillerson, should not be seen as an admission that somehow State cannot be made to work. It was simply an admission that the president and his chief foreign policy advisor no longer saw eye to eye. While in recent years it has been common to see Secretaries of

State remain in place for a much longer period of time, Tillerson is by no means the first such cabinet officer to leave office after serving only briefly. A similar president to Trump in terms of his transformation of American political life was Ronald Reagan, and he too had a problematic Secretary of State—in Alexander Haig. Haig served only eighteen months before being replaced. Woodrow Wilson saw his Secretary of State, William Jennings Bryan, resign over policy concerns early in his administration. If we look at such Secretaries of State as William Rufus Day (who served only six months in 1898), Edward Everett (four months in 1853), Robert Bacon (thirty-seven days in 1909), and especially Elihu Washburne (only *five days* in 1869), Secretary Tillerson seems like a real survivor.

The president should have someone representing him in foreign policy who shares his concerns—at least in broad strokes. The cabinet members, at the end of the day, represent the president. The mass of diplomats at State, however, just like the mass of soldiers at Defense, carry out the orders no matter who is in charge. Likely plenty of the Foreign Service Officers who have remained with State since 2017 are not enthusiastic about President Trump, but I would be genuinely shocked if any significant number of them do not do the jobs they are instructed to do. This is especially true of my former colleagues in Consular Affairs, who are passionate about the protection of American lives abroad. In any case, there is no realistic alternative to maintaining a diplomatic corps. I remember a number of years ago hearing a critic of the State Department say that with all the news media we had in the world, we did not need to send diplomats abroad. Even if they have reservations about State, I don't think many Americans would be comfortable entrusting their foreign policy to the editorial board of the *New York Times.*

Protecting American lives is the paramount national interest, but it is not the only one. True, no right can exist without the right to life, but we all want to do more than just survive. We may have differing opinions as to the role of government in that equation, but I believe that most of us would agree that government does have a role in preventing attempts by outside actors to threaten our prosperity. The protection of American well-being should be seen as the second great national interest upon which our foreign policy should be based.

Again, as in the protection of American lives, our national interest in protecting and promoting American well-being can be and usually is best pursued by means short of war. But that does not mean that war is off the table. One of our earliest international conflicts had at its root the protection of American well-being, even if there were elements of the protection of American lives as well. In the early 1800s, the Barbary States of North Africa, which were officially a part of the Ottoman Empire but behaved with so much autonomy as to be de facto independent, were demanding ransom from Western shipping engaged in trade in the Mediterranean. Those who refused or were unable to pay had their ships confiscated, and the crews were often sold into slavery. President Thomas Jefferson refused to allow the payment of tribute, on the principle that no third party should be allowed to interfere with free trade between nations. He called the Barbary States by their proper name: pirates (if Jefferson had had access to the technology we have today, he might have even tweeted that). A military force was sent to teach the Barbary pirates a lesson, and while the job required follow-up under both Madison and Monroe, attacks on international shipping by the Barbary States came to an end. Incidentally, the section in the U.S. Marine hymn that mentions "the shores of Tripoli" is a reference to the Barbary Wars. Today Tripoli is part of Libya—some of the world's hot spots have a habit of flaring up again and again.

While the Barbary Wars can be seen as actions to prevent attacks on Americans, they were not primarily fought for that reason. American lives could have been protected by paying ransom, but that would have meant accepting that a third party could dictate when and where we could trade, with increased costs to Americans as a result. War was seen as necessary to ensure that Americans could be engaged in trade, which contributed to the prosperity of all our fellow citizens.

A number of tools far short of war exist to protect American well-being. The idea of punitive tariffs, for example, is being discussed for the first time in years—and many Washington talking heads have nearly exploded, as if such talk were unprecedented. But protective tariffs are a tool that was used by Republican administrations all through the nineteenth and early twentieth centuries. A punitive tariff is just what its name says: a tax on imported goods designed to punish the exporter of those goods for engaging in unfair trade practices ("dumping"), or for promulgating other policies that negatively impact American well-being. It differs from a revenue tariff, which is a tax on imported goods not directed against any particular country but rather designed simply to raise revenue. Before we had the income tax, the federal government was funded largely through revenue tariffs. And while nineteenth-century Democrats tended not to support tariffs designed primarily to punish foreign producers or to protect American industry, they did support the concept of tariffs in general—there was no other way to finance the federal government. Historically, therefore, criticism of tariffs has been on the grounds of how they are applied rather than a philosophical opposition to the whole concept of taxing imported goods.

Tariffs are most effective when there is a domestic source for the imported goods being taxed. If, for example, Chinese tires cost fifteen percent less than American tires, many Americans may choose to buy Chinese tires due to the competitive price. But if our government determines that the Chinese price is artificial, either because of dumping of goods below cost in order to seize the market, because of unfair labor practices, or by some other measure, it may choose to place a tariff of, say, twenty percent, on Chinese tires. This would mean that Chinese tires would now cost more than American tires, and the American consumer would likely switch his preference based on the relative price— unless there were some perceived quality advantage to Chinese goods, which is not generally the case. In theory, the Chinese would then correct their unfair trading practices in order to regain a share of the American market. Of course, they could retaliate by imposing their own tariff on American tires or even on some other good, such as wheat, but whether or not they would do this largely depends on how much they are willing to sacrifice in order to maintain the market share that their tires previously held. Besides potentially changing the behavior of the offending country, this tariff could have another benefit: it would be increasing demand for U.S. tires domestically and thus potentially create new manufacturing jobs. But it would also have a negative effect: tires would cost more money for all Americans, who would be forced to forego other goods or savings to afford them. All of these implications should be carefully balanced before imposing such a tariff. That being said, tariffs are nothing new; they have been used with great success by both developed and developing nations for centuries.

Sanctions—a sort of halfway house between tariffs and war, in terms of severity—are another tool in our arsenal. While tariffs are interventions in the market that still respect the market itself—they simply add to the price of an imported good and make it less profitable to sell in the United States—sanctions are a form of punishment that is direct rather than market-based. Sanctions prohibit certain (or all) types of trade and restrict (or prohibit) certain transactions. They are theoretically designed to change the behavior of the offending nation by depriving that country of vital trade. But that can be a tricky proposition, especially when only one or a few countries are in on the sanctions. In that case, another country may step in and gain for its own people the business that would have gone to American companies. Typically, therefore, sanctions are generally not used to protect our prosperity so much as to make a political statement.

For sanctions to be effective, they must be painful for the country targeted. But if they are so painful as to threaten that nation's very existence, they may lead to open conflict. The attack on Pearl Harbor, while part and parcel of Japan's aggressive expansionist policy, can also be seen as a response to crippling U.S. sanctions that had been imposed on Japan starting in 1937. The lesson here is that sanctions, like war, should be used only when our vital national interests are at stake. When the sanctioned country is incapable of effective military response, though, there may be other circumstances in which sanctions could work. If a group of nations with ample resources imposes sanctions against a smaller country with few resources, for example, that smaller country will face the prospect of its quality of living drastically declining if it does not comply with the demands set forth by the group of sanctioning nations. This worked in the case of Rhodesia. In 1966, during a time when black majority governments were coming to power across Africa, the white-led minority government of Rhodesia made its unilateral declaration of independence and was thus seen as an international pariah. The international community imposed sanctions against that country. While many other factors—including a weak global economy and a vigorous insurgency inside the country—contributed to the fall of the white-led government and the creation of the country of Zimbabwe in 1980, at least some scholars believe that sanctions had a decisive effect.[2] If that is the case, it is one of the few examples of the successful use of sanctions. Even here, though, the long-run results have been mixed. The creation of Zimbabwe did eliminate a white-minority government, but the new leaders of Zimbabwe created in its place a socialist hell-hole that no longer can feed its own people, despite Rhodesia once having been the breadbasket of Africa.

In most cases, sanctions will not be that effective. For a large country with large amounts of natural resources, sanctions may only serve to increase tension rather than compel the kind of behavior we seek. If a large country with abundant resources is hit with sanctions, the result will be far less convincing, particularly if the sanctioned country still has plenty of trading partners. One example would be the 1973 oil embargo. In this event, Middle Eastern oil exporters decided to punish the United States for its support of Israel by withholding petroleum from the U.S. market. This had a devastating effect on the U.S. economy in the short term, and I can still remember the long lines for gasoline across the nation as people sought to fill up their cars. In the long term, however, it backfired. The United States became less dependent on foreign oil by increasing domestic production, by exploring alternative fuel sources, and by conservation. Since the short-term economic pain stretched into the administration of Jimmy Carter, and his policies were unable to prevent economic stagnation, one might even say that the oil embargo indirectly led to the election of Ronald Reagan, which is certainly not an outcome that the Middle Eastern oil exporters would have foreseen or desired.

Another weakness of sanctions is that they can, for political reasons, outlive their purpose—in some cases, going on seemingly forever. I would argue, for example, that sanctions against the Communist Cuban regime have been counterproductive, as they have given the Cuban government a convenient excuse for the failure of their pathetic economic policies, even as nearly every other country in the world has engaged in open trade with them. We will go into this case in detail in chapter thirteen, but suffice it to say that if sanctions have not produced regime change in the fifty-odd years that they have been in effect, it is unlikely that they will produce that change anytime soon.

Up to this point we've been discussing broad-based economic sanctions, which typically serve as a symbol of our displeasure, a displeasure deep enough that we are willing to take an economic hit in order to express it, even though it is unlikely to have any effect—or at least not the effect we seek—on the party upon whom the sanctions are imposed.

There is also a case to be made for more limited sanctions directed at the protection of American lives and prosperity. In the case of a country that is seeking to build a nuclear bomb, for example, cutting off its supply of fissionable material might at least delay its development of atomic weapons. In another case, a country seeking to undermine America's technological superiority in a certain industry might be denied access to advanced computer components by specifically targeted sanctions. In these cases, we would be seeking not to change another nation's policy but to deny it, at least in the short term, needed materials for carrying out actions that would put our safety or our welfare at risk.

So, there are a number of tools for protecting Americans' lives and promoting their well-being. How those tools should be used in pursuit of our national interests depends on an infinite variety of concrete circumstances. But there are typical scenarios that have tended to repeat again and again, from which we can derive some rough and ready principles.

From the Barbary Wars, we can see that one of our long-standing interests is to ensure that outside actors do not interfere with Americans' right to trade. This does not mean we go to war with every nation who restricts American trade in some way, although we may consider treating the goods from that country in a like manner, through tariffs or quotas. But the general principle is clear: America has always supported "the freedom of the seas." It is in our national interest that international water and airways be kept clear for all countries to use. This issue has come up repeatedly in our history. International conventions to which the United States is a signatory, or whose content is recognized as part of the body of international law, allow a nation to claim waters no more than twelve (originally three) miles off its shore. Beyond that is *mare liberum*, Latin for "free sea"— international waters where anyone can freely sail. This principle has been tested on a number of occasions in recent years. In 1981, U.S. forces entered the Gulf of Sidra, the part of the Mediterranean off the coast of Libya. Libya, then under dictator Muammar Qaddafi, claimed the entire gulf as its territorial waters, a claim that no one else recognized and that was not consistent with international standards—but a typical measure for a man who wore satin tablecloths as a fashion statement and claimed that his country was the only real democracy in the world. Qaddafi had tested previous American presidents, but Reagan refused to back down. When two Libyan jets fired on American F-14s on patrol, the Libyans quickly got the worst of that exchange and went crashing into the sea. After a similar incident eight years later (with identical results), Libyan claims to this vast area of international waters were largely ignored.

In more recent times, China has asserted claims to substantial portions of the South China Sea that in some cases are claimed by other nations, and in other cases are considered by most to be international waters. U.S. forces have operated in this area, not without controversy, to assert our recognition of these waters as international and thus free for shipping. This is not so much an assertion of American power as a stand in support of international law. But in taking that stand we are acting in our own national interest, as the vital underlying principle of freedom of the seas—which makes international trade and travel possible—is one we hold to be crucial to our national interests.

But trade is not the only foreign policy issue fundamental to our national well-being. Control of our borders, while often seen as a purely domestic issue, has a dramatic impact on our bilateral and multilateral relationships. As someone who was once head of the Consular Section at our Embassy in Dublin, Ireland, a country with a long history of immigration to the United States, I can attest to the importance that foreign leaders place on U.S. visa policy—as I used to get regular telephone inquiries from parties high up in the Irish government every time some aspect of our policy changed. While the question of whom we decide to let in to our country has a great impact on every country in the world, it primarily affects the people of the United States, as decisions in this sector shape not only our economy but even who we are as a people.

There is a certain mythology about how our borders were controlled in the past. The prevailing narrative is that we were open and generous and took all comers until evil rich white men decided they did not want to share anymore and began closing things down. Like much of the progressive narrative, this view is simplistic where it is not completely false. A little bit of history is necessary to better comprehend the realities of U.S. border security.

It is true that at the very beginning, immigration—or, rather, colonization—was not subject to quotas and explicit regulations. America was seen as an essentially empty land of vast resources.

Native Americans might have disagreed with that assessment, but in terms of population density, what is now the United States was vastly under populated compared to much of the rest of the world, not to mention compared to levels of population density today. And while there were not laws on the books saying who could go where and when, the practical matter was that the original colonists tended to be homogenous when seen against the rest of Europe, let alone the rest of the world. Most white settlers came from northern and western Europe, and blacks, who came originally as indentured servants and then as slaves, were with few exceptions drawn from one particular region of western Africa. This was because, in practice, the governing powers would have had something to say if vast numbers of, say, Spanish colonists started arriving and setting up communities in British North America. It would rightly have been seen as invasion and would have likely led to war. In fact, Spanish attempts to establish missions and communities in what is now the State of Georgia were largely unsuccessful, in part because the English encouraged pirate attacks on these settlements, which they saw as an attempt to stretch Spanish territory in the New World. The original colonizers understood that the nation which sent the most people into the New World would control the destiny of America long into the future.

Once the thirteen colonies gained their independence from Great Britain, there were no explicit restrictions on immigration, but the nature of travel in that era necessarily limited settlement to the hardy few. This would change over the course of the nineteenth century, as technological advances in sail- and then in steam-powered travel made the trip to America less daunting than

PUTTING AMERICA FIRST
Theodore Roosevelt Edition

"In the first place, we should insist that if the immigrant who comes here in good faith becomes an American and assimilates himself to us, he shall be treated on an exact equality with everyone else, for it is an outrage to discriminate against any such man because of creed, or birthplace, or origin. But this is predicated upon the person's becoming in every facet an American, and nothing but an American.

"If he tries to separate from the rest of America, then he isn't doing his part as an American. There can be no divided allegiance here. Any man who says he is an American, but something else also, isn't an American at all. We have room for but one flag, the American flag, and this excludes the red flag, which symbolizes all wars against liberty and civilization just as much as it excludes any foreign flag of a nation to which we are hostile. We have room for but one language here, and that is the English

it once had been. And, contrary to popular belief, once large numbers of people who appeared not to share American values began to arrive in the United States, Congress acted quickly to put in place the first official restrictions on who could enter our country, beginning with the Chinese Exclusion Act of 1882. I am not planning on defending it and subsequent restrictions on immigration; I only bring it up to illustrate the point that control of our borders is not a new policy that came up sometime in the 1920s when we all decided to put on white sheets and shut ourselves off from the rest of the world. From the very beginning, the people who arrived here helped to determine who we would become, and that continues to be the case today. Unrestricted or, at least unregulated, immigration in an era of easy and inexpensive travel would transform our country into something we would not recognize. Some people would argue that that would be for the better—that our racist, white, rich, homophobic, cisgendered, patriarchal, meat-eating, Founding Fathers left us nothing worthy of preservation, and that we would be better off in a globalist free-for-all. But for those who wish to conserve the political, social, and cultural heritage we have received from our forefathers, control of our national borders is vital not only to our security but to our identity and well-being.

Of course, we don't have controls at our borders solely to protect our cultural and economic well-being, but also to protect our right to life itself. Open borders mean that *anyone* can cross, for any reason, including those who wish to do us harm. It is not racist or xenophobic to prevent people harboring criminal or terroristic designs against our fellow citizens from coming into the United States. Still less is it somehow unenlightened to prevent people who have actually committed crimes or acts of terror from entering. In order to keep these people from coming in, we need to control access to our country, just as we control access to our homes to keep out people who would rob us, or worse. As President Trump said in his speech to the people of Poland in July 2017, "While we will always welcome new citizens who share our values and love our people, our borders will always be closed to terrorism and extremism of any kind."[3] This means more effective controls at our land borders and trained officers at our other ports of entry, as well as continued screening by consular officers overseas for those requiring visas, so that the problems can be identified before a malefactor arrives on our shores.

President Trump's immigration proposals are the most far-reaching of any president in recent history, as they focus

> language, for we intend to see that the crucible turns out people out as Americans, of American nationality, and not as dwellers in a polygot boarding house; and we have room for but one soul loyalty and that is a loyalty to the American people."
>
> —**THEODORE ROOSEVELT**, Letter to the President of the American Defense Society, 1919

primarily on the well-being of Ameri-can citizens—and not the elite among us, but especially on working-class Americans hardest hit by policies that have seen their wages driven down or even their jobs disappear. In fact, many of the so-called elite are those yelling loudest about Trump's proposals, which would prevent companies from importing cheaper labor—legally or illegally—and require them to focus their hiring efforts on those already here, whether American citizens or Legal Per-manent Residents ("Green Card" holders).

Much ink has been spilled on the proposed border wall with Mexico (and I will spill even more in chapter twelve), but Trump's proposals go far beyond the vital step of securing our southern border. The proposed requirement for employers to verify the legal status of their employees ("E-Verify") will increase job opportunities for Americans. An increase in stateside enforce-ment—augmenting immigration police forces such as ICE (Immi-gration and Customs Enforcement) and the Border Patrol and ending the old "catch and release" policy, in which arrested illegal aliens were turned loose and naively expected to show up voluntarily at deportation hearings—will make it less attractive to enter the country without the proper permission and to over-stay or misuse visas.[4] The primary beneficiaries of these policies will be our own poor and lower middle classes. When it is no longer economically or politically feasible for companies to hire undocumented aliens, they will begin looking at the people who are already here.

This seems to be already playing out. According to the 2017 *CBP Border Security Report*, issued December 5, 2017, over the past year, we have seen the lowest number of illegal border crossings *on record*, along with a gradual increase in apprehensions of those who do make it across. It seems that—as both the enforcement and the rhetoric have been stepped up—thousands of potential clandestine border crossers are deciding that it is simply not worth the risk. And then, guess what happened? Unemployment rates for African Americans dropped to their lowest levels *in history*,[5] while rates for Hispanics fell to similar lows. Just a coincidence? I think not. And yet the so-called mainstream media continues to trumpet the false narrative that our president's policies are based on nothing more than racism and ignorance, or even more sinister motives. It is understandable that the media moguls would fail to understand the positive impact that tougher border policies have on American workers. Living as they do in their gated communities and their Manhattan high-rises, their only contact with the working class comes when their maids show up to change the sheets.

People are not the only thing we control at our borders. Anyone who has tried to enter the United States with illicit drugs, certain types of weaponry, or even raw meat and fruit will likely agree that those decisions caused some delays in their travel plans when they attempted to clear U.S. Customs. We could choose to let everything that anyone wanted to bring in into the country— a position supported by some radical libertarians—but as a society we have determined that certain restrictions serve to benefit the common good. In the case of illicit drugs, we may even go further, by working with supplier countries to try to dry up that trade at the source, either by "carrot" methods (granting favorable trade status on non-narcotic goods to create a bigger market for legitimate crops and materials produced in those countries), or by "stick" methods (tariffs, sanctions, or even military action against countries seen as recalcitrant). Again, we take these actions because we believe it is in our national interest to promote the well-being of our populace. Some rogue nation may one day decide that it is in its national interest to flood the U.S. with cheap heroin or cocaine, but this is why we use all the tools available to us to convince those kinds of nations that helping stem the tide of illicit drugs is the wiser course of action in the long term.

Access to vital raw materials is another important national interest tied to the promotion of American well-being. Lest I hear some readers begin to chant, "No War for Oil!" keep in mind that war is by no means the only tool at our disposal for pursuing our national interests. We orient our entire foreign policy to ensure that those interests are served. And access to important raw materials is one of those interests.

The United States has been richly blessed with abundant natural resources. That is something for which we should constantly give thanks to our Creator. For generations our waterways have been harnessed for cheap power, and fossil fuels are abundant under the surface of our land. We have large amounts of mineral deposits for use in industry, and our agriculture is some of the most productive in the world. That being said, we are no longer resource-independent. We trade with other nations to get materials that we lack or, in some cases, that are more cheaply produced or easily extracted in other countries than at home.

This we do to ensure our economy booms, jobs are created, and Americans continue to maintain a high standard of living. So we make trade deals with nations that have materials we desire.

Related to ensuring access to raw materials in other countries is promoting American exports abroad. I believe that creating markets for American goods should be one of the primary goals of our diplomatic efforts overseas. When foreigners buy our goods, American producers directly benefit. Trade deals are also one of the oldest forms of diplomatic interaction, as they address mutual needs. Those who see trade deals as inherently exploitive understand little about human history and nothing about human nature. To be fair to these critics, however, it can be difficult to see how humans truly interact in the larger world when one's activities outside of academia are confined to trips to Whole Foods and Starbucks.

The promotion of peace throughout the world is also clearly in our national interest. Not only is a more peaceful world a safer world for all of us—a peaceful world is also more likely to be a prosperous world, and a prosperous world is more likely to want to buy goods, including American goods. Conventional left-wing "wisdom" would lead us to believe that the captains of industry crave war because it leads to greater markets for things like guns and planes and poison gas. In the real world, however, markets crave stability more than anything else, and there is far more money to be made from a people at peace than one at war. What's more, progressive mythology aside, most Americans— even CEOs—recoil at the thought of human suffering. We want folks to get along and are often willing (sometimes too willing) to offer advice. But the opportunity for America to act as an impartial arbiter in international disputes to which she was not a party did not arise much before the early twentieth century. When it did, starting with the Russo-Japanese War, it was the logical result of general American disinterestedness. America was known not to be invested in anything beyond her immediate national interests. A party with no stake in the game is generally preferred as a mediator over one that has a stake. Just as, to avoid the appearance of partiality, we call upon officials of a different athletic conference to referee a championship game, so too was it natural for countries to look to the United States to help guide the parties involved to a fair decision. This is not an example of unwarranted interference in the affairs of other countries; it is not meddling where we don't belong. It is simply being a good neighbor to our fellow global inhabitants, offering advice where requested. Not until the United States came to be seen as a global hegemon did our peace-making efforts come to be seen with distrust. And we did not help that perception when we began to take sides in disputes that clearly had nothing to do with our national interests—as has been the case in recent years in the Balkans, Eastern Europe, and the Caucasus. Our interventionism has not necessarily doomed all of our efforts at peace-making, but America would be much more effective if she were seen as an impartial observer—objective when her own national interests are not at stake.

If ensuring American safety and American well-being are what national interest is all about, then what about "making the world safe for democracy" or promoting universal human rights? The fact is, as our foreign policy has evolved to take on less tangible goals and objectives, it has become frayed and incomprehensible. While we may differ on the question of by what means we should defend American security against specific threats, defense at least has a measurable outcome: the reduction or elimination of the threat. We may choose different policies to promote American well-being, but, again, we have a measurement for success—an increase in or at least the maintenance of our standard of living. More "idealistic" policies, on the other hand, such as promoting democracy across the globe or guaranteeing human rights, inevitably set us up for failure. For one thing, the outcome is often not measurable. What exactly constitutes the successful promotion of democracy? Do free elections count—even when they result in an anti-democratic regime coming to power, as happened in Gaza with the victory of Hamas?

And how about human rights? We Americans are divided amongst ourselves on the question of what even constitutes a human right. Consider the right to life—from conception to natural death. In the traditional Judeo-Christian view, life is the most fundamental human right. But many in the human rights business would balk at it. In fact, they promote abortion and abortifacient birth control, not to mention euthanasia, for what they see as unproductive members of society.

Do human rights include freedom of religion? Most educated people in the world would have said yes as recently as 1948, when the Universal Declaration on Human Rights was adopted. But now some in the progressive movement see certain new "rights"—to have your gay marriage celebrated, to be called by your preferred transgender pronouns—as trumping freedom of religion. If we make things we cannot even agree on amongst ourselves the goals of our foreign policy, we cannot expect any-thing resembling success. And when we put ourselves in the position of dictating to other countries what they should believe, we create resentments that not only make the accomplishment of those goals unlikely but ultimately jeopardize our real national interests.

So, the principle is simple, at least in theory. Our foreign policy should be dictated by our national interests. Period. In other words, *America First*. This is not because we see ourselves as having entitlement that no one else has; it is because we are *Americans*. I have no problem with a French political leader coming up with a France First foreign policy, or a Mongolian leader coming up with a Mongolia First foreign policy or a Rus-sian leader coming up with a Russia First foreign policy (oh wait! We already have one of those—more on that in the next chapter). No one in the world can judge what is best for us as well as we can. And even if they could, we would resent them for it. What America First means is that we conduct our policy to look out for our own national interests and expect every other country in the world to do the same. We balance our interests against those of others in order to achieve mutually beneficial goals.

And there's a lot of mutual benefit to go around. Contrary to popular belief, looking out for ourselves is the best way to guarantee peace. We should not seek to dominate but rather, as Confederate President Jefferson Davis said in an address to the Southern Congress, "All we ask is to be let alone." A foreign policy directed to the pursuit of our true national interests, in contrast to a foreign policy seeking to remake the world in our own image (or whatever image happens to be in vogue at that particular moment), is the true guarantor of peace and, with it, of American prosperity.

In the rest of this book we will divide up the world for a concrete examination of where and why American interests lie, and, just as important, where they do not. In nearly every case, we will see that our original instincts are often our best ones.

THREE

RUSSIA

OUR ETERNAL FOE?

Let us begin our examination of the countries of the world with Russia, once, back in the days of the Soviet Union, the "other" superpower—and, if many in the media and Congress are to be believed, our eternal adversary. The truth is, though, that America's relationship with Russia has not always been adversarial. Consider the observations of Prince Gortchakoff, Russian Minister of Foreign Affairs in 1861 on the special kinship between the two countries. As he wrote to the Russian Minister at Washington, "The two countries, placed at the extremities of the two worlds, both in the ascending period of their development, appear called to a natural community of interests and of sympathies, of which they have already given mutual proofs to each other."

In fact, almost alone among European powers, the Russian Empire supported the Union cause during the American Civil War from the very beginning. Those of us with ancestors who fought on the Southern side might not necessarily see that as a positive thing, but it is easy to understand why they made that decision. Russia in the nineteenth century was still an expanding empire, pursuing its own manifest destiny to dominate the great landmass stretching from Eastern Europe to northern Asia. It saw the United States in a similar light, as a rough and tumble country taming the wilderness and bringing Christian civilization to the savage and primitive peoples who inhabited the fringes of the world. The two countries had a lot in common in character, and their interests were not in conflict. The United States and Russia even shared common enemies and common concerns. Most Americans of the mid-nineteenth century still saw Great Britain as a power to be wary of. We had, after all, fought two major wars with Britain—one them less than fifty years before the outbreak of our own Civil War (this book is being written at about the same distance in time from the Vietnam War, which many readers will see as not so far away in time or memory). Russians had even more reason to fear John Bull, as they had just finished fighting a major conflict against British, French, and Turkish forces during the Crimean War.

The friendly relations between the United States and Russia would pay dividends immediately after the War Between the States. Russia's possessions at that time included Alaska, a sparsely populated colony that had been settled about a hundred years before but had never been an integral part of the Russian Empire. Russian activities there were confined to the fur trade and to the preaching of the gospel (to this day, large communities of Russian Orthodox Christians exist among Alaska's Native population). Being detached from the mainland of Russia, Alaska was vulnerable to being snatched away by some foreign power, and the most likely candidate to do so was the master of the adjacent landmass then known as British North America, now called Canada. So to thwart any attempts by their British adversary to enrich themselves at Russian expense, the tsar's government entered into negotiations with the United States for the sale of Alaska. A formal treaty was entered into in 1867, Alaska became a territory of the United States, and in a few short years—with the discovery of gold in the 1890s and early 1900s—would bring untold wealth to America. The discovery of oil deposits in Alaska would continue the flow of wealth to the lower forty-eight. And in 1959 what had once been "Russian America" became the forty-ninth state of the Union.

Cordial relations between the United States and Russia continued for many years after the purchase of Alaska. During another war scare between Russia and the United Kingdom, in 1878, Russian sailors arrived in American ports ready to board ships there in case of the outbreak of conflict. At the conclusion of the 1904–05 Russo-Japanese War, the belligerents approached the United States—as we have already seen—as an impartial intermediary to assist in bringing that conflict to an end. The Treaty of Portsmouth (New Hampshire), which brought an end to that conflict, was shepherded by our own president, Theodore Roosevelt, who won a Nobel Peace Prize for his efforts.

Our cozy relationship with Russia would come to an end only after the Bolshevik Revolution of 1917. Our relationship changed not because we suddenly had aims on the Russian mainland, and only partially because of our unprecedented direct involvement in a European war (World War I), but rather because an ugly and insidious philosophy had taken root in Moscow. That philosophy demanded nothing less than the destruction of everything we held dear, the elimination of thousands of years of Western civilization and values. With the triumph of Bolshevism in Russia, Moscow became the headquarters where plots for the world dominance of international Communism began to be hatched.

Today it is fashionable to downplay the evils of Communism. Many in American academia sympathize with Communist thinking—not necessarily of the economic kind, comfortable as they are in suburban homes, driving Swedish cars, and eating imported European delicacies—but rather of the cultural sort. They are enamored of the idea of overthrowing Western civilization and replacing it with something radically different. Communism, despite its manifest failures in every realm of human endeavor, remains attractive to those on the Left precisely for its hatred for Western Christian norms. As the enemy of their enemy, modern academics figure Communism can't be *that* bad.

In fact, it was more than just bad. Communism was and remains *evil*. It is condemned out of the mouths of its own leaders. As Felix Dzerzhinsky, founder of what would become the KGB, said, "We stand for organized terror—this should be frankly admitted. Terror is an absolute necessity during times of revolution. Our aim is to fight against the enemies of the Soviet Government and of the new order of life." Lenin himself wrote, "Attack, not defence, must be the slogan of the masses; the ruthless extermination of the enemy will be their task." And Trotsky bragged, "As for us, we were never concerned with the Kantian-priestly and vegetarian-Quaker prattle about the 'sacredness of human life.'"

We could go on and on, especially if we started citing the numerous quotations that demonstrate Josef Stalin's complete disregard of human life. Suffice it to say that Communism was rightly seen as a threat to the whole world from the very beginning, as it promised nothing less than the complete overthrow of the old order—a goal even the most naïve of the Communists' dupes are forced to admit. The idea of this insidious philosophy having a base from which to launch its goal of world revolution was a frightful prospect indeed.

However, for all of its long-range goals, the most immediate threat of the Bolshevik Revolution was that it took Russia out of World War I and thus furthered German war aims. During peacetime, we might have simply kept a wary eye on the Bolsheviks and did what we could to prevent their subversion from spreading to our shores. But 1917 was not peacetime. The United States was already involved in the First World War at this time, and we joined in sending an expeditionary force to Russia to help defeat the Soviets and re-open the Eastern Front. As it turned out, that was not a necessary step for defeating the Central Powers. But with our forces already there and a civil war erupting as non-Communist parties sought to stop the Bolsheviks, the West collectively decided that this would be a low-cost option to stopping Marxism in its tracks. Whether this was a good opportunity is still up for debate. While the declared purpose of Communism was visible for any to see, the earnestness with which they would carry out their murderous program over the next eighty years or so could not have been foretold. In any event, with the end of World War I there was very little enthusiasm for a long anti-Bolshevik campaign that could last years and potentially cause millions more deaths. Still, American forces remained in Russia until 1920, engaging Red Army troops in a number of battles that led to the deaths of some five hundred U.S. soldiers—truly among the most forgotten in our history.

That the U.S. withdrew its forces from the Soviet Union should not be seen as an admission that Communism was not all that bad after all. Rather, it should be seen as an admission that we were primarily concerned with the threat of Communism at home, rather than on some distant shore. Liberal commentators would have us believe that "the Red Scare" was just ignorant Americans overreacting to a threat that did not really exist. As a matter of fact, organized cells of left-wing radicals—Communists, anarchists, and others—not only preached the violent overthrow of American society but actually sent waves of letter bombs to numerous public and press officials across the United States. A bomb hit Wall Street, causing numerous deaths, and many Americans feared that these were just the preliminary stages to revolution. The U.S. had already banned anarchists from immigrating to America (partly in response to William McKinley being assassinated by a foreign-born anarchist in 1901), and they gradually extended the ban to members of communist parties. These measures were popular with the American people, as they excluded those whose stated purpose was to bring violent revolution to the United States. It was not thought necessary to make a distinction between "peaceful" Communists and "radical" Communists, nor did we have prominent members of Congress or the presidency lecturing us on how real Communism was always a philosophy of peace. The primary concern was the safety of the American citizen, and if this meant denying certain foreigners admission to the United States, so be it.

Overseas, we kept an eye on the Soviet Union. After the death of Lenin and the consolidation of power under Stalin, opportunities for Soviet expansionism were minimal. Subversion, led by the Comintern and its member organizations (including the Communist Party, USA) would continue, but Russia and her associated territories were a shambles—at least in part as a result of Stalin's policies of forced collectivization and his purges, which were responsible for tens of millions of deaths within the Soviet Union.

By the early 1930s, most countries of the world had established diplomatic relations with the USSR, and the United States, under Franklin Roosevelt, decided to do the same. This should not be seen as a stamp of approval of the regime, but merely an acknowledgment of political reality—plus, in the midst of the Great Depression, it presented an opportunity to open up Russian markets to American goods. Again, our policy has traditionally been not to seek out "monsters to

PUTTING AMERICA FIRST
John Quincy Adams Edition

"She has, in the lapse of nearly half a century, without a single exception, respected the independence of other nations while asserting and maintaining her own. She has abstained from interference in the concerns of others, even when conflict has been for principles to which she clings, as to the last vital drop that visits the heart. She has seen that probably for centuries to come, all the contests of that Aceldama the European world, will be contests of inveterate power, and emerging right. Wherever the standard of freedom and Independence has been or shall be unfurled, there will her heart, her benedictions and her prayers be. But she goes not abroad, in search of monsters to destroy. She is the well-wisher to the freedom and independence of all. She is the champion and vindicator only of her own."

—**JOHN QUINCY ADAMS**, Speech to the House of Representatives, July 4, 1821

destroy." By the 1930s the Soviet regime in Moscow was an established fact, whether we liked it or not. Failing to acknowledge it by this point would have hurt no one but ourselves.

Another actor posing a threat to peace and security had appeared on the European stage: Nazi Germany. Like Communism, National Socialism was an ideology both collectivist and expansionist. While the Nazi movement was initially opposed by Communist parties across the world as a potential rival for the same base of support, the opposition between Nazis and Communists vanished overnight when Stalin and Hitler reached an accord, the Molotov-Ribbentrop Pact, dividing Eastern Europe into spheres of influence. Germany invaded Poland, and the USSR got in on the act by attacking the Poles from behind and incorporating large swaths of Polish territory into the Soviet Union, as well as annexing the previously independent Baltic States, which had been part of the Russian Empire before the Bolshevik Revolution. All of Europe was on the brink of war as two collectivist totalitarian empires appeared to join hands to divide up the spoils of their conquests. Many Americans worried that the U.S. would somehow be sucked into yet another European war—even as political leaders assured the electorate, as they had in the First World War, that America would remain at peace.

Hitler brought about his own demise when he broke his treaty with Stalin and attacked the Soviet Union in the summer of 1941. Tens of millions of people perished on the Eastern Front, including some twenty million Soviet citizens.

By the time Hitler attacked the Soviet Union, Roosevelt had already quietly ended our policy of strict neutrality and begun supplying Allied forces with war materiel under the "Lend-Lease

Program." When the Soviet Union was attacked by erstwhile ally Germany, the USSR became a recipient of American aid as well.

The story of the oddly warm and chummy relationship between FDR and Stalin is beyond the scope of this book, but it merits a brief mention. That Stalin and Roosevelt got along so well would be understandable if it had been merely a relationship of the-enemy-of-my-enemy-is-my-friend sort, but Roosevelt seemed to genuinely trust Stalin and see him as a viable partner in the creation of a peaceful post-war world. In his autobiography William C. Bullitt, the American ambassador to the Soviet Union, quoted FDR saying in 1943 that Stalin "won't try to annex anything and will work with me for a world of democracy and peace." This was the man who had initiated extermination on the basis of ethnicity long before Hitler ever did, and who ranks with *Der Fuehrer* as one of the worst mass murderers in history. Franklin Roosevelt did not live long enough to see how hopelessly naïve his trust was, but his relationship with Stalin is an illustration that the United States was not always at odds with Russia, even under the worst of Soviet leaders. (It is also an illustration of the blind spot that many Americans on the progressive end of the political scale have when it comes to atrocities committed by progressive leaders in other parts of the world.)

It did not take long after the guns fell silent in 1945 before the two new world powers—the United States and USSR—were at odds. An emboldened Communist empire was on the march, soon dominating much of Eastern and Central Europe, as well as expanding into Asia with the fall of China to Communist forces in 1949. With the explosion of Soviet nuclear weapons, the confrontation between the West and the East became an existential one; we were in it not just for the preservation of our way of life, but for the preservation of life itself. So America took a new and unprecedented stance. Rather than retreating across the Atlantic as we did in 1918, the United States remained on the front lines in the fight against international Communism. This struggle would eventually find us committed by treaty to the defense of countless countries around the globe and see us engaged in actual combat in places such as Korea and Vietnam.

Was America finally, once and for all, abandoning our policy of national interest-based foreign policy in favor of taking on all the evils of the world, even where they did not affect our security and well-being? Many people in our foreign policy establishment would have us believe so. To this very day they are adamant about the "need" to project U.S. power wherever some injustice occurs—or, at least, where something happens that we don't happen to like. But the Cold War was not so simple and clear-cut. True, many liberal internationalists were overjoyed to see the United States a player on the world stage, viewing our new willingness to intervene across the world as a first step in the elimination of the nation-state and the creation of an international world order led by—well, people like themselves. But some of the most vociferous supporters of America's new role in the world were those who had been previously so jealous of our neutrality— Western Republicans and conservative Southern Democrats (the latter an almost completely extinct species of politician today). They had not had a sudden road-to-Damascus experience converting them to internationalism. Instead they saw America's own security and well-being as under direct threat from the Soviet Union. In other words, the Soviet Union, because of its goal of world domination, threatened our national interests. The people of the heartland had no interest in some sort of progressive new world order. They did, however, wish to maintain the old order they had always enjoyed, with the freedoms they had. They knew that the expansion of Communism threatened those very freedoms—and not just in the abstract, because the Communist adversary they faced had the weapons to carry out its threats if America was not vigilant in her own defense. The Cold War was not really a new departure for American foreign policy so much as the exception that proves the rule—a rare period of time in which it was necessary for the United States to operate globally in order to preserve those freedoms she enjoyed locally.

For nearly fifty years, therefore, our greatest enemy was the Soviet Union. Absent the threat of nuclear annihilation, we would probably have gone to war with each other at some point during those fifty years—we almost did anyway, on a couple of occasions. We spent two and a half generations parrying and thrusting across the global arena, building up arsenals and institutions, and the related bureaucracies to run them—for a war that, thanks be to God, never came.

And we triumphed. Not merely through force of arms, although that did play a role, but also through force of ideas. Nations have long built walls to keep out foreign invaders, but the idea of building a wall to keep one's own citizens *in* was one of the starkest illustrations of the moral bankruptcy of the system imposed on much of the world by the Soviet Union. Until recently, we would have also pointed to Communist restrictions on free speech and religion as equally abhorrent to the mind of modern man, but since many of our progressive colleagues in the

West now advocate those very things, this indictment of the Soviet regime is a bit more problematic these days.

The bottom line is that we won the Cold War, and as in the period following victory in any conventional war, it was time for us to re-evaluate our position in the world and move on. At a minimum, it was certainly a time to re-evaluate our relationship with Russia now that the Soviet Union was no more. And for a time, it appeared that a new era of harmony in U.S.-Russian relations would begin, similar to the period before the Bolshevik Revolution. Perhaps we would go back to highlighting the "natural community of interests and of sympathies" that Prince Gortchakoff pointed out in 1861. Indeed, the time was ripe for such a re-adjustment. According to the Chicago Council on Foreign Affairs, American "warmth" toward Russia was at its highest point in recorded history in the early 1990s.[1] Russian views of America were equally rosy. As recently as 2002, nearly twice as many Russians had favorable opinions of America as unfavorable ones.[2] Needless to say, those were more hopeful days. Since that time the level of mistrust between Russians and Americans has returned to levels not seen since the worst days of the Cold War. By 2006, Vladimir Putin was reduced to arguing, in an interview with the French television channel TF-1, "I see that not everyone in the West has understood that the Soviet Union has disappeared from the political map of the world and that a new country has emerged with new humanist and ideological principles at the foundation of its existence."

What happened? Before the Bolshevik Revolution the United States and Russia were never in a state of competition, let alone conflict. Initially we feared the installation of Communism in

Moscow, but really only intervened as a war measure, deeply invested as we were in the Allied effort to win World War I. Despite the undeniable evil of the Communist Russian regime, we came to an accommodation with them, and even became the Soviets' allies for a time before the relationship broke down at the end of World War II, poisoned by Soviet aggression. But at the end of 1991 the Soviet Union ceased to exist. What's more, the massive empire that the USSR had controlled broke into fifteen separate sovereign states with only localized bloodshed. So much for the Soviet hymn declaring, "Unbreakable Union of freeborn Republics, Great Russia has welded forever to stand!" I became a Foreign Service Officer eleven days after the fall of the Soviet Union, and I remember fondly the great feeling of optimism among my colleagues that the future would bring about great cooperation between Russia and the United States, as we also worked for trade and good relations with the new countries once ruled from Moscow. It was as if a great shadow that had darkened our entire lives had been lifted and we could finally move on to a more hopeful future.

Old habits die hard, though. Used as we were to defending the free world, too many Americans—especially in the diplomatic community—had come to presume that we had been anointed to right all wrongs, wherever they might take place. We had a president—a Republican at that—who spoke of a "New World Order." At the head of this order would naturally be the United States of America, because we "see further into the future," as a Democratic Secretary of State once famously said. In short, America decided that defending our true national interests was not nearly as exciting as attempting to remake the world in our own image. But in so doing, we abandoned our role as the model democracy and became the new Soviet Union—a freer, lighter, and happier version, to be sure, but similar in one important respect: we would not rest until everyone shared what we viewed as the proper values.

So rather than abandoning or at least, re-thinking, the NATO alliance, whose very reason for being was to keep Soviet troops from crossing the Fulda Gap on the border between East and West Germany, we expanded it right up to the backyard of Russia. Some American politicians wanted to place even former Soviet Republics like Ukraine and Georgia under the NATO umbrella. Given later developments in those new countries, we can now see that had we done so we would likely have gone to war with Russia long since— something we avoided in the nearly fifty years of Cold War, when our national interests really were at stake. Through our support of the so-called "color revolutions" in several of the countries once part of the U.S.S.R, in which pro-Moscow parties were overthrown in favor of those toeing a more Western line, we generated a lot of resentment where goodwill had ever so briefly reigned. And all the while we could not articulate how America and Americans would be made better off by taking sides in issues that were once none of our concern. It came to the point where we reflexively took the anti-Russian position in every dispute, no matter the merits of the case. Crimea, for example, is populated primarily by Russian speakers and was a part of Russia from the time of Catherine the Great until Soviet Premier Nikita Krushchev decided to award the peninsula to the Ukrainian Soviet Socialist Republic—a relatively meaningless gesture at the time, since it was all controlled from Moscow anyway. When the Soviet Union broke up in 1991, new national borders were largely determined by the pre-existing boundaries of the former Soviet Republics. Locals had little say-so in the matter, except in areas such as Transnistria (Moldova) and South Ossetia and Abkhazia (Georgia), where the mostly Russian inhabitants rebelled and created de facto independent enclaves, which are still functioning as mini-states more than a generation later but not recognized by any nation. More than 90 percent of Crimean voters opted for regional autonomy, and Crimea became part of the new nation of Ukraine. This was never an easy fit, and on several occasions protests against Ukrainian rule erupted in Crimea. Annexation to Russia was sought after protests against a 2014 revolution backed by the United States ousted Victor Yanukovych, the elected president of Ukraine. In the unrest that followed, Russian troops intervened, Crimea declared its independence, and federation with Russia was announced.

That is a necessarily very condensed, not to say simplistic, reading of the 2014 Crimean crisis. Reasonable minds can differ over whether or not Crimean annexation by Russia was proper, especially in light of the Budapest Memorandum of 1994, in which Ukraine gave up its nuclear arsenal in exchange for certain guarantees, including territorial integrity and no interference in its political autonomy.[3] This agreement was signed not only by Ukraine and the Russian Federation, but also by the United States and the United Kingdom. But most experts do not believe that it commits any of the signatories to military assistance, nor does it include enforcement mechanisms.[4] What is more, it does not directly address the issue of Crimea or any other region whose inhabitants no longer wish to remain within Ukraine. Finally, even if one held that Russia violated this agreement by allowing for the annexation of Crimea to its Federation, an argument can be made that the United States had already broken it when we provided support to the overthrow of the elected Ukrainian government of Viktor Yanukovych during the 2014 Ukrainian Revolution.

Still, whether or not the Budapest Memorandum has any teeth, it can be argued that it is in our interest to protect the territorial integrity of recognized states. Standing up for Ukraine could protect us in the long run by bolstering the principle that larger nations cannot redraw national borders—that it is unlawful to carve out a territory that has been recognized as being an integral part of another nation. The problem with this analysis is that we failed to respect that principle in the 1990s when we engaged in a bombing campaign to force Serbia to relinquish Kosovo, a region that had been a part of that country since medieval times. Perhaps because we are "the indispensable nation," we are allowed to follow a different set of rules from anyone else. Even so, the question we must ask ourselves is what vital national interest was served when we decided to make support for Ukrainian sovereignty over Crimea a keystone of our policy in that part of the world. Does Russian control of Crimea put American lives at risk? I have not seen any argument advanced that would suggest that either Russian *or* Ukrainian control over Crimea would have the slightest effect on our security as Americans. The argument could be raised that by antagonizing a major regional player—Russia—in that part of the world, we actually raise the threat to American citizens and thus act *against* our own national interests. What about American well-being? Does a construction worker in Des Moines or a cafeteria worker in Newark or a farm worker in the Mississippi Delta see a change in his lifestyle when the blue, white, and red of the Russian Federation flies over Sebastopol in place of the blue and gold of Ukraine? One could, in the interest of encouraging the peaceful resolution of all disputes, express concern over violence that has taken place in the region and encourage all parties to find a peaceful solution, since the maintenance of peace can be generally seen to be in the interest of all parties. But why is it our place to take sides? Even if I believed that Russia was completely in the wrong in this affair, I see no national interest of the United States threatened by this act, and certainly not threatened to the point at which we are justified in alienating Russia over the incident. Contrary to the beliefs of Democratic political hacks and Republican neo-conservatives, making Russia our enemy for no reason is detrimental to both our security and our well-being.

To hear the story from much of the political class, however, Russia represents an existential threat to the United States. According to Hillary Clinton, Vladimir Putin is to be compared to Adolf Hitler, and according to John McCain, today's Russia is our "moral opposite."[5] The evidence of substantial Russian interference in our 2016 elections in favor of one particular candidate appears to be dubious, and in any case anti-Russian voices in both the Democratic and Republican parties were spouting bellicose language long before the 2016 election cycle even began. So what is it about Russia in 2018 that generates such spittle-flecked hysteria among much of our political class?

For some Republicans, including McCain, the answer appears to be a rather simple one. If I had a neighbor who was a violent alcoholic for years and years and I suddenly heard that he had decided to change his ways, I would probably be skeptical at first—not from a lack of charity, but out of prudence. I certainly would not lend him my car keys right off the bat. Over time, however, as I noticed his progress, my trust in him might grow, and I would hope that I would do what I could to encourage him along his path, maybe even offering a hand of friendship. Another person might have a different approach and, depending on how much havoc had been wreaked by this alcoholic neighbor, it might be that those around him would never trust him, even if he stayed on the wagon for thirty years. That is human nature, I suppose.

So for those of John McCain's generation, who lived through real evils emanating from Russia for nearly the entirety of their adult lives, it is naturally difficult to accept that a government based in Red Square can be anything but malignant. Russia was our foe and will always remain our foe. It's all black and white, and no amount of new evidence will ever change that equation. McCain's hatred for Russia is certainly understandable. He entered Congress, after all, when the Cold War was still at full throttle, and it may very well be hard for him to make a mental adjustment to changed circumstances. I have heard of older Southerners who refused to vote for a Republican even into the 1970s on the grounds that the GOP was the party that started the Civil War under Abraham Lincoln—since whose time quite a few changes had taken place in both parties. I can certainly understand holding fast to a worldview that no longer corresponds with reality. It creates problems, though, when the person clinging to such a worldview still holds a great deal of power in determining U.S. foreign policy. It certainly adds fuel to the argument in favor of term limits.

But what about fanatical opposition to Russia among Democratic leaders? After all, even before there were any signs of changes in the Soviet Union, Democratic luminaries such as Alan Cranston, Gary Hart, and Jesse Jackson, all 1984 presidential candidates, supported the idea of a nuclear freeze, trusting that the Soviet government would do the same, based on mutual goodwill. For this they were praised by name in a pamphlet put out by the Soviet Novosti Press Agency.[6] Why is it that we could trust the leaders of one of the world's worst totalitarian regimes back in the days of the Cold War, but now that things have changed in Moscow, we have to isolate Putin's Russia at all costs?

This is a more difficult question to answer. While back in the day when the Democratic Party truly embraced diversity of thought, there were a great number of genuinely anti-Communist Democrats, the liberal leaders castigating Russia today are not cut from that cloth. Mental sclerosis is not to blame here—at least not the kind that prevents one from modifying one's opinion in response to a change in circumstances. What is the explanation, then?

The answer may lie in Vladimir Putin's public stances on some issues most dear to the modern liberal heart. Regardless of whether or not one believes that Putin is sincere in his public statements (he is a politician, after all), in recent years he has expressed support for views that were once mainstream in the Western world but are now considered anathema by progressive leaders. He calls himself a Christian and enjoys a close relationship with the leadership of the Russian Orthodox Church. Not only that, but he is one of the few political leaders who talks about protecting Christian minorities in areas where they are oppressed, such as the Middle East. On so-called LGBT rights, Putin's views are even more at odds with those of our bicoastal glitterati. In a series of interviews with Oliver Stone for the Showtime Network (aired in June 2017), Putin stated his support for the idea of marriage as between a man and a woman, defended Russia's ban on adoption by same-sex couples, and even expressed discomfort at the idea of showering with a homosexual man (gasp!). He can sound an awful lot like our elites' worst nightmare: the dreaded religious right. As he told *Time* magazine in his "Person of the Year" Q&A, "First and foremost we should be governed by common sense. But common sense should be based on moral principles first. And it is not possible today to have morality separated from religious values."

Today's Left is united by their dedication to the overthrow of traditional Western values. Viewpoints on marriage and sexuality that were considered commonplace a generation ago are now "hate speech"; we have already seen people lose their livelihoods as a result of beliefs well within the mainstream as recently as the beginning of Barack Obama's first term. Christianity bears special opprobrium among liberals, despite the fact that it is the origin of our fundamental beliefs concerning human rights. That a major world leader would obstinately hold to Western tradition in these areas triggers deep-seated hatred among those on the Left. Because he stands for the things they are working so hard to destroy, Putin must be brought down.

Thus, many Democrats see the Russians as enemies in the Culture Wars, while some Republicans still seem to be fighting the Cold War. Neither are pursuing America's national interests.

Of course, there will always be a divergence of interests between the U.S. and Russia, as is the case with any other country. And our history of mutual antagonism adds a special twist to any problem that may come up between us. But we must not let events of the past dictate how we form our current policy, especially when those events are not tied to present reality. Vladimir Putin is first and foremost interested in promoting Russia's interests, and he has enjoyed very high public approval ratings in Russia as a result. In the most recent Russian elections, which saw extraordinarily high turnout by American standards, he was re-elected with over 75 percent of the vote. But the fact is, any good leader looks out first for the interests of his own country, and if we have leaders in Washington who are equally vigilant in promoting an America First policy, we won't have major problems between our two countries, located, as we are, "at the extremities of the two worlds."

What are our interests vis-à-vis Russia? First and foremost, we have an interest in maintaining a peaceful relationship. Russia's nuclear capability means that it is one of the few countries, if not the only one, that can literally annihilate us. This does not mean we should act on the basis of appeasement or, even less, servile fear, but it does mean that we should bring a healthy dose of respect to our dealings with Moscow. We should eschew needless antagonism. We should be outspoken in the defense of our own rights and interests, but where those interests do not lie, we should not get involved. Who sits in the presidential seat in Kiev or who flies their flag in the Crimea is, frankly, none of our concern. To make those things our concern suggests that our foreign policy is first and foremost anti-Russian—an impression that is unlikely to make friends and influence people along the banks of the Volga River.

Second, Russia represents an enormous market for U.S. goods. According to the most recent statistics posted by the Office of the United States Trade Representative (2013), Russia was America's twenty-third largest goods trading partner, with $38.1 billion in two-way goods trade, among which were large amounts of American agricultural products, such as poultry meat, tree nuts, soybeans, and live animals. In addition, Russia remains one of the world's largest oil exporters, and fuel oil was the largest item on the menu of goods imported from Russia to the United States. In a time when other sources of foreign fossil fuels are areas subject to political volatility—not just the Middle East, but also Venezuela and Nigeria—a stable, friendly relationship with Russia gives us a secure source for imported petroleum.

The third national interest that arises in our relationship with Russia is in our fight against international terror sponsored by radical Islamic nihilists. Because of the multi-ethnic nature of its Federation, Russia has long had its own domestic problem with this kind of terror and has developed a certain expertise. While we may have issues with some of the Russians' friends in the Middle East, Russia also faces similar enemies. Cooperation rather than confrontation in places like Syria can serve both countries in the short and the long term. If Russia wants to commit her resources in crushing Middle Eastern terrorist cells that also seek to inflict mayhem on our interests, why should we object?

With the election of Donald Trump as president of the United States, a further common interest ties our two countries together:

a realization that Western civilization itself may be on its last legs—not so much as a result of outside pressure but because of enemies within who would love nothing more than to see the work of thousands of years come crashing down, and who, Taliban-like, are already actively engaged in destroying the symbols of that civilization they find most "offensive."

Unfortunately, the first year of the Trump administration saw decidedly mixed results in terms of resetting our relationship with Russia. Hamstrung by so far unconfirmed allegations of "collusion," President Trump has not yet been able to bring on a thaw in what is becoming Cold War II. He caved in to Congressional pressure in August 2017 when he signed a new round of sanctions against Russia,

PUTTING AMERICA FIRST
Donald Trump
Edition

"The fundamental question of our time is whether the West has the will to survive. Do we have the confidence in our values to defend them at any cost? Do we have enough respect for our citizens to protect our borders? Do we have the desire and the courage to preserve our civilization in the face of those who would subvert and destroy it? We can have the largest economies and the most lethal weapons anywhere on Earth, but if we do not have strong families and strong values, then we will be weak and we will not survive."

—**DONALD TRUMP**, Remarks to the People of Poland, July 6, 2017

even while complaining of the legislation's flaws.[7] It is almost as if the alliance of liberal and neoconservative Russophobes in Congress and the media has been successful in thwarting Trump's positive instincts in this matter through the mantra-like recitation of the bizarre canard that Vladimir Putin actually brought about the election of Donald Trump. They have painted this administration into a corner; at this point anything anti-Russian action will be seen as evidence that the charges are valid.

Even so, Trump, at least initially, wisely held back from the chorus of voices automatically blaming Putin for the attempted assassination of former Russian military intelligence officer Sergei Skripal, saying that he would wait for the facts in this case to be clear before determining who was to blame. It is a sign of the ideologically-driven madness in Washington and in our media that this reasonable position was painted as yet more evidence that Trump is not suited to be president. Real leaders, you see, make decisions that forever affect our foreign policy before any of the facts are in.

But despite sanctions under both Presidents Obama and Trump, Russia's economy appears to be doing better than it has in years.[8] And whether we like Vladimir Putin or not, barring some unforeseen event he is likely to be our main interlocutor in that part of the world for years to come. As has been our historic policy, we should work with the person who actually holds the reins in Moscow, rather than lamenting that a person more to our liking does not sit in the Kremlin.

Even as many media outlets, perhaps in what they hope is a self-fulfilling prophecy, predict that U.S.-Russia relations will continue to deteriorate,[9] all is not lost. As we have seen, we have no existential beef with Russia. Highlighting the things we have in common with the Russian Federation, as well as pointing out our mutual enemies, can only serve to improve our bilateral relationship. In addition, we must make clear to Russia that we do not seek to tread in her backyard, just as we expect her to refrain from involvement in our own. We would certainly have something to say were Russia to attempt to subvert the governments of Mexico or the Bahamas, for example. We should make it clear to countries that were once a part of the Soviet Union that we seek their friendship and will work with them on areas of mutual concern, but that we will not take sides in policy and territorial disputes they may have with Russia or other neighbors in the region. That is something for them to resolve as sovereign states, without bringing in outside pressure. We will always urge parties to work toward peace, since that is in all our interests, and we will offer our counsel when it is sought out by *both* parties, but beyond that we will hold to Jefferson's maxim of "commerce with all nations, alliance with none."

FOUR

EUROPE

THE ORIGINAL ENTANGLING ALLIANCE

In the American mind, Europe has long represented the place where they do things differently. American politicians have traditionally held up the American way of life as the superior of the two—though that is changing. In the case of President Obama, for example, it wasn't clear which he preferred. Most of us Americans, however, as much as we may love Europe—and I confess that there is a special place in my heart for Italy and Ireland, where I spent significant portions of my career—generally believe that we do things better in the New World. This is despite the fact that millions of Americans can trace their ancestry back to the Old Continent (I am leaving out the United Kingdom at this point as it is, in more ways than one, a special case). According to records by the United States Census Bureau, some 15 percent of the population claim German heritage, the largest of any ethnic group, while 11 percent claim Irish origin, nearly 6 percent Italian, just over 3 percent Polish or French, and between 1 and 2 percent each the Netherlands, Norway, or Sweden.[1] Significant populations of ethnic minorities like these could lead to tension in many nations, but our European immigrants have tended to assimilate very well. It is not uncommon to see an American from Boston claim to be "Irish" (much to the amusement of people actually born in Ireland). New Yorkers call themselves "Italians," and Minnesotans talk about being "Norwegian." But if pressed, nearly all of these people will say that they are first and foremost Americans. In the case of most European-Americans, ethnic identity is a matter of ancestral pride, not a determinant of policy—and almost never a basis for allegiance. Our origins help us to understand who we are and how we got here, but they have little influence on what we do—except for a tiny minority of us.

All that being said, Americans and Europeans have a lot in common, and I am not referring primarily to race. Americans who travel to Europe generally feel a sense of familiarity with the culture there, at least at a surface level, that they do not feel when traveling to more "exotic" climes—unless they grew up in an insulated ethnic community. While we Americans have a very distinct and separate identity as a people, the basis of our culture is European. We are a part of the West, regardless of our own racial DNA, and notwithstanding academic and media protests to the contrary. The values we see as distinctly American first evolved from two thousand years of Christendom and thousands of years of Roman and Greek civilization before that and then were adapted to the climes of a new continent. We may hate this shared culture or even work to destroy it—as some are doing—but that does not change the fact that it is a part of who we are.

This line of argument may seem to be in tension with the principle that we are first and foremost Americans. But there is no contradiction at all. Understanding what created American culture does not take away from the distinctiveness of it, any more than understanding that wine comes from grapes means that we think a bottle of Chardonnay is the same as a box of raisins. We should appreciate, understand, study, and even celebrate our European heritage (at least until they deem that to be a "hate crime")—all the while realizing that what has arisen out of that heritage on the American continent is something special.

Leaving the United Kingdom aside (until the next chapter), the focus of our European policy throughout the first hundred years or so of our national

PUTTING AMERICA FIRST
Herbert Hoover
Edition

"We were challenged with a peace-time choice between the American system of rugged individualism and a European philosophy of diametrically opposed doctrines—doctrines of paternalism and static socialism."

—**HERBERT HOOVER**, campaign speech in New York City, October 22, 1928·

existence was France, and to a lesser degree Spain. That makes perfect sense, as they were two of the leading world powers at the time. European powers such as Germany and Italy—not to mention nearly the whole of Eastern Europe, Greece, Ireland, and Norway—did not even exist as nations for much of this period, either because they were part of a larger whole, under Austro-Hungarian, Ottoman, or other rule, or because they comprised a number of smaller states, as in the case of the German principalities of Central Europe and the various nations of the Italian peninsula. We generally enjoyed good relations with these other powers on the basis of the principle that guided our original foreign policy—our national interest. The United States and these European peoples all engaged in commerce with each other and sent diplomats to each other's capitals, and there was little cause for tension between us.

Things were different with France and Spain because they were not simply distant European powers, but also empires maintaining colonies in our own neck of the woods. This was a matter of concern, but it could also play to our advantage, as in the case of our War for Independence, in which the New World interests of France and Spain were among the causes that led those two countries to support our efforts at secession from Great Britain. While we did sign a treaty of alliance with France in 1778 in the midst of our independence struggle, it was effectively annulled with the outbreak of the French Revolution, although not formally abrogated until the 1800 Treaty of Mortefontaine. And our country did not automatically become a permanent ally of either France or Spain as a measure of thanks for their assistance. We appreciated their support, and many scholars believe that we could not have achieved our independence absent their assistance, especially in the case of France. But we also realized that these countries had come to our assistance as disinterested benefactors, not because they sympathized with the ideas that came to dominate our independence movement. (Americans would become avowed republicans during this period, while both the French and Spanish kings ruled by divine right.) Rather, Spain and France aided the infant American nation because they felt it was in their national interests to do so. We signed a treaty with France as the price of this assistance, during a time when our own existence as a nation was at stake. It is not clear what would have happened had the French Revolution not effectively dissolved our treaty obligations, but the takeaway from this period is that, once we were on our own two feet, we would not sign another treaty of alliance for over a century. During our struggle for independence, our leaders were willing to take help from any quarter and pay almost any price, but once independence was achieved we would stand by Spain and France when it suited our interests to do so—and against them when it did not.

And soon enough that would be necessary. America's "Quasi-War" with France took place during the presidency of John Adams.

A number of leading lights on the American political scene, distrusting monarchical government, had expressed support for the French Revolution. Thomas Jefferson, who was our minister (the equivalent of an ambassador) to France when the Revolution broke out, was enthusiastic about it. Even in 1795, after the worst excesses of the Revolution, he would write that "this ball of liberty…will roll round the world…it is our glory that we first put it into motion."[2] But Jefferson left France not long after the Revolution began in 1789, and he had not been present for the Reign of Terror. Perhaps naïvely, he believed that the excesses of the French Revolution were but a passing phase and that France would become a strong Republic after the initial growing pains.

Not every American leader was taken in by a revolt that would later serve as an inspiration for such tragic episodes in world history as the Paris Commune and the Bolshevik takeover of Russia. Alexander Hamilton, writing during the same period, noted that most Americans had been heartened by the French Revolution when it first broke out, and were even willing to overlook some of the atrocities that occurred, but began to lose their enthusiasm when they witnessed "one volcano succeeding another, the last still more dreadful than the former, spreading ruin and devastation far and wide—subverting the foundations of right security and property, of order, morality and religion sparing neither sex nor age, confounding innocence with guilt, involving the old and the young, the sage and the madman, the long tried friend of virtue and his country and the upstart pretender to purity and patriotism—the bold projector of new treasons with the obscure in indiscriminate and profuse destruction."[3] Whether or not the initial revolution against French King Louis XVI had any merit, it became clear within a few short years that the radical leaders of the French Revolution, like their spiritual descendants to the present day, were more motivated by class hatred, envy, anti-religious bigotry, and self-promotion than they were by a thirst for justice.

Regardless of any sympathy that American leaders may have had for the new order of things in France at the beginning, the

vast majority of Americans were unwilling to give the revolutionaries anything more than moral support. President Washington officially declared the United States neutral in the conflict
between Revolutionary France and the United Kingdom. And
when "Citizen Genêt," the ambassador that the revolutionary
government had sent to the United States, recruited American
ships and sailors to fight for the French Revolutionary cause
against Britain and Spain, even Jefferson (at that time serving as
President Washington's Secretary of State) agreed that Genêt
must be recalled by France. Regardless of our sympathies, it was
not in our national interest to join with France in her attempt to
export the Revolution by force.

And it was not long before events soured us on Revolutionary
France. During the administration of John Adams, tension
between the U.S. and France broke out into violence when U.S.
officials refused to pay the "tribute" (bribe) required by corrupt
French officials as a price for entering into negotiations on matters
of mutual concern. "Millions for defense, not one cent for tribute," was the national reply, and American and French vessels
engaged in the undeclared naval Quasi-War, with dozens of casualties on both sides before an agreement was reached ending
hostilities in 1800. By this time, Napoleon Bonaparte had seized
some of the mechanisms of power in the French Republic, and he
had other things on his mind—such as becoming emperor—that
took precedence over financing a naval war with a young nation
so far away from the European mainland. We would never again
come so close to war with France, and our relationship eventually
evolved into one of friendly indifference—the standard in those
early days for our relationship with every foreign country.

This "isolationism"—as our long term of non-interference would later be branded—would soon lead to dividends for the young United States. Napoleon, wishing to divest himself of further American headaches (and eager to acquire European ones), sold to the government of the United States, now led by President Thomas Jefferson, a vast plot of land known as the Louisiana Purchase: the nearly 900,000 square miles of land that would make up all or part of the states of Louisiana, Arkansas, Texas, New Mexico, Colorado, Kansas, Missouri, Wyoming, Nebraska, Iowa, Montana, North Dakota, South Dakota, and Minnesota, as well as some that today is part of Canada because we eventually ceded it during much later negotiations on our northern border with Britain.

What can we learn here? France, our ally in our War for Independence, reverted to being simply one of many nations with whom we enjoyed good relations. During the upheavals of the French Revolution, while some American leaders expressed their approval, we did not take sides. When tensions neverthe-less eventually escalated, leading to a state of warfare, they were soon enough resolved when both parties saw the futility of continuing the fight. In short, acting as a reasonable nation primarily concerned with our own interests, America showed France that we were a worthy partner with whom to conduct business. And so the United States was able to promote the well-being of the American people by pursuing our national interest in expanding across North America. The treaty with Napoleon that made this possible came about because France no longer had ambitions in that part of the New World, and we did. We could reach a bargain because there was no larger agenda on either side. Had we become an eternal ally of Louis XVI in appreciation for his assistance, we would have become anathema to Republican elements in France. Had we officially taken sides in the French Revolution in favor of those revolutionaries, Napoleon might have been concerned that we would work to prevent his own rise to power as subversive of those revolutionary aims. Instead we supported our national interest, and our national interest alone, and this enabled us to make what was likely the most important deal in the history of the United States—one that was a direct cause of our evolution from an insignificant young republic to the dominant power in the Americas and, eventually, the world.

In the early years of our Republic, our relationship with Spain featured much less prominently than that with France. Our dealings with Spain were largely confined to questions regarding our respective borders, since Spain, until the 1820s, controlled the vast majority of territory south of our border, including what is now Florida and the Southwest. After the Louisiana Purchase, there was some dispute over where to draw the border between the U.S. and Spanish possessions in North America, with both countries claiming what came to be

PUTTING AMERICA FIRST
Thomas Jefferson
Edition

"I know that the acquisition of Louisiana had been disapproved by some from a candid apprehension that the enlargement of our territory would endanger its union. But who can limit the extent to which the federative principle may operate effectively? The larger our association the less will it be shaken by local passions; and in any view is it not better that the opposite bank of the Mississippi should be settled by our own brethren and children than by strangers of another family? With which should we be most likely to live in harmony and friendly intercourse?"

—**THOMAS JEFFERSON**, Second Inaugural Address, 1805

known as West Florida (roughly the Gulf areas of what is now Mississippi, Alabama, and northern Florida). In addition, the remaining peninsula of Florida was coveted by American settlers as being the last "open" land on the Eastern Seaboard.

The calls to purchase Florida from Spain increased as Seminole and Creek Indian attacks on border settlements began to pick up and Spanish authorities seemed unwilling or incapable of doing anything to stop them. This was the early nineteenth-century version of a neighboring country being seen as a harbor for terrorists, so political pressure on Washington to resolve the issue of Florida was quite high. (An aside here is necessary. I am not judging the legitimacy of Native American attacks on the Florida frontier. I am merely explaining how those attacks were seen by most Americans at the time. One has to work to understand historical events by trying to see the world the way the people saw it at the time. Only then is it possible to comprehend what took place and why and use the lessons from that understanding to address contemporary concerns. It is really easy—and very popular—to sit back and make judgments on the actions of our ancestors in order to make ourselves feel oh so superior. But in doing so, we not only understand little, we learn even less.)

Eventually the Spanish government yielded to American entreaties. Spain was exhausted and bankrupt. Spanish government under the Bourbons had only recently been restored after more than a dozen years of occupation by Napoleonic forces. Many of Spain's colonies in America either were in revolt or had already achieved their independence. Spain couldn't afford to sink money in an unprofitable colony that was causing problems with its northern neighbor. In 1819, the United States and Spain signed a treaty awarding the whole of Florida to the United States and making adjustments to the borders. Instead of paying Spain directly, the United States assumed responsibility for claims by U.S. citizens against Spain. This treaty effectively ended—for nearly eighty years—any tensions between the two countries. True, there would be voices calling for a U.S. annexation of Cuba for much of the nineteenth century, but internal American tensions that led to the Civil War would effectively shelve the whole Cuba question.

It would come back in 1898, though, and lead to war between U.S. and Spanish forces. We will review that history in detail in chapter thirteen because even though the United States and Spain were the principal belligerents, the Spanish-American War was less about Spain as a European power than it was about America's relationship with Latin America—and, to a lesser degree, the place of the United States in the world at large, as we took responsibility for the Philippines as well. In other words, while we went to war with a European power in 1898, it was for reasons that had little or nothing to do with European politics. Regardless of the wisdom of entering into war with Spain and whether or not it represented a departure from traditional American foreign policy goals (for the record, I believe it did), our decision to do so did not change our long-held commitment to the advisability of staying out of European affairs. The Old Continent was still seen as a place of ancient and irresolvable prejudices that could easily suck in anyone who chose to take sides in any dispute there.

Our confrontations with other European nations (again, setting aside the United Kingdom) were practically nonexistent for the first one hundred forty years of our national odyssey. There were some negotiations with Germany over territories in the Pacific in the late nineteenth century. And there were occasional areas of international cooperation during crises (such as the response to the Boxer Rebellion in 1900), but by and large we were content with friendly relations and good trade. We had no designs on other nations, and they had none on us, and therefore we all had ample space to look out for our own national interests. This does not mean that we were truly "isolationist"—a canard that conjures the image of a nation shut in on itself, wanting nothing at all to do with the outside world. On the contrary, we were actively involved in world affairs. A quick glimpse of the "Index to United States Documents Relating to Foreign Affairs, 1828–1861," put out in three volumes by the Carnegie Institute of Washington around 1920, shows that our diplomats were quite active during this period, which does not even cover the years after the Civil War. Each volume is hundreds of pages long and consists of little more than lists of treaties and other diplomatic actions between U.S. and foreign interlocutors. No, we were not isolated from the world. We were actively engaged in doing what was necessary to protect American interests abroad, whether that involved trade, maintaining security for the homeland, or ensuring the safety of Americans abroad. But what we were not doing was telling other countries how they needed to run their internal affairs. During this time, despite it being interrupted by the most brutal war in American history—the Civil War—America continued to grow, both literally in terms of territory and also in wealth, going from an economic backwater to the richest nation in the world. Now one can't pin all of this on our decision to pursue an America First foreign policy, but it certainly didn't hurt. Just sayin'.

The American policy of staying out of European affairs came to an end when we entered the First World War in 1917. But the change did not happen overnight. Following the Spanish-American War, the United States acquired overseas territories that we had no intention of incorporating into the Federal Union, and some political theorists, particularly within the Republican Party, pushed the idea that truly great nations—like Great Britain and France—are colonial nations. They conquer and civilize and extend their influence across the globe by the force of their military might. This was the popular and mainstream "modern" view at the time. For America to be great, these pundits argued, we must be involved everywhere, and we should put down any who stood in our way with our military might. Those who argued differently, they claimed, were holding to an outdated view of what America was all about. Most Americans didn't buy this "jingoism," or extreme nationalism, but it had its adherents in the press and among some of the political elite. They couched their views in terms of the national interest, but unlike traditional supporters of an America First foreign policy they had difficulty in pointing out specifically how Americans would benefit by adopting a more militaristic tone in our relations with other countries. In their way of seeing things, it was simply more "manly." Theodore Roosevelt, who despite being right on any number of issues concerning American national interests had a weak spot in his heart for military adventures, can be counted as chief of the "jingoes"—including when it came to U.S. involvement in World War I.

But it wasn't "Teddy" who got us into that war. It was a Democratic president whose life prior to politics had been spent in academia, an effete man in comparison to someone like Roosevelt, who led the charge and sent our doughboys "over there." In doing so, Wilson initiated a wholesale transformation in Democratic Party politics with regard to the national interest.

Before Wilson, Democrats were widely regarded as the conservative party, both in foreign and in domestic policy. Grover Cleveland's view of foreign affairs is one that would have been shared by George Washington, John Adams, Thomas Jefferson, and all of the Founding Fathers. William Jennings Bryan, who was the Democratic candidate for the White House in 1896, 1900, and 1908, was an outspoken opponent of American interventionism anywhere in the globe.

Woodrow Wilson, however, did not share in this reluctance to increase American involvement in the world. He, like many future Democratic presidents, strongly believed not only that he was right but that the world would be a better place if everyone thought like he did. This was not intolerance, or narrow-mindedness, you see, because the values he wanted to promote were those of fairness and international cooperation and freedom and respect—at least in his mind. Wilson was a strong idealist, and like many idealists, really could not fathom how anyone could object to his policies when they were so self-evidently good. Wilson's certainty about the rightness of his views would eventually lead to his signing legislation in 1918 that criminalized speech putting the government in a bad light—legislation that was opposed by many Republicans, including Theodore Roosevelt.

But despite Wilson's academic background, he had worked long enough in the political world to know that it is often inexpedient to show one's true colors. Thus when he ran for re-election in 1916 in a very tight race with Republican Charles Evans Hughes, Wilson campaigned on the slogan, "He Kept Us Out of War." World War I had been going on for two years by that point, and Americans recoiled in horror from the unprecedented casualties of industrialized warfare and the prospect that, despite the wishes of the citizenry, our political leadership might somehow get us involved.

But Wilson knew what he was doing. He was an admirer of Great Britain—a real Anglophile—and thus ready to believe the propaganda emanating out of London about German "atrocities," which included unfounded claims that Belgian babies were being pinned to church doors by bayonet-wielding German troops (for those conditioned by twenty-first-century norms, substitute the word "kittens" for "babies," and you can understand the moral outrage).

As it turned out, Germany would help Wilson get America into the war. Unrestricted German submarine warfare, in which all boats owned by Allied powers were seen as fair game, led to the loss of American lives on ocean liners such as the *Lusitania*. Americans saw these attacks as the height of barbarity. And British propaganda exacerbated Americans' indignation. The attack on the *Lusitania* was portrayed as an unprovoked, callous act of murder perpetrated on innocent civilians. The fact that the British government was using these same civilians as a shield to transport munitions across the Atlantic was covered up. In fact, Britain hid this fact from the world until modern times, when it finally admitted the presence of munitions on the *Lusitania* and similar British ships carrying American passengers.

Then, when Americans learned of the Zimmermann Telegram—a message from German authorities to Mexico, promising that country large portions of the American Southwest if Mexico would join the Central Powers—it was the final straw. In 1917, Wilson asked for and received a declaration of war from the U.S. Congress.

When the U.S. entered World War I as part of the Allied powers, for the first time we were engaged in a war in which our interests were not paramount. As part of a coalition, we could no longer operate simply in pursuit of what we thought was best for America. Still, once the decision to wage war was made, it was our duty to prosecute that war effectively. Once our nation is at war, there is no substitute for victory and no accolades for half-measures. Even William Jennings Bryan, who had resigned his post as Wilson's Secretary of State back in 1915 in protest over his boss's pro-British leanings, offered his support to the war effort once war was declared. Our soldiers performed admirably and probably saved the Allied cause.

Once the war was over, the question was whether America had reached a real turning point in her approach to foreign affairs. Would we go back to the interests-based foreign policy that had served us so well before 1917, or would we take the

world stage as one of the "Great Powers," engaged in that particularly European pastime of redrawing maps and settling on
"spheres of influence"? This was a
matter of considerable debate in post-
war America. Those who advocated a
return to the status quo antebellum (I
have always wanted to use that phrase,
which just means the way things were
before the war), were derided in terms
that will be very familiar to modern

> **PUTTING AMERICA FIRST**
> Douglas MacArthur
> Edition
>
> "In war there is no substitute for victory."
> **—GENERAL DOUGLAS MacARTHUR**

readers—as selfish, isolationist, backwards, uncharitable, the
same insults applied to anyone wishing to buck the "wisdom"
of the foreign policy elite today. Back then, the big cause our
supposed intellectual betters championed was that of the League
of Nations, joining which would have meant an unprecedented
reduction in American sovereignty for no clear good purpose.
Despite that, even today we are told that American refusal to
join the League was the cause of every manner of evil, probably
even the Great Miami Hurricane of 1926. The League went on
without our participation, and while it was singularly unsuccessful in its goal of keeping world peace, it did make a strong stand
against the use of Esperanto as a universal auxiliary language,
choosing English and French instead.[4]

In 1920, despite the urgings of the now internationalist elites
and their allies in the press, the voters spoke loud and clear when
they elected a candidate—Republican Warren G. Harding—who
promised to return Americans to "normalcy." That included a
modest foreign policy based on the promotion of American interests first. For the rest of the decade and into the thirties, we once

PUTTING AMERICA FIRST
Hiram Johnson
Edition

"It is rare, indeed, that any speech is made in favor of the league which does not bitterly condemn Americans who think of their own country first. We who would protect and preserve our own nation, who loyally and patriotically would hesitate to involve its sons and its future generations in perpetual and continuous warfare, are designated as 'little,' 'selfish,' and 'provincial' Americans—even men without international human sympathy and bereft of world vision. For the first time in our history the jealous guarding of our own, the love of our traditions and our institutions, the passion for our land and our liberty, have become venial sins. We are told that our past affords no precedents; that our history contains no lessons; that all of those who have passed before whose names we revere, spoke but empty words, and that their counsels give no guide. This strange psychological phenomenon, apparently accompanying war, is an unnatural

again pursued the policy bequeathed to us by our forefathers and were scrupulous in staying out of European affairs. Of course—and this became more fuel for the interventionist argument—it was during this time that the Fascists took control of Italy and the National Socialists came to power in Germany. We are told that this is what happens when America stays aloof from throwing her weight around in international political affairs. But I have yet to see a coherent argument for the assumption that American participation in the League or other active involvement in European affairs would have stopped the March on Rome in 1922 or prevented the German people from voting for the Nazi Party in sufficient numbers to give it control of the government in 1933. It seems that resentments arising out of the First World War had more to do with the rise of extremism in between-the-wars Europe than a lack of American representation in Geneva, where the League was based. If anything, a case could be made that U.S. involvement in World War I—guaranteeing, as it did, a clear-cut Allied victory—led especially to the rise of National Socialism. By this argument, it was not America's retreat from European affairs that messed up the world, but rather the fact that we got involved in the first place.

distortion of human intelligence which time alone will heal. May it be cured before the injury it threatens is done to the nation."

—SENATOR HIRAM JOHNSON
(R-Calif.), *Vardaman's Weekly*, June 26, 1919

America began to inch away from neutrality again during the early administration of Franklin Roosevelt, a president whose ideas on international affairs were not dissimilar to those of Woodrow Wilson, who had been Roosevelt's boss when he served as Assistant Secretary of the Navy. But the U.S. was attacked directly on December 7, 1941, and for better or worse Pearl Harbor brought us into a new European war. Judging by our national interests, whether or not the U.S. should have taken the steps it did to lend support to the Allied cause before Pearl Harbor largely depends on whether or not one believes that U.S. involvement in World War II was inevitable. From a present-day perspective, it is a bit of an academic exercise. Once American lives were directly targeted by a member of the Axis powers, like it or not we were at war. Once at war, we had but one duty, and that was to win, and this we did convincingly.

As we have already seen, America stayed involved in Europe after the close of World War II because of the new threat emanating out of Moscow. But this was not, contrary to popular opinion, a radical change in our priorities, but rather a national interest-based policy that sought to defend the Western world (and with it, ourselves) from the threat of annihilation. (Avoidance of annihilation is a pretty basic national interest.) Because the front lines of the Cold War were drawn across Europe, we remained militarily committed on the Old Continent for as long as that existential threat remained.

But Europe did not sit still while our troops, along with some of theirs, sat facing the Warsaw Pact. In 1951, six of the countries that had been most affected by the two most horrendous wars in history—France, (West) Germany, Belgium, Luxembourg, the Netherlands, and Italy—sat down in Paris to create the European Coal and Steel Community. The idea was that strong trade links between the core nations of Western Europe would make it difficult for war to break out between them in the future, while at the same time helping all members of this economic alliance to mutually benefit through increased trade. This economic agreement came to take in more than just coal and steel; a few years later it was transformed into the European Economic Community (EEC), and more countries came to be members. While economic concerns remained at the heart of the EEC, it gradually began to assume a political dimension, eventually becoming what we now know as the European Union (EU), which currently has twenty-eight members—although one of them, the United Kingdom, is in the process of becoming the first country to leave the EU.

I mention the European Union only in passing not because I think it is somehow unimportant for any discussion of Europe. On the contrary, what the EU eventually becomes and who remains to be a part of it is vitally important to the future history of Europe. Will more power from European parliaments be given up to unelected bureaucracies in Brussels, or will power begin to devolve back to the national assemblies deemed to have surrendered it in the first place? Will decidedly non-European countries like Turkey and Morocco become a part of the mix? Will other nations follow the UK out of the EU, or will Great Britain be the "odd man out"? These and other questions concerning national defense, immigration, and what constitutes European values are crucial for any discussion of the future of that continent. But we are not concerned here with Europe's future, as that is rightly a question for Europeans to decide. We are concerned with what America's interests are in Europe, and what we need to do to defend those interests.

When the Communist bloc collapsed in Eastern Europe in 1989–90, leading to the end of the Warsaw Pact and then to the end of the Soviet Union itself in 1991, the reason for U.S. troops to be stationed in Europe came to an end. We had gone to Europe to fight the Nazis and remained to protect ourselves from the Communists. Left-wing media reports to the contrary, the Nazis were decisively defeated in 1945 and would never again serve as a threat to any nation, let alone the United States, even if assorted losers and malcontents have learned that they can magnify their importance far beyond their numbers by attaching a swastika to their arms. Communism as a military threat was neutralized in the early 1990s, even if the political version is making a comeback on college campuses and among those whose historical conscience is primarily formed by Snapchat and Instagram. With the demise of these two threats to our well-being, our need to maintain a military presence in Europe also disappeared. Figures as diverse as Democratic Representative Patricia Schroeder of Colorado and columnist and former Republican presidential candidate Patrick J. Buchanan argued convincingly that while NATO had served our country—and Europe—quite well, the need for this alliance had passed.

But alliances, like all bureaucracies, have a tendency to develop lives of their own. While U.S. troop strength in Europe was reduced in the 1990s and early 2000s from a Cold War high of 400,000, there were still 62,000 active duty U.S. personnel in Europe as of 2016, according to U.S. European Command.[6] Much of this reduction was due to a recognition of the changes in circumstances in Europe as a result of the fall of the Soviet Union, but part of it was due to more pressing U.S. military responsibilities elsewhere. After all, a typical Army brigade is probably more useful someplace where war is actually being waged rather than sitting in Germany waiting for non-existent Warsaw Pact forces to come streaming across the plains of central Europe.

The question remains: Why do we have *any* active duty U.S. military personnel in Europe? The answer lies not in a somehow evolving notion of national interest, but rather in our abandonment of the whole concept of national interest as a basis of foreign policy. The new rationale for America's foreign policy, when one is articulated at all, has come down to something along the lines of "we have the power, so let's use it." National interest is banished to the back of the room. Thus, it is unthinkable to remove troops from Europe, because, well, they are already there. And since they are there, our policy becomes driven by their presence, despite the potential for conflicts in areas that have no bearing on U.S. national interest.

For example, the presence of U.S. troops in Europe was a contributing factor to our leadership in the bombing campaign against Serbia in 1999, during which anywhere from two hundred to five hundred Serbian civilians were killed, depending on which source is consulted. This bombing campaign was not to neutralize a threat to our people nor to advance a vital national interest, but to force Serbia to allow for the secession of one of her historic provinces, Kosovo. (Incidentally, Kosovo is home to a majority Muslim population, and Serbia is Orthodox Christian. This seems to be forgotten in the Left's narrative that the United States' policy is always anti-Muslim at its core. Of course, the fact that we supported a secessionist movement in a territory made up of Muslims seems to be largely forgotten in the Muslim world as well, with the possible exception of Kosovo itself.) Had we been forced to deploy our bombers from the U.S. mainland, rather than from bases in Italy and Germany, we might have reconsidered our active participation in that campaign. Instead, it was too easy to be swept up in emotional claims of atrocities committed, and since we had bombers handy, why not use them?

That we were victorious in forcing Serbia's hand just encouraged the voices of those who envisioned a new role for the United States—righting all the world's wrongs. This is the policy that eventually led to the transformation of our war in Afghanistan

---

PUTTING AMERICA FIRST
Donald Trump
Edition

"If we cannot be properly reimbursed for the tremendous cost of our military protecting other countries, and in many cases the countries I'm talking about are extremely rich.... we have many NATO members that aren't paying their bills."

—**DONALD TRUMP**, *New York Times* interview, July 20, 2016

from one of punishing and deterring would-be aggressors to one of "nation-building"—and to our interminable involvement in Iraq. The problem with a foreign policy based on capability, rather than interest, is that it soon becomes one of perpetual war for ever-elusive peace.

In the post-Cold War world, what are U.S. interests in Europe? Because so many Americans can trace their ancestry back to European countries, there will always be a sort of nostalgic interest in the Old Continent, and that is fine—so long as we remember that our policy should be based on our interests alone. That being said, our politicians, journalists, artists, and popular culture icons will continue to look to Europe for inspiration, just as many Europeans feel a commonality with their cousins' culture across the pond. Good relations with all countries is in everyone's interests, and we should do all we can to encourage friendly relations built on the everyday encounters of real people. Trade, exchanges, study abroad programs, and tourism should all be promoted, as these not only enrich Americans' well-being but also contribute far more to mutual understanding at a grassroots level than any public policy pronouncement ever could. Most of these initiatives are private; they don't cost the government a dime. Where there is government involvement, as in the area of certain exchange visitor programs, we should evaluate them on a case-by-case basis to determine if a particular program serves our interests. It does not need to serve our national interests in a direct way; anything that promotes around the world a more correct view of what America is all about and who the American people are can help to dispel myths that lead to anti-American actions. But we do need to get rid of programs that are actually antithetical to our interests. For example, bring-ing foreign scholars with expressed anti-American sentiments over to meet with similarly-minded radicals is not likely to con-vince these scholars that America is not so bad after all. It merely gives them an American audience for their anti-American views.

Tourism and trade are the big interests that we need to defend in our relationship with Europe. If we take just the coun-tries of the European Union, our trade amounts to $2.7 billion *per day* by 2012 United States Trade Representative estimates. Obviously, both sides benefit from this arrangement, and this gives us flexibility to ensure that the trade is both free and fair. We could do better on the export side, and this is where our people, both in Washington and abroad, should examine how to better open European markets to U.S. goods.

Tourism can be seen as another type of trade—of ideas and impressions, and even (temporarily) of people. In concrete terms it contributes to our well-being by creating profits and jobs. Eight of the top twenty countries sending tourists to the United States are in Europe, and even during the early months of 2017 when the press told us that foreigners were staying away from the United States because, you know, Trump, some two and a half million visitors arrived from Europe alone. Tourism is a major contributor to American prosperity, as tourism is one of the top revenue generators for countless American cities. We need to ensure that legitimate travelers can easily arrive in the United States while at the same time keeping our borders secure. Thus, it is in our national interest to continue strong relation-ships with European police forces and to exchange data on suspected terrorists and other radicals, so that the travel process for legitimate tourists and business visitors is a seamless one. Right now, we have visa-free travel arrangements (the Visa Waiver Program, first established under President Ronald Reagan in 1986) with most European countries, and this has by and large worked well, especially with the implementation of the Electronic System for Travel Authorization (ESTA). There are a few loopholes that could be tightened (I do not want to share those with a broad audience, for obvious reasons), but we can protect our safety and our well-being under the current system, given a few tweaks. Some conservatives have talked of abolishing the Visa Waiver Program because it makes it too easy for illegitimate travelers to slip through. There is no question that a face-to-face interview by a consular officer overseas adds a layer of scrutiny not present when a traveler goes through the Visa Waiver Program. But we should understand that any change from the current system would drastically impede tourism and cause chaos; we simply do not have enough people nor infrastructure to conduct the visa interviews that would be necessary to accommodate our current level of travelers from Visa Waiver countries. With all the goodwill in the world and unlimited funding, it would be years before we could train the personnel and build the buildings necessary for them to do their work. In the meantime, wait times for visas would skyrocket, and we would likely see a dramatic decrease in tourism to the U.S., with a corresponding loss of jobs and revenue in the parts of America dependent on tourism. There may come a time when we hold that to be necessary in order to safeguard our security, but I do not think we are anywhere near that point, and I hope we never are. Rather, continued information sharing—a result of good diplomatic relations especially with European countries—combined with diligence at our borders and an analysis of trends on the ground in each of these countries by our diplomatic and intelligence officials will serve to keep us both safe and prosperous. Rather than abolishing the system, we can suspend it for individual countries if changed circumstances warrant that action. Argentina, for example, used to be a Visa Waiver Country, but changes in that nation's economic situation led to an increase in overstays, which disqualified it from participation in the program. Suspending or eliminating Visa Waiver travel for any country is a tool we can always consider should our security needs outweigh our economic ones. We can also winnow out selected travelers who may otherwise qualify for VWP travel, but who deserve the extra scrutiny that comes with a face-to-face consular interview. For instance, nationals of VWP countries who have also visited one of several "countries of concern," in recent years could be ineligible to travel without a U.S. visa in their passport. This does not mean they could not travel to the U.S., but that our security concerns outweigh the inconvenience to the traveler in having to apply for a visa—and the possible loss in tourist revenue, should he decide not to visit the U.S. as a result. The key here is that the executive branch of our government needs to have the flexibility to respond to real-world threats in real time. We have a good system, overall, but it can always be improved. One of the best ways to improve it is to not second-guess (and clog with endless lawsuits) the motives of the executive when it places restrictions on certain categories of people in the interest of national security. Not only does such second-guessing put our country at greater risk, it creates havoc and confusion among those officers, both from State and Homeland Security, who have to execute the law.

At the same time, we should be hesitant about plans to increase the number of countries that participate in the Visa Waiver Program. Strict requirements, put in place by Congress to ensure border security, apply to any country that the Department of Homeland Security (DHS), in conjunction with the Department of State, declares eligible for VWP travel. Occasionally there are calls by members of Congress or foreign governments to waive those requirements for certain "friendly" governments. This would be a mistake. The current legislation includes requirements that VWP countries agree to report stolen passport information through the proper channels, that they allow our DHS officials to regularly evaluate their security, law enforcement, and immigration apparatus, and that their people who travel to the U.S. do not overstay their welcome in large numbers. To waive any of those requirements is at best a recipe for adding to the numbers of illegal immigrants in our midst; at the worst, it could lead to serious criminal aliens or terrorists being able to establish themselves in the United States. The fact that we hold to these standards has been a point of contention in our relationship with the European Union, since not all members of the EU qualify for visa-free travel. EU officials have several times threatened to force Americans to apply for visas to visit any European country if we don't let all Europeans travel visa-free to our shores, but this is a bluff. EU countries such as Germany and France are, if anything, even less prepared to return to the old way of doing business than we are, and they are far more dependent on international tourism. And the size of our country means that reverting to the old visa system would have a proportionately greater impact on European than American tourism: because in many instances Americans would have to travel hundreds of miles just to get a visa for their two-week trip to Italy, many of them would decide it wasn't worth the trouble, so European tourism would take an even greater hit than American tourism would should we impose a similar requirement on the Europeans. So, we should let the EU continue to bluster and politely but firmly hold to our standards for Visa Waiver travel.

On a side note, one of the ways our Bureau of Consular Affairs at the Department of State works to protect American citizens abroad is through the publication of Travel Alerts and Warnings. These provide valuable information to Americans who are abroad—or planning to go abroad—on potential threats and dangers to their well-being. Needless to say, these safety warnings are not always viewed favorably by the nations that are targeted by them. Not only can they have an adverse effect on tourism; they are sometimes seen as an affront to a nation's honor. But we should resist any and all pressure foreign nations exert on us to water down the information we give our American travelers. Consular Affairs has largely done a good job in keeping politics out of our Travel Alerts and Warnings, and we should make sure that that is always the case.

Where our interests in Europe do NOT lie is in the maintenance of large bodies of troops to protect the European continent. Western Europe is home to some of the world's wealthiest nations, and, until recently, almost none of these nations spent even 2 percent of their Gross Domestic Product (GDP) on national defense. It was far too easy for them to entrust their own protection to their old Uncle Sam across the Atlantic and save their money for other things.

Many European leaders were aghast at the prospect of an American president who did not blindly swear allegiance to the concept of an eternal NATO forever subsidized by the American taxpayer. While Trump has (regretfully) moderated some of his earlier rhetoric about the need for NATO (and under his administration, the alliance increased by one, with the accession of Montenegro), his tough talk has paid off. Prior to Trump's election, only three countries—the U.S., the United Kingdom, and Greece—met the NATO target of spending a minimum of 2 percent of GDP for defense. Since then a number of other countries—Poland, Latvia, Romania, Estonia, and Lithuania—have joined the ranks of those spending at this level for their defense, and according to NATO Secretary General Jens Stoltenberg half of all NATO members should be in compliance by 2025.[7]

This is an admirable start, due in large part to European fears that President Trump might just pull us out of NATO altogether if changes were not made. It shows that looking out for our own interests can lead to positive results in the international arena. During the 2016 presidential election, the conventional wisdom, as articulated by candidate Hillary Clinton, was that any questioning of the need for the NATO alliance was "dangerous."[8] A Clinton presidency would likely have seen NATO member states continue with the same free ride, subsidized by the U.S. Treasury as before. Trump's willingness to look at NATO from the standpoint of America First has already paid dividends, as European states seem to be lining up to show their willingness to make a greater financial contribution to their own defense.

But it is not enough. We need to make it clear that European defense must be taken care of by Europeans. We should of course cooperate in matters of intelligence, and joint training exercises can be mutually beneficial, but we are no longer in the Cold War. American troops should defend American interests. Those will occasionally overlap with European interests, but sometimes they won't. If a crisis arises in, say, the Balkans or the Baltics, it should be the primary responsibility of those who actually live in the region to confront it, rather than depending on Uncle Sam to do the job for them. This means that we should gradually reduce U.S. troop levels in Europe, just as President Eisenhower envisioned during the middle of the Cold War. This should be the case even if we decide—for some unaccountable reason—that participation in NATO still serves our national interest. It is one thing to promise to come to the aid of an ally. It is quite another to assume the majority of defense responsibilities for our allies, regardless of whether or not those responsibilities serve our national interests.

Another area where our interests do NOT lie is in the future of the European Union. As its name implies, this is a European project, not an American one. It should remain so. We don't need our leaders pushing for greater European integration—or, for that matter, lesser. If the European Union leads to some kind of United States of Europe, so be it. That would pose certain challenges, but it would also carry certain advantages. If, on the other hand, the whole experiment of European integration fails and Brexit is followed by Grexit, Italexit, Germexit, Frexit and so forth, then so be it. That outcome would also lead to certain challenges, but also confer certain advantages. We need to respect European space and abide by whatever decision they make for themselves, adjusting our policies accordingly. Whatever circumstances we find ourselves in, our policy pronouncements must be based on what is best for the United States, and not what we in our wisdom think is best for our European brethren or for the world at large. And we should expect the same from the leadership of Europe. They will look after their interests, and we will look after ours, but we will do so as good neighbors, each respecting the other, even where we may not agree.

American agnosticism towards European integration is especially advisable during an era when Eurosceptic movements are on the rise, and not just in the UK. Governments in many of the former Eastern Bloc nations now part of the EU, such as Poland and Hungary, are retreating from blind adherence to dictates coming out of Brussels, seeing them as remarkably similar to dictates coming from their previous Soviet overlords.[9] Again, this is a European issue and thus beyond the scope of this book, but the growth of Euroscepticism serves to underline the complications involved in taking sides in issues that are none of our concern. We should work to maintain good relations with some hypothetical United States of Europe—or with a post-EU Europe broken up into any number of independent nation-states. The choice is the Europeans', not ours.

Our history and culture mean we will always pay more attention to Europe than most other parts of the world. There is nothing wrong with that, so long as we don't succumb to the delusion that our future is somehow determined by the future of Europe. Our forefathers never forgot where they came from, but they also remembered that they were now part of something new.

FIVE

THE UNITED KINGDOM

MATER SI, MAGISTRA NO

The United Kingdom deserves its own stand-alone chapter—not just because of the "special relationship" between the US and the UK that has been so touted over the last seventy years or so, but because much of who we are as Americans originated in Great Britain. We should be cognizant of that fact and even celebrate it, but we should not get it in our heads that we necessarily have to follow the British example in our national development. Specifically, the end of the British Empire should not be seen as justifying the creation of an American one.

I will not go into a long discussion of our War of Independence, nor

> **PUTTING AMERICA FIRST**
> Thomas Jefferson Edition
>
> "That these United Colonies are, and of Right ought to be Free and Independent States; that they are Absolved from all Allegiance to the British Crown, and that all political connection between them and the State of Great Britain, is and ought to be totally dissolved."
>
> —**THOMAS JEFFERSON**, Declaration of Independence, 1776

recount the events that led to our second conflict with Great Britain, the War of 1812. This history is generally well known, at least among people who have actually read books. (I realize that excludes large segments of the crowds currently clamoring for eliminating our national and regional symbols, but they probably won't read this either.) Suffice it to say that the people of our part of the North American continent went from being British subjects to citizens of their respective states and the United States in rather short order. Our relationship with the Mother Country would remain quite acrimonious for a long time. As I mentioned before, for several generations from the founding of our country, most Americans would see the United Kingdom as the greatest threat to American security.

But circumstances change, and yesterday's enemy can be tomorrow's ally. By the late nineteenth century, most Americans no longer saw Britain as an adversary. Many prominent Americans, in fact, looked on British imperialism with approval, believing that a duty to civilize the "dark" corners of the globe was "the white man's burden." Once America acquired her own small empire after the Spanish-American War, Anglophiles of various stripes created the narrative of the "special relationship." A quick survey of the last names of most U.S. politicians at the time shows that Americans of English ancestry still predominated in the halls of power. A kinship of blood, plus a shared language and a mostly Protestant culture, led many prominent figures of the time to believe that America and Britain could stand side by side in bringing peace and prosperity to the benighted peoples of the world. When the First World War broke out, many of these men prayed for Allied victory, and a few particularly Anglophile

Americans even volunteered in Canadian and French units to do their bit.

The man in the street, however, did not automatically feel kinship with the British. We had, after all, fought two wars against them. In addition, certain groups of Americans—notably those of Irish and German origin—had no reason to look on the people of Britain as blood-brethren even if our overall culture owed much to England. But once we became involved in World War I, American attitudes toward the British began to change. Our alliance soon passed to friendship. Ever since then, most Americans put the United Kingdom in a special category occupied by no other nation, with the possible exceptions of Canada and Australia.

This is all well and good. Friendly relations with any country are desirable, especially one with whom we share so much history and from whom we derive so many of our basic civic values. The fact that we share a native language also helps—even if we sometimes mean different things by the same words.

But we should not let close ties lead us to believe that we have identical interests. Even in the post-World War II period, the U.S. and Great Britain have been at odds on foreign policy. One rather dramatic example of this was the 1956 Suez Crisis when, in a surprise move, Egyptian leader Gamal Abdel Nasser nationalized the Suez Canal. In response British forces, working with the French and the Israelis, intervened militarily against Egypt and sought Nasser's overthrow. The United States, in the midst of the Cold War with the Soviet Union, feared that this attack on Egypt could turn the entire Arab world to the USSR So working together with our Soviet adversaries, we pressured the invading nations, including Britain, to withdraw their forces from Egypt.

We can take important lessons from the Suez Crisis. To Americans of 1956, only eleven years removed from World War II, the British were, in the overall scheme of things, the "good guys." If we as a nation had had to choose another nation with which to share a beer (assuming that nations could drink beer), Britain would have been high on the list—would certainly have beat out Egypt every time. But even though the British were our "friends," it was not in our interest to back them in 1956. Almost simultaneous with the Suez Crisis was the Soviet invasion of Hungary, in which the USSR forcibly put down dissent in that Soviet satellite country. An expanding Soviet threat needed to be curtailed in any way possible short of war (since all-out war between the nuclear super-powers would have had catastrophic consequences for every person on the planet). Reigning in our British friends was a necessary measure to thwart Soviet expansionism into the Middle East. In short, it was not in our national interest to back the British, despite our alliance with them and our cultural and ideological ties.

At other times our interests have indeed meshed. Early in our history President James Monroe, in an unabashedly bold move for such a young country, declared the entire Western Hemisphere off-limits to European powers, with the exception of those colonies and dependencies already in existence at the time of his declaration of what came to be known as the Monroe Doctrine.

A century and a half later, in 1982, Argentinian forces asserted an early nineteenth-century claim to the islands the

Argentines called the Malvinas—known in the rest of the world as the Falkland Islands—and launched an invasion of that British dependency. According to Miles S. Pendleton, Deputy Director of the Office of Northern European Affairs at the U.S. Department of State, then–Secretary of State Alexander Haig initially cited the Monroe Doctrine as the basis for American efforts to prevent a British military response.[1] But when Argentina refused to negotiate, US support quickly swung to the United Kingdom. Many observers attribute the change to the close personal relationship between President Ronald Reagan and British Prime Minister Margaret Thatcher, but the main reason for our rejection of the Argentine claim was that it was in our national interest to do so. Despite Argentina's attempt to establish an historical right to the Falklands, Britain had ruled the islands for over one hundred and fifty years. What is more, the residents of those islands, many of whose families had been there for generations, almost uniformly supported British rule. When Argentina refused to negotiate its claim and resorted to military force, it was not in the United States' interest to be seen as rewarding aggression, especially in the midst of a Cold War with the Soviet Union. In addition, our support for the United Kingdom was not a violation of the Monroe Doctrine, despite the fact that it was a conflict between a European and an American power, because back to the time of President Monroe himself we had allowed for European powers to maintain those possessions they had in the Western Hemisphere that had not agitated for independence. There is no evidence that the Falklanders ever wished to be independent of Great Britain, let alone become a part of Argentina.

Popular mythology aside, we don't automatically back the British whenever they face a challenge. We have supported the UK and will continue to do so when our mutual interests coincide, and that is how it should be. Sentimentalism has no place in foreign affairs, as it leads us into conflicts that are none of our concern and puts American lives and well-being at risk.

All of that being said, our relationship with the United Kingdom will likely become ever more important in the coming years, especially as the UK pulls out of the European Union. It will become a more normal, bilateral relationship without the bothersome filter of a bloated continental bureaucracy to complicate things. Our views of the rule of law are similar—the common law is, after all, a British invention—and in recent years our people have been targeted by some of the same radical Islamic terrorist forces. We differ on how we deal with those threats at home—Americans would be nervous at the level of CCTV monitoring that exists in Britain, for example—but we are more likely to come to agreement with the UK on common policies to deal with threats outside our borders than we would with most other countries. We should continue close cooperation with British police officials and military forces to combat the powers seeking to do us harm. This includes offers of assistance in the wake of terrorist attacks, since the perpetrators involved are likely to be our enemies as well.

Another area of national interest in our relations with the United Kingdom is in foreign trade. Not only is our mutual trade substantial but—as is unfortunately not the case with many other nations—it is balanced. That is to say, our imports to Britain and exports from the British nearly match each year, according to

U.S. Census Bureau figures. The United Kingdom is not only a valuable trading partner: it is by and large a fair one. With the UK's departure from the European Union, a well-negotiated trade deal that continues this trend is in both of our countries' interests.

Tourism is another big factor in our bilateral relationship. Nearly 10 percent of British jobs are related to tourism, and Americans are number one when it comes to the amount of money spent on British holidays.[2] Likewise, more Britons visit America than any other country besides Canada and Mexico (with whom, after all, we share land borders), with nearly five million of them making temporary visits to the US in 2015 alone.[3] Our common English language and similar cultures will likely always keep these numbers high, but we should do all we can as a country to promote tourism from the United Kingdom.

> **PUTTING BRITAIN FIRST**
> Margaret Thatcher Edition
>
> "We have not successfully rolled back the frontiers of the state in Britain, only to see them re-imposed at a European level, with a European super-state exercising a new dominance from Brussels."
>
> —**MARGARET THATCHER**, speech to the College of Europe, Bruges, Belgium, September 20, 1988

We should recognize, however, that the UK, like the United States, is a highly diverse country. There are small but significant home-grown terror cells within the radical Islamic community in Great Britain. It should be noted that many of the attackers in the worst terrorist actions on British soil since 9/11 were, in fact, citizens of the UK. They may also target America. For example, the infamous "shoe bomber," Richard Reid, a.k.a, Abdel Rahim, was born in England. We need to continue our strong relationship with British security forces to ensure that those responsible for border security are alerted to potential threats such as these. We also need not be afraid to revisit the categories of people we exclude from participation in the Visa Waiver Program, as has been done in the first months of the Trump administration. We can't let mindless "fairness" to foreigners overrule the safety and security of our own citizens, to whom we owe our first allegiance. In a relationship as close as ours is to the United Kingdom, there is sometimes a hesitancy to enact policies that might be perceived as "hurtful" to the pride of a friendly nation. However, our primary responsibility is to our own citizens and to their safety.

And we should be wary of the siren song that portrays the United States as some sort of replacement for the British Empire. Current supporters of this view are not explicitly racialist and colonialist, as the jingoes a few generations ago who talked about taking up "the white man's burden" were. Today's boosters of American imperialism (thought they don't typically call it that) hold that the Anglo-American values of democracy and rule of law should be promoted at the four corners of the world. This was once the job of the British Empire, but since it no longer exists, the torch has been passed to Britain's eldest daughter, the United States. We have an obligation to promote this secular gospel everywhere, even to those who do not want to hear it.

Leaving aside the fact recent events in the United States have shown that Americans no longer even agree among ourselves what democracy is, the belief that we are somehow endowed with the duty of bringing democratic rule to an unappreciative world population is a recipe for continuous conflict—and hatred for our country in every distant land. That has been amply demonstrated in the decade and a half since we first went to war in Afghanistan and Iraq. In a 2007 column, Patrick J. Buchanan accurately labeled this belief "democratism" and said that it, like Communism and Fascism, was an ideology doomed to failure.[4] Democratism poses as a national interest–based foreign policy: the justification being that once "the People" are in charge every-where, all will be Peace and Universal Brotherhood—just as Socialism promised Utopia once the Workers finally controlled the Means of Production (all capitalized, because, well, it is just so Sincere!). But pie in the sky is not a reasonable basis for a foreign policy. Democracy promotion by the United States should cease, as it is counterproductive to our interests. It creates resent-ments, and these resentments put real live Americans (as opposed to abstract ideas) at risk. The creation of an American Empire, even an informal one, is not in our national interest.

SIX

CHINA

THE SLEEPING GIANT

China is the most populous country on Earth, with well over a billion people living within its borders. It is a wealthy country. According to 2016 figures from the World Bank, it has the second largest GDP of any single country, after the United States, and those numbers are expected to grow.[1] Its history goes back thousands of years, and its culture has fascinated people from around the world for almost as long. Officially Communist, its people are unabashedly consumerist. There are nearly forty Gucci stores in China, for example. While it bills itself as an atheistic state, Buddhist and Taoist temples are crowded with worshippers at all hours of the day, and Christian churches, both officially sanctioned and underground, are growing by leaps and bounds—so much so that experts speculate that by 2030 China may have more churchgoers than the United States.[2]

To say that China is a highly complex society marked by contradictions would be an understatement, and the history of our relationship is equally complex. America's first diplomatic agreement with the Chinese government, the Treaty of Wangxia, dates back to 1845. Like most of our early dealings with China, it mainly concerned trade. Unlike the European powers of that time, the United States had no territorial designs on China, and we were not interested in monopolizing Chinese trade, but rather preferred an open door policy. Thus by and large we were not sucked into the European-Chinese wars of the nineteenth century, except for a few minor actions during the Second Opium War (1856–1860) during which the U.S. Navy and Marines engaged Chinese troops near Guangzhou (Canton) while they were in the area providing protection for U.S. citizens.

Americans began to pay more attention to China in the years just before and after our Civil War. The California Gold Rush of 1849 and similar events brought in tens of thousands of Chinese, some seeking their fortune in the mines and others setting up shop to cater to the needs of the new settlers. Many went into the laundry business, even in the older Eastern states, while others opened restaurants, leading to the creation of a distinctive American Chinese cuisine that is different from the food eaten in China itself. Uncontrolled immigration from China led to tensions in the Western States, which in turn led to the passage of the Chinese Exclusion Act of 1882. This law did not completely cut off Chinese immigration to the U.S. but reduced it to a trickle. While it was a sore point with the Imperial Chinese government, there was little China could do about it, and it would remain in effect until the 1940s, when the exigencies of World War II, in which China was an ally, led to its repeal.

Despite cutting off the flow of Chinese workers to the U.S., Americans continued to trade with China, and we maintained diplomatic relations with the Imperial Chinese government. As we have already seen, in 1900 U.S. troops joined an international coalition of forces to rescue our diplomats from probable murder by the Society of Righteous Fists, otherwise known as the Boxers. But compared to our British, French, German, Russian, and especially Japanese counterparts, we stayed largely aloof from the internal affairs of China. These countries, noting the decline of the Imperial Chinese government, took advantage of China's weakness for their own gain. The United States, despite taking on Pacific territories after the Spanish-American War, did not see it as in her interest to establish a beachhead on the Chinese mainland, as so many other countries were doing. (Incidentally, the most famous Chinese beer in the world, Tsingtao, was actually created by German settlers in one of those foreign enclaves, the modern Chinese city of Qingdao.)

When the Chinese monarchy was overthrown in 1911, the United States recognized the new republic and continued its largely disinterested policy towards China. America was focused on trade and friendly relations with all nations at the time. And China was in no position to make strong alliances or play an important role in world affairs. In fact, China was not fully unified until the late twenties, following more than a decade of instability and infighting within China after the fall of the Imperial government. But World War II and its aftermath would dramatically change U.S. policy towards China.

The Second World War effectively began in China in 1937, when Japanese troops launched a full-scale invasion of the

Chinese mainland. Chinese and Japanese troops had battled off and on all through the decade of the 1930s, with Japan making territorial inroads, but from 1937 to 1945 it was all-out war between these two Asian powers. When the United States entered World War II in 1941, China became our ally in the fight against the Axis.

Complicating matters was a Chinese Communist insurgency that sought to take control of the Chinese government from Nationalist forces. Occasionally fighting together against the Japanese, they also battled each other from time to time, and after the end of World War II full-scale civil war erupted and lasted until the end of the 1940s, leaving millions dead and leading to the establishment of a Communist government in Beijing, with Nationalist forces establishing a rump regime in Taiwan. The birth of "Red China" at the beginning of the Cold War was of great concern to American policymakers, as it was seen as part of international Soviet-inspired expansion of Communism at the expense of the free world. Even so, the United States did not intervene to save the Nationalist government of China, as the cost would have been too high. The American public was not ready to enter such a conflict so soon after World War II, especially as doing so would have meant running the risk of open war with the Soviet Union. Our actions, therefore, were reminiscent of our decision to bring U.S. forces home from Russia in 1920, even though we would have liked to see the demise of Communism there as well. We did, however, recognize the Taiwan government as the legitimate government of China for the next thirty years. During a period of time when mainland China was an economic basket case, we could effectively register our displeasure with the Communist take-over of China by simply refusing to acknowledge it. This hurt no national interest of our own and signaled our unwillingness to lend legitimacy to the worldwide Communist movement then on the rise. This too mirrored our actions after the Bolsheviks came to power in Moscow, when we held on recognition until we saw that the Revolution was a fait accompli .

It would not be long, though, before U.S. and Chinese troops came to blows. In the neighboring Korean peninsula, only recently granted independence after years of Japanese domination, the country had been split into two halves as a Communist insurgency there, inspired by China, took control of the north. In 1950 North Korea invaded South Korea and came very close to unifying the peninsula under Marxist rule. The United States, as part of its strategy of containing Communism (and thus protecting America from eventual Communist takeover), led a United Nations coalition of forces that inflicted decisive defeats on North Korea and could have unified the peninsula under democratic rule—had not China intervened as well. For the next two years, American and allied forces battled Chinese troops. Nearly forty thousand Americans perished in that conflict, as well as perhaps two hundred thousand Chinese. The result of that war is the situation we have today: a return to the division of the peninsula into two halves.

Despite our official non-recognition of Communist China, following the Korean War we kept our diplomatic channels open with Beijing, and this led to warmer ties in the late 1960s and early 1970s. For one thing, the Chinese government was largely inwardly-focused during this time, as the horrors of the Cultural

Revolution were being inflicted on the Chinese populace. For another, Soviet-Chinese tensions (which led to a brief border war in 1969) meant that the forces of Communism were no longer monolithic, so that a softening of our position towards Beijing could serve our interests in further containing a still powerfully aggressive Soviet Union.

Under the administration of Richard Nixon, once a vehement opponent of Red China, the United States began to open up to Beijing. The thaw in relations began with trade deals and later led to an exchange of athletes, first in the field of table tennis—so that this overture was referred to as "ping-pong diplomacy." The culmination of Nixon's efforts came about in 1972 with his visit to China, a gesture so dramatic that it even inspired an opera (*Nixon in China*, by John Adams). That a life-long anti-Communist like Nixon should be the first American president to visit the People's Republic is an illustration of national interest foreign policy in action. Because China had parted ways with our principal adversary, the Soviet Union, it was important for us to normalize our relations with China, both for reasons of national security and to take advantage of the opportunity to open the Chinese market to American goods (and vice versa—unfortunately more vice versa, as it has turned out; trade between our two countries is seriously unbalanced in China's favor, not least because of the Communists' many unfair trade practices). Just as we gave up our hatred of Great Britain in the nineteenth century when the United Kingdom was no longer seen as a threat and as, in more recent times, Germany went from enemy to ally during the course of the 1940s, so too our hostility to China was lessened as we realized that it was no longer in our interest to keep the Chinese at arm's length. The opening to mainland China culminated a few years after Nixon's visit with the recognition of the People's Republic of China as the legitimate government of that nation. At the time many conservatives blasted our switch of recognition from Taipei to Beijing—coming, as it did, under the generally feckless administration of Jimmy Carter. But this move was consistent with our earliest foreign policy initiatives, in which we recognized the de facto government rather than the one we wished was in place. Again, sentimentalism has no place in the formulation of foreign policy, which must be based on what is best for the American people.

The opening up to China continued through the 1980s. In 1989, as pro-democracy forces brought an end to Communism in the former Warsaw Pact nations, China took no chances and bloodily suppressed its own dissident movement, with massacres in Tiananmen Square and elsewhere across the country. This caused a period of renewed frosty relations, but ties warmed up again in the 1990s and 2000s, even though disputes over trade and Chinese currency manipulation (which allows Chinese products to be sold at artificially low prices), have led to tensions on the economic front.

The election of Donald Trump focused a spotlight on U.S.-China relations because of Trump's claims that China was not playing fair when it came to trade, allegations that bear

PUTTING AMERICA FIRST
James Monroe Edition

"Our policy...is...to consider the government de facto as the legitimate government for us; to cultivate friendly relations with it, and to preserve those relations by a frank, firm, and manly policy, meeting in all instances the just claims of every power, submitting to injuries from none."

—**JAMES MONROE**, 1823 Address to Congress

more than a kernel of truth. Trade deficits with China run in the hundreds of billions of dollars each year.[3] While lower Chinese wages certainly play a role, at least until recently currency manipulation was also to blame. When Trump assumed office and became the first president since 1979 to directly contact the president of the Republic of China (Taiwan), he was telegraphing to the Chinese government that everything was on the table if the Chinese did not work with the United States to ensure a mutually beneficial trade relationship.

There is no question that China today is a major economic powerhouse seeking to expand its influence across the world. During my time in southern Iraq during Operation Iraqi Freedom, the common perception was that Iran was dumping goods in order to gain control over the local economy. As a matter of fact, it was not the Iranians but rather the Chinese whose goods were the most predominant in the local markets, and their national petroleum company (CNPC) was soon setting up shop in the oil fields. The Chinese are also operating in a big way in Africa.[4] Unlike U.S. efforts in Africa, which tend to be more overtly political, China's efforts at promoting goodwill appear to be almost entirely economic in orientation, and thus are often seen in a more positive light by the Africans themselves. China works to develop African infrastructure in order to create more markets for Chinese goods but doing so betters the lives of the

PUTTING AMERICA FIRST
Donald Trump
Edition

"It's not like I'm anti-China. I just think it's ridiculous that we allow them to do what they're doing to this country, with the manipulation of the currency.... "

—**DONALD TRUMP**, accepting the presidential nomination at the Republican Convention, July 21, 2016

Africans in the meantime. Each side gets something from the deal, and this is an equation that people from trading cultures understand.

Of course, the more Chinese goods that are bought across the world, the less opportunity there is to sell American goods. It would be in our national interest to take a page from the Chinese model and shift some of our foreign aid efforts away from things such as democracy promotion and women's empowerment, focusing instead on projects that will both benefit the recipients in the short term and also serve to make the United States a more prosperous nation in the long run. I am not talking about neo-colonial operations that work only for our own benefit, but rather projects where it is clear from the outset that each side is getting something from the deal. That's the kind of outreach to developing countries that the Chinese have been engaged in for some time.

In our own commerce with China, we must, as President Trump has stated repeatedly, seek a fair deal. We need to look beyond the short term and not rule out any economic weapons we have in our arsenal, including tariffs. Should we determine that any portion of our trade deficit is caused by unfair Chinese trade practices—currency manipulation, protectionism designed to artificially support state-owned industries, or dumping of underpriced goods—we must not be afraid to impose tariffs on Chinese products. This will lead to Chinese products becoming less desirable and cut into Chinese profits while at the same time giving a boost to American-made goods in the same categories. Yes, it will lead to a short-term increase in prices, but this should be more than made up for by an increase in American manufacturing jobs.

In any event, knowing that the United States is willing to take such steps would likely ensure that Chinese trade practices with the United States become more transparent. Because of the better pay and more humane working conditions of the American laborer, we may never completely eliminate our trade deficit with China, but we should not be content to allow our manufacturing base, and with it, good blue collar jobs, to be permanently off-shored.

On the security side, we do not face an immediate conventional threat from China. The possibility of Chinese and American troops facing each other, as we did in the Korean War, seems remote, as it is in neither of our interests to do so. That being said, we should not underestimate the capability of the Chinese military, especially in the area of sensitive technologies. We should continue to monitor the types of technologies we allow to be sold to China or to companies doing business in China, realizing that anyone operating in China is likely to have no secrets from the government in Beijing—as any foreigner who has ever visited China will confirm. We need good intelligence on Chinese military capabilities and how those capabilities may be effectively countered, not because we foresee war with China—God forbid!—but because the best way to keep our people safe is to be prepared to defend them in any eventuality, however remote.

A particularly tricky area in this regard involves our historical commitment to the freedom of the seas. China claims large swaths of ocean that are recognized by the rest of the world community as international waters or as territory belonging to China's neighbors. As I mentioned in chapter two, the United States has deployed our naval forces to some of those areas in dispute on various occasions over the past several years. As one of the world's largest trading nations, it is in our national interest that the international sea lanes of the world remain open. We do not need a permanent presence in those areas, but we need to remind China—and her neighbors—that we will not stand idly by when any nation threatens to appropriate to herself that which belongs to all. We don't do it as the "world's policeman," and still less as the protector of the weak and powerless, but rather because maritime trade is intrinsically dependent on freedom of navigation. Allowing other nations or non-state actors to limit that freedom puts our entire way of life in the hands of those who do not necessarily look out for our own best interests. Hence, we cannot acquiesce to China's threats to the freedom of the seas. We need to make our intentions clear—and also keep the channels of communications with the Chinese open.

We should maintain good diplomatic relations with Beijing. We must defend our rights and prerogatives, whether in the area of trade or in security or in the freedom to travel in international waters, but we should also remain engaged with the Chinese government. Our worldviews may be dramatically different, but we do share some common concerns. China has a large Muslim minority, many of whom reside in the Xinjiang Region in China's Northwest, and this province has seen jihadi violence in recent years, some of which has spilled over into other parts of China. As we work to neutralize threats by Islamic extremists against our own security, we should remember that we have a potential partner in a China that faces similar threats.

Another area of mutual concern is an aggressive North Korea. China is about the only friend North Korea has these days, and that "friendship" is based more on mutual fear than shared values. Should China turn its back on North Korea, Pyongyang would be even more destitute than it is now. (Then not only would their people be literally starving to death, they might not even have enough resources to build important things like missiles and huge monuments!) China fears that collapse—economic or political—in North Korea would lead to a refugee crisis that would have a negative impact on the Chinese economy. So China tolerates North Korea, but there are signs that that toleration will go only so far. According to media reports, the Chinese recently—in the context of the latest round of threats coming out of Pyongyang—made it clear that they would defend North Korea from American aggression but were quick to add that they would remain neutral in the event of a North Korean first strike. Since the lunatics that run North Korea do on occasion listen to the Chinese, it is in our interest to keep channels of communication open.

President Trump seems to understand the vital role that China plays in keeping the cauldron that is North Korea from overflowing. While cracking down on unfair trade practices has been a cornerstone of the president's economic policy and China is among the worst offenders in this area, Donald Trump realizes that the benefits of fair trade with China would be swiftly negated by the outbreak of war with North Korea. "China's hurting us badly on trade, but I have been soft on China because the only thing more important to me than trade is war," President Trump declared in an interview with the *New York Times* at the end of 2017.[5]

Far from being a retreat from principle, this is merely an acknowledgment that war, especially nuclear war, would unleash far greater evils than the temporary tolerance of unfair trade. Just as the right to life supersedes other rights, the preservation of peace counts for more than obtaining a fair trade deal. First things first—if the Chinese work as responsible partners, effectively quarantining North Korea's threat to the region, we can hold off on punitive measures for their unfair trade practices, at least for now. But we should also make it clear that the trade issue is not off the table, and that we will revisit it at the appropriate time. For example, while not specifically directed at China, Trump's recent tariffs on foreign steel and aluminum show the administration's continued commitment to a fair deal for American workers and manufacturers in the trade arena. Regarding the U.S.-China trade relationship, if we determine that China's actions are not contributing to reining in the excesses of the Pyongyang regime, then all bets are off. Putting American First does not mean blind adherence to a pre-set program, but rather pragmatically assessing what course of action will likely bring the greatest good for our people.

China and the United States will probably view each other with great suspicion for the foreseeable future. Simply put, we do not trust each other. But a lack of trust need not rule out good relations in ordinary times, and even cooperation where we each can derive an advantage from it. We should always let China know where our national interests lie and refrain from the temptation to interfere where they don't. We don't have to like each other, but it is in our national interest that we get along.

SEVEN

JAPAN AND KOREA

NICE PEOPLE, COOL CARS, TRENDY CUISINE. ANYTHING ELSE?

There are few if any Asian countries that Americans view as favorably as South Korea and Japan. They are seen as non-threatening—despite the fact that, in the last seventy-five years, we went to war against one of them and on behalf of the other. Not only that, but we have had serious trade issues with both countries in more recent years. Part of our good feelings toward the Japanese and South Koreans is due to the Cold War, during which both countries were seen as stalwart anti-Communist allies, particularly South Korea, which was nearly taken over by its Marxist neighbor. Japan was also seen as "safe." With an exploding capitalist economy and an ancestral aversion to China, the largest Communist country in the neighborhood, the chances of the Japanese being lost to the free West seemed slim ("Japanese Red Army" terrorists in the 1970s notwithstanding).

Our close relationship with both of these countries is a recent phenomenon, though. Before the 1850s, we did not even have a trade relationship with either, as both Korea and Japan maintained insular policies of closure to the world, allowing only limited trade with selected partners. The voyages of Commodore Matthew Perry in 1853 and 1854 led to the signing of the first U.S.-Japanese trade agreement. Korea remained hostile to Western trade for another twenty years or so, even firing on American ships that were in the area to protect U.S. interests in the early 1870s. The attack led to a punitive expedition by U.S. Navy and Marine forces in which American and Korean troops came to blows for the first time. This expedition did not lead to an opening of Korea, but later in the decade the growing influence of Japan, which had once dominated the Korean peninsula, led to an end to Korean isolation from the world. Shortly thereafter we signed a trade agreement with the Koreans—which became moot when the Japanese once again took over; Japan occupied Korea until the end of World War II.

U.S. forces utterly defeated Japan, our original enemy in World War II, in a decisive way rarely seen in history. Two atomic bombs incinerated tens of thousands of Japanese men, women, and children. There is disagreement over whether the United States had a moral right to use such a weapon against civilians, but little dispute over the results of the bombing, which ended the war and had a profound effect on the Japanese psyche. We occupied Japan until 1952, imposing a parliamentary democracy that endures to this day—one of our few successes in "nation-building." By the time sovereignty was restored to Japan, it was a completely different place from the aggressive nation of Tojo and the warlords. In any event, the new threat from international Communism allowed both sides to let bygones be bygones and stand together as allies through the Cold War, an alliance cemented by the signing of the U.S.-Japan Treaty of Mutual Cooperation and Security in 1960.

U.S. action was even more decisive in the case of South Korea. Absent U.S. involvement in the Korean War, there would likely be no South Korea today. That helps explain why, according to a 2014 BBC poll, some 58 percent of South Koreans have a positive impression of American influence, versus just over a quarter who have negative views.[1] These numbers are down from polls done in previous years, but still represent a lingering appreciation for the United States in the mind of the average Korean.

And Americans don't just view Koreans and Japanese positively—we think they're hip. Americans—especially our young people—have been captivated by one trend after another from Japan: sushi, Pokémon, and anime cartoons. Korean culture has also been making inroads in recent years, at least in larger American cities, where "bibambap" is no longer the sound a ball makes when bouncing off a hard surface but rather a tasty Korean rice bowl dish. Appreciation for all things Japanese and Korean is rife among sophisticated young Americans. And it is hard to dislike someone you consider to be cool.

It is certainly laudable that our countries have good relations and that our people get along. Huge revenues are generated by Japanese and South Korean tourists to the U.S. In 2016, more than two and a half million Japanese and nearly two million South Koreans came to the United States, making Japan fourth and South Korea seventh in the number of visitors to the U.S.[2]

We should continue to promote the United States as a destination in those countries. This is another example of where the Visa Waiver Program works quite well. While we should always be vigilant, Japanese and South Korean visitors pose a very low threat to our security or well-being. Since their citizens tend to comply with the terms of their admission into the United States, they do not overstay their welcome and contribute to the problem of illegal aliens in our midst.

But we should not let smiling faces and happy relationships blind us to defending our national interest in our interaction with these two countries. We run a trade deficit with both South Korea and Japan. While not nearly as dramatic as our trade deficit with China, these imbalances are a matter of concern, especially in light of the U.S.-South Korea Free Trade Agreement (KORUS) that entered into effect in 2012 during Barack Obama's administration. President Trump has been critical of this trade deal, which appears to have been made with the idea of aiding multinational corporations and key South Korean industries, rather than safeguarding our own economic interests. Opposition to the deal is particularly vehement in the U.S. textile industry, which fears it could sink this vital U.S. manufacturing sector.[3] Some economists estimate that over 150,000 jobs could be lost as a result of this agreement.[4] It was hoped that lower Korean tariffs would benefit U.S. automakers, but sales of American cars in South Korea are dwarfed by the number of Korean vehicles sold in the United States. The reduction of Korean tariffs on certain American goods has not made a big difference in terms of American jobs, and some sectors, such as rice, remain protected. This appears to be a case where free trade ideology—and crony capitalist reality—have interfered with the safeguarding of our national interest. Trump's insistence that we should get a better deal for American workers than was offered by this accord caused South Korean officials to fear that we would pull out of KORUS altogether. In a victory for an America First trading policy, Seoul agreed to renegotiate this agreement with Washington, and preliminary talks were held in January 2018. A new deal will not happen overnight, but even the opening of these negotiations is solid evidence of Trump's commitment to trade that is both free *and* fair—and the power of an "America First" foreign policy to change facts on the ground.

Seeking to renegotiate to get a better deal for America represents a dramatic break with the orthodoxy that has governed both parties in recent decades. A key takeaway here is that nothing stops us from doing better than we have in the past. The media narrative peddled by the free-trade-über-alles crowd and their allies in the stop-Trump-at-any-cost camp is that other countries won't play ball with us if we insist on trade agreements that directly benefit American workers and manufacturing. The fact is that, in the same way that other countries have things we want—whether it be in terms of goods or markets—we have things they want. Just as we should expect them to act out of their own national self-interest, it should come as no surprise to them when we wish to do the same. Somehow, the conventional wisdom has been that other nations can take protectionist measures for their own benefit but the sky will fall on the United States should we follow their examples. Under Donald Trump, however, our position on trade is no longer a passive one, marked by resignation to America losing her position as an industrial power, with the role of government merely to "helping people understand the realities of the world in a positive way," as former president George W. Bush once remarked in reference to NAFTA.[5] As Donald Trump seems to understand, we should make trade agreements—or any agreements, for that matter—if and only if they serve our national interest.

In the case of Japan, tariffs are not the key barrier to trade, according to the U.S. Department of Commerce.[6] Instead American manufacturers face subtle forms of discrimination against foreign-made goods, such as the requirement that a company demonstrate prior experience in the Japanese market. In addition, certain Japanese regulations favor goods produced domestically. It is certainly within Japan's rights to do all it can to promote its own industry, and if I were Japanese I would likely applaud these efforts. The key thing to remember, though, is that we all too often turn a blind eye to these kinds of trade obstacles when opening up our own country to imported products. Free trade is well and good, but not when it is only practiced by one side. Formal or informal trade barriers to American companies selling on the Japanese market should be brought down, or, if they can't be, we should erect similar barriers for the benefit of our own industries and the workers who produce our goods.

Countless trade "experts" tell us that responding in kind will be devastating for the American economy, but they never seem to be able to explain why these kinds

PUTTING AMERICA FIRST
Donald Trump Edition

"I want trade deals, but they have to be great for the United States and our workers. We don't make great deals anymore, but we will once I'm president."

—**DONALD TRUMP**, remarks on withdrawing from the Paris climate agreement, June 1, 2017

of protectionist measures seem to work very well for countries like Japan.

Defense is another one-way street in our relationship with both Japan and South Korea. During the Cold War it was in our national interest to keep troops defending both countries in order to prevent either China or the Soviet Union from gaining a bridgehead from which to better attack our interests. We were not there out of the goodness of our hearts, but because we believed that, should World War Three break out, it would be better to do the fighting in Seoul or Tokyo than in San Francisco or New York. And we were concerned that the weakness of these two countries in the wake of World War II and the Korean War made them easy targets for Communist aggression.

We are no longer in the Cold War, no matter what some U.S. senators would have us believe. This does not mean that threats to the security of South Korea or Japan do not exist, merely that the calculus with respect to confronting them has changed.

Everyone would agree that North Korea poses the greatest threat to South Korean security, just as it did in 1950. However, unlike in 1950, South Korea is a wealthy country today. According to the World Bank, it spends 2.6 percent of its vast GDP on defense and has a well-developed military that could stand up to North Korea on its own. While we hope that no new conflict breaks out between Pyongyang and Seoul, there is no reason why Americans should be the first casualties in any replay of the Korean War, especially when a portion of the South Korean public is ambivalent about our presence in their country. Obviously, we cannot pull out our troops overnight lest we send the wrong signal to both Koreas, but this should be our long-term goal.

That being said, there is no reason why we cannot talk with North Korea if North Korea is open to doing so. Sitting down with one's adversaries to see if an agreement can be reached confers no legitimacy on the positions of that adversary. We are not in a war where we are demanding unconditional surrender (and should we settle for nothing less than unconditional surrender, then war is likely to be the only result). While President Trump has been outspoken in his criticism of the North Korean leadership, he stunned many observers in March 2018 when he expressed his support for a face-to-face meeting with Kim Jong Un. Liberal commentators, who in the past had excoriated Trump over his bellicose statements on North Korea,[7] put in a quandary by this decision, expressed cautious support for the idea of talks—but hinted that they did not think Trump could pull them off.[8] Some Republican members of Congress, on the other hand, expressed alarm that the president would even consider sitting down with the North Korean leader before North Korea yielded to key demands, suggesting that Trump was naïve or ill-advised in agreeing to such a summit.[9] In their view, I suppose, talking to North Korea is only effective if we already have what we want ahead of time—a curious approach to diplomacy. All of this chatter reminds me of another transformational president, Ronald Reagan, who agreed to sit down with Soviet leader Mikhail Gorbachev at a time (1985) when the Soviet Union was still very much the "Evil Empire," and the dismantling of the East Bloc was something no one would have predicted.

The key takeaway is that we must do all we can do to look out for American interests, and this includes the unconventional. As of this writing, we cannot know if a summit with North Korea will be successful, but the fact that it is being talked about as a possibility is a hopeful sign that the man now in the Oval Office understands that pragmatism in practice does not contradict firmness in principle. A deal that lessened tensions in that part of the world would serve American interests not only by preventing possible bloodshed but also by setting the stage for our eventual withdrawal, entrusting South Korea's security to the South Koreans themselves.

Turning back to troop levels, the case for maintaining troops in Japan is even weaker than the one for the Korean Peninsula. The Japanese, too, are threatened by North Korean belligerence, but they have completely relied on U.S. protection rather than taking responsibility for their own defense. Since the Second World War, Japan has traditionally spent less than 1 percent of their GDP on defense. This is their right, of course, but it is also our right to let them know that we no longer wish to pay that expense on their behalf, especially when we are paying other costs in terms of our trade deficit. Furthermore, our defense pact, dating to 1960, is completely one-sided. We are obligated to defend them, but they have no obligation to defend us. It is time to scrap this agreement. We need to gradually withdraw our forces from Japan and allow them to provide for their own protection, as any normal country does.

In the meantime, President Trump is already taking steps to allow Japan to be more responsible for her own defense. Early in 2018, the administration approved the sale of anti-ballistic

---

PUTTING AMERICA FIRST
Donald Trump
Edition

"You know we have a treaty
with Japan, where if Japan is
attacked, we have to use the
full force and might of the
United States. If we're attacked,
Japan doesn't have to do anything. They can sit home and
watch Sony television."

—candidate **DONALD TRUMP**,
Iowa, August 2016

---

missiles with an estimated value of $133 million to Japan, to help protect that nation against any threat arising in the region, especially North Korea.[10] Selling the Japanese weapons to provide for their own defense is not an example of overseas intervention by other means. On the contrary, it is America First foreign policy in action. We sell defensive weaponry to help keep the peace and by so doing not only generate goodwill, but also provide jobs for American workers and dividends for American investors. Selling weapons to friendly nations is something we have been doing since at least the 1850s, when British officials put in their first orders for Samuel Colt's famous revolvers, and it is something we should continue to do, as it provides benefits for both parties. It makes no sense to acknowledge a nation's right to defend itself from unjust aggression as legitimate but then brand those who provide the tools to make that defense possible as immoral.

One objection to turning over South Korean defense to the South Koreans and Japanese defense to the Japanese is that both North Korea and its benefactor China have nuclear weapons. As we withdraw our troops, we should make it clear that we expect China to prevent North Korea from utilizing its nuclear arsenal. Should the Chinese be unwilling to give us such a guarantee, we should let them—and the North Koreans—know that we will withdraw any objections we have to Japan and South Korea being able to defend themselves by all means possible, including developing their own nuclear defense capability. It is in our national interest, for reasons of both security and economy, that our troops are not deployed in such a manner that any war automatically becomes a U.S. war, whether or not it is in our interest to take part. It is in China's interest that her neighbors, particularly Japan, do not join the nuclear club. By working together diplomatically, we can begin to shift some of the responsibility for keeping the peace in that region to the regional powers most affected by developments in the area.

Under our tutelage, both South Korea and Japan have developed vibrant, market-based economies under well-established democratic rule. On the economic side, they have done so well that they now often beat us at our own game. They no longer need to be propped up. We can maintain the same cordial relations we have enjoyed over the past half century by treating them as grown-ups who can be trusted to look out for their own interests just as we look out for ours.

EIGHT

INDIA

THE BIGGEST COUNTRY IN THE WORLD THAT WE NEVER TALK ABOUT. I'M OKAY WITH THAT.

India is one of the world's most ancient societies, with roots going back to the dawn of time. The Indus Valley civilization was a contemporary of Sumer, in Mesopotamia, and the oldest kingdoms of Egypt. While the peoples of the ancient Indian civilizations were eventually displaced by invaders, the influence of the bygone Indus Valley settlements can still be felt on contemporary Indian culture. Modern India is a "vibrant, modern nation built on an ancient civilization," as President George W. Bush put it.

The entity we know today as India, however, now with over a billion inhabitants, is a very recent creation. Throughout much of India's history, the subcontinent was occupied by various kingdoms made up of many different peoples, speaking different languages and expressing different beliefs. Various efforts were made to unify this part of the world—under the Macedonian Empire of Alexander the Great, the Gupta Empire in the fourth century A.D., and the Mughal Empire in the sixteenth century. But India remained divided into a cornucopia of smaller states—which was one of the contributing factors to the success of European colonialism.

The Raj, the British colonial regime that controlled India until its independence in 1947, included present-day Pakistan and Bangladesh and gave the modern world its concept of India. While many Westerners tend to think of "Indians" as being Hindi-speaking Aryan people who practice the Hindu religion, that particular group is only one of the vast number that make up modern India. While Hindi is widespread in India—and so is English—nearly a dozen major languages and probably close to one hundred minor languages and dialects are spoken there. Indians are diverse in terms of race, and while Hinduism is the predominant faith, six other religions have "national minority status": Christianity, Islam, Sikhism, Jainism, Buddhism, and the Zoroastrianism of the Parsis. There is also a large Baha'i population, relative to the number of Baha'is in the world, and a tiny but ancient Jewish community. The only thing that ties these very different people together is the fact that they live in what is now the modern Republic of India.

The U.S.-Indian relationship really only goes back about seventy years. Because India was part of the British Empire for most of our history, we had little reason for interaction with the peoples of the Indian subcontinent. Distance coupled with immigration restrictions meant that the Indian-American population was insignificant until 1965, when our immigration policy swung the doors of the United States wide open to the entire world. (Perhaps not coincidentally, 1965 was also the year the first

Indian restaurant opened in Washington, DC—the now-defunct Taj Mahal, which used to be on Connecticut Avenue. I mention this because our foreign policy elites often see unrestricted immigration only in terms of all the new tasty cuisines they will have the opportunity to sample, and thus can't fathom why anyone would have an objection to open borders.) Since the changes in our immigration policy, Indian-Americans have been one of the fastest-growing segments of our population. No longer an invisible minority, Indian-Americans include former Republican governors Bobby Jindal of Louisiana and Nikki Haley of South Carolina (now our ambassador at the United Nations); U.S. Senator Kamala Harris, a California Democrat; and writers Dinesh D'Souza and Fareed Zakaria, as well as a whole host of academics, scientists, musicians, religious leaders, and representatives of popular culture. Even so, Indian-Americans have tended not to organize politically on ethnic lines, meaning that our policy towards India has been remarkably free from the kind of pressure groups that have arisen in the past as communities of newcomers looked as much to their countries of origin as to their current country of allegiance.

The distance between America and India, our lack of historical interaction with the Indian subcontinent, and a relatively young Indian immigrant community in the U.S. all mean that our policymakers have not spent a lot of time focusing on India. While we supported Indian independence from the United Kingdom as part and parcel of the general wave of decolonization that took place after the Second World War, our support was more in words than in deeds—similar to the traditional lip-service we gave to republican movements from the earliest

---

PUTTING AMERICA FIRST
Ulysses S. Grant Edition

"As the United States is the freest of all nations, so, too, its people sympathize with all people struggling for liberty and self-government; but while so sympathizing it is due to our honor that we should abstain from enforcing our views upon unwilling nations and from taking an interested part, without invitation, in the quarrels between different nations or between governments and their subjects."

—**ULYSSES S. GRANT**, First State of the Union Address, 1869

---

moments of our history. Our relationship with India was strained during the Cold War as India, seeking to distance itself from both the United States and the Soviet Union, became a leader of the so-called "Non-Aligned Movement." This was partly a response to our close relationship with Indian rival Pakistan—another new nation that had been born out of the same movement that produced Indian independence—though the United States remained largely aloof from the four wars that India and Pakistan fought in the latter half of the twentieth century.

Except for brief periods of rapprochement, such as during the short Sino-Indian border war of 1962, the Indians tended to view U.S. Cold War policy with suspicion, and India did not participate in attempts to isolate the USSR when that country invaded Afghanistan in 1979.

Following the end of the Cold War, our relationship has been a mixed bag. Since 9/11, common concerns about Islamic extremism have led to closer ties between our two nations, especially during the presidency of George W. Bush, but political rhetoric aside, one would be hard-pressed to call India a major partner of the United States, let alone an ally. We both have a republican form of government, substantial populations, and powerful military capabilities, but beyond trade there is little to bring us together. Incidentally, while George W. Bush does not have a huge cadre of fans around the world, he was extremely popular in India, with approval ratings remaining steady at 70 percent for much of his term of office.[1] I think one of the reasons behind President Bush's popularity on the subcontinent is that he treated India as an equal partner on the world stage, rather than a country that needed to be lectured. Contrast that with President Obama's 2015 speech in which he said that religious intolerance in India would have shocked Mahatma Gandhi. Imagine an Indian leader telling us that we are not living up to Jefferson's ideals.

The fact that our nations have never been close is not necessarily a bad thing. Without the baggage of a common history or the complications of previous strife, it is easier for us to identify our national interests dispassionately. Most Americans are aware of India, but very few could point to any incident in the last fifty years of U.S.-India relations that has had any impact whatsoever on the lives of average Americans, with the possible exception of our visa policy. That is an indication of a successful bilateral relationship. We will know that our interactions with India have been well-managed if, fifty years from now, Americans are equally ignorant of the details.

As a well-developed democratic nation, India has shown herself capable of self-government. But how she governs her own people should be no concern of ours. India, despite having a nuclear capability, has never been a security threat to the United States, and we should ensure that she never becomes one. The best way to do that is to refrain from telling India what to do in matters that do not directly concern us. We do not need special ambassadors roaming the world, as has often been the case, to ascertain whether or not other sovereign nations live up to our standards, especially in areas such as the "LGBT" agenda, where Americans themselves are deeply divided. No one has made the United States the arbiter of what constitutes universal human rights, especially at a time in Western history in which such determinations now appear to be arbitrary rulings of a tiny self-anointed cultural elite.

This does not mean that there are no matters of concern in our relationship with India. As with many nations in the world, the United States has a trade deficit with India that has steadily increased in recent years, largely due to American insistence on free trade ideology even where it is detrimental to American industry—for example, when it's free trade only on our side, and protectionism on the other side. Since U.S.-India trade is relatively small, this is not a high-priority problem, but we should keep in mind that India is a rapidly developing country. As its people become more affluent, they will not only be a growing market for imported goods, they will also develop further capabilities to create industries that are in direct competition with our own. We should ensure that our negotiators strike the right balance between trade and protection to ensure the best deal possible for both of our peoples. We should also continue to take care that sensitive technologies are closely safeguarded.

Another area of major concern regards work visas issued to Indian nationals. The H1B visa is a work visa that was originally designed to allow foreign nationals to work in the United States in highly skilled professions where there was a shortage of Americans able to fill those jobs. In practice, it has been used as a way to find cheaper imported labor to avoid paying the kinds of salaries that Americans are used to receiving. And it is also a kind of indentured servitude for the foreign workers, since the H1B holder cannot work for any other company besides the one that initially hired him without going through a change of status or a new visa application. Indian nationals make up a large number of H1B holders, especially in the IT industries. They are oftentimes employed in the U.S. by the American branch of multinational corporations actually based in India!

President Trump, to much wailing and gnashing of teeth, has pledged to cut back on H1B abuse, but how much of an impact this will have on our overall immigration policy remains to be seen. As of this writing there are several proposals on the table, including one that would raise the wage paid to workers on H1B visas to $100,000 per year.[2] This would make it more likely that firms would only use the H1B for its original purpose—to bring in talented professionals who offer skills in short supply in the United States. In the meantime, at least anecdotally, the Trump administration appears to be giving existing applications for H1Bs greater scrutiny; the approval rate for applications, which was around 90 percent in the past, has dropped.[3]

Our visa policy, like all of our foreign policy, should be primarily concerned with protecting the safety and well-being of Americans. Another nation's concerns over the loss of livelihood to its nationals working in the United States should not be a driving factor in our visa decisions. We need fair, transparent visa policies that are open to everyone but that benefit America first.

The best word to sum up our national interest in India is non-interference. India has emerged as one of the leading nations of the world—on the strength of its own people. In a world of "failed states," we should applaud that. An India that is successful and independent—non-aligned, if you will—is in our national interest. It creates stability in a part of the world that has been racked by strife in recent years and in doing so eliminates the perceived need for our country to get involved where it does not belong. We should continue to trust that India will do what is best for her people while we do what is best for our own.

NINE

THE REST OF ASIA

TWO AND A HALF BILLION PEOPLE, BUT WE REALLY NEED ONLY ONE CHAPTER

This chapter will cover the Asian countries that were once part of the Soviet Union (including the so-called "Stans"), those of Southeast Asia including the islands around there—Australia and New Zealand (I know, geographically their own separate continent!), Mongolia, Nepal, Bhutan, Bangladesh—and, what the heck, everything else around the Pacific and Indian Oceans that we have not already discussed. Another title for this chapter might be "A Whole Collection of Countries that Don't Fit Anywhere Else and Have Little Impact on U.S. Foreign Policy."

There are vast areas of the world that are simply not crucial to Americans' national interests. This does not mean that they never played an important role vis-à-vis the United States, nor that they never will. It just means that at the present time they are not that important to U.S. foreign policy. It does not mean we should completely ignore them. We trade with all of them, and our balance of trade with some of them is a matter of concern. That is one of the reasons America has embassies and consulates overseas, so that we have people on the ground who can examine the peculiarities of each country's economic circumstances. These include our State Department Economic Officers who provide analysis and our Foreign Commercial Service Officers who look for ways to promote U.S. exports.

If you come from one of these countries, please don't be offended. The fact that I don't mention your country by name does not mean that I think you have nothing to offer the world. In fact I am sure that your people are the smartest and friendliest on the planet and that your national history is not only truly fascinating but has so much to teach us in the twenty-first century. But this book is not about the glories of Sri Lanka, to name a country I won't bring up again. It is about defending U.S. national interest in the world. In fact, rather than being offended that I don't talk at length about your country, you should be flattered. It simply means that your nation is not a source of major problems for the U.S. and that we generally get along. If we ever had a truly successful national interest–based foreign policy, we would one day be able to put every country in the world in this particular chapter.

Let's start the discussion with the countries of Asia that were once part of the Soviet Union: Georgia, Armenia, Azerbaijan, Kazakhstan, Uzbekistan, Turkmenistan, Tajikistan, and Kyrgyzstan. These countries have dramatically different histories, with some of them dating back thousands of years while others never really existed as separate national entities until the dissolution of the USSR Most of them have substantial Muslim populations, but two of them—Georgia and Armenia—have large Christian majorities, with Armenia holding the distinction of being the first officially Christian country in the world. Armenia is also the only one of these countries with a significant diaspora outside her geographic boundaries—including a very visible one in the United States, which has given us such prominent figures as former California governor George Deukmejian, tennis player Andre Agassi, singer Cher (Cherilyn Sarkisian), and Kim Kardashian, who is famous for being famous.

What all of these countries have in common, however, is that they did not exist as sovereign entities in the modern world before 1992. We have only had to develop a separate Uzbek policy or a separate Kazakh policy over the last twenty-five years. Before that, our policy toward Moscow would have also covered the peoples who live in what are today Uzbekistan and Kazakhstan and all the rest, since they were a part of one country. While that is no longer the case, I would suggest that it still makes perfect sense to consider them as one entity. I don't mean that we should dismiss their claims to sovereignty, but that we should acknowledge that whatever happens in, say, Turkmenistan is far more likely to have an impact on Russia than on the United States. And we should not seek international influence out of proportion to our genuine needs. Instead, the maintenance of good bilateral relations with the major regional power—Russia—should be the lynchpin of our approach to these countries that once belonged to the Russian Empire.

How would this work in practice? It would not mean shutting down our embassies or tuning out the leaders of these countries. There is ample opportunity for us to work with these nations in areas of mutual interest. An example is the fight against radical Islamic terror. We had a very good working relationship with Uzbekistan in the early stages of our efforts to defeat the Taliban in Afghanistan. Unfortunately, we overplayed our hand there, involving ourselves in the internal affairs of Uzbekistan itself, and that cooperation was scaled back. But as transnational jihadi groups seek to infiltrate nations with sizeable Muslim populations, there may come a time when we can work together with some of these countries in an effort to both provide protection to our own people and, at the same time, ensure stability in these countries—working together to secure mutual national interests.

But we should not be taking sides in disputes between Moscow and the countries of the region, unless our national security or the well-being of our citizens is clearly threatened. Since we have tended, almost as a reflex, to take the anti-Russian side in every dispute, our involvement erodes our relationship with Russia and does little to gain us support in the countries of the region. Oftentimes the people of those countries are themselves divided. Therefore, putting our nose in these disputes is self-defeating. We make enemies where none existed before, and that adversely affects not only our well-being (in terms of money diverted to supporting our policy there that could better be spent elsewhere), but also our security, as now we have to look at the offended parties as potential adversaries.

Russians constitute a large minority in nearly all of the countries of the former Soviet Union. Tensions between ethnic Russians and others have often fueled disputes between these countries and Russia, leading in extreme cases to Russian-dominated areas breaking away—as they did in Georgia, with the establishment of the rump republics of South Ossetia and Abkhazia. In the abstract view, we may decide that one party or the other has the greater amount of law and justice on its side. But foreign policy should never be about abstract views of anything. Rather, we should ask ourselves how Americans will be concretely affected by our actions or lack thereof. Consider the most visible of these disputes: in the secession crises in Georgia (and we ain't talkin' Atlanta here), we can see that the question of which flag flies over Sukhumi really does not impact the lives of any Americans anywhere. The fact that most of you probably had never even heard of Sukhumi until I mentioned it here—it is the capital of the breakaway Abkhazian Republic, in case you were wondering—only proves my point.

This question *does* impact the lives of Georgians and of Russians, though. So they are the ones who should be worrying about it. We have a tendency to think we should have a policy on every international question that arises. That is absurd. Some things are simply none of our concern. Imagine that you live in a neighborhood and try your best to get along with all of your neighbors (and I hope that is the case). One day, one of your neighbors begins complaining that another neighbor plays his music too loudly at inappropriate times, while the other denies it. You can't hear the music from your house, so you can't say who is right. You have a number of options here. You could take the side of the complaining neighbor, on the principle that loud music is a bad thing, and that, even if the music really isn't that loud, you want to take the side of those supporting peace and tranquility, to establish a precedent in the neighborhood. You could, on the other hand, take the side of the alleged music-playing neighbor, on the grounds that the freedom to play music is a vital component of one's autonomy and that we don't need overly sensitive neighbors reacting to every perceived slight. You could spend a lot of your own time and money—maybe even hire a private investigator—to look into the facts of the case and definitively determine which of your neighbors is in the right. Or you could just stay out of the dispute and let the two neighbors work it out on their own. I don't know about you, but I would be inclined to take the last option—because my own interests are not directly affected. Sure, I want to see harmony among my neighbors, but unless they have appointed me to be the arbiter of all neighborhood disputes, my input is likely to be unwelcome, if not by both, then certainly by one of the parties involved. Similarly, there are many instances in which disputes arise in the world that do not affect us directly. We should maintain relationships with both sides while remaining neutral on the underlying dispute. We can offer mediation if both sides request it, but, at least in the part of the world we have been discussing, that is extremely unlikely to happen.

To sum up, we should continue to strive for good relations with all the countries of the former Soviet Union, but we should do so in the context of our more important relationship with Russia. We must balance all the things we do on the basis of what benefits our people. Acting as a disinterested third party goes against what we have been doing ever since the advent of the Cold War, but it is a natural condition for a normal country that seeks peace with its neighbors and well-being for its citizens. It is a role that we as a country would do well to re-learn.

Moving on from the "Stans," let us take a look at Southeast Asia. This is a prime example of a part of the world that was vital to our national interest less than fifty years ago. We were involved in a war in Vietnam that was part of our overall struggle against Communist expansion. Whatever the merits or demerits of the Vietnam War, what happened in that neck of the woods just a few decades ago had a direct effect on both our security and our well-being. U.S.-Vietnam relations, as well as our relationships with neighboring countries, were crucial to the development of our foreign policy in, say, 1969. That is no longer the case. The end of our military effort in the area in 1975, coupled with the end of the Cold War less than twenty years later, relegated this part of the world to peripheral status in terms of our national interest. That is a good thing for all parties involved. Currently, our focus in the region is on trade—with some Southeast Asian countries also sharing common concerns about security.

That is the case with Burma, also known as Myanmar, with which we have had a strained relationship for many years. Burma has suffered almost constant political instability since independence from Britain in the late 1940s, and a coup in the late eighties led to sanctions being imposed on the new regime by the U.S. and European countries. As is usually the case with sanctions, the government was not toppled and the initial outrage in the international community lessened over time. Our relations with the Burmese government eventually improved. Peace and stability are far from returning, and, as of this writing, Myanmar is seeing renewed conflicts between the government and certain Muslim groups within the country. Despite that, we have decided that it is more in our interest to engage with the government there than to keep it isolated. After all, the issues in dispute do not have a direct bearing on U.S. national interests. We do, however, insist on calling the country by the name Burma—its official name before the coup (when it became Myanmar)—which just shows that while our foreign policy is sometimes activist, sometimes it is downright passive-aggressive.

The Philippines is a special case. This nation of several thousand islands was an American colony from the time we took it from the Spanish in 1898 until its independence after World War II. We fought a bloody war against pro-independence insurgents in the early years of the twentieth century and several shorter wars against Muslim separatists (the Moros) on the island of Mindanao. Even after independence, the United States continued to play a dominant role in the Philippines, which was a major U.S. partner in Asia during the Cold War, with American bases there serving an important role in the Vietnam War.

The end of the Cold War marked the end to our permanent military presence in the Philippines, but the two countries still continued close defense cooperation until recently, up into the era of the Global War on Terror. The presence of an historic Muslim insurgency within the Philippines makes that country one of special concern. It is in our interest, for example, to see that that insurgency does not become infiltrated by

---

PUTTING AMERICA FIRST
Grover Cleveland Edition

"That foreign policy commended by the history, the traditions, and the prosperity of our Republic.... is the policy of neutrality, rejecting any share in foreign broils and ambitions upon other continents and repelling their intrusion here."

—**GROVER CLEVELAND**, First Inaugural Address, 1885

outside forces, especially considering the large number of people of Filipino origin now resident on the U.S. mainland. While respecting the sovereignty of the Philippines, we should strive for close cooperation in security matters that have the potential of affecting both of our countries. Beyond this, however, we should not view with alarm recent declarations by Filipino authorities of a "re-orientation" of their policy toward other nations in the area, notably China. There is no evidence that the Filipino government intends to actively combat our interests, and its people have an overwhelmingly positive view of the United States. In fact, after reaching its lowest ebb under the previous administration—when Philippine President Rodrigo Duterte famously told Obama to "go to hell"—our relationship with the Philippines appears to be on an upswing since President Trump's visit to Manila in November 2017.[1]

Part of the improvement is no doubt due to similarities in personal style between the two leaders, but the thaw in our relations also demonstrates how an America First foreign policy not only advances our own interests but can serve to smooth our relationships with other countries. Filipino President Duterte's notorious anti-drug policy, in which many of the niceties of the rule of law have been dispensed with in order to combat criminal narcotics enterprises in that country, has met with much criticism. It was American criticism under President Obama that caused cracks to erupt in our relationship. President Trump, on the other hand, did not bring up that controversial policy during his visit—no doubt seeing it as an internal affair of the Philippines, rather than any of our business. In so doing, he showed a respect for the sovereignty of that nation rare in the annals of

U.S. history. I find it ironic that the supposedly "racist," "boor-ish," and "ignorant" president we have now (if the left-wing media is to be believed) knew better how to connect with the leader of a major Third World country than the supposedly eru-dite, sensitive, and welcoming president we had before.

Just to the south lie a number of countries with dramatically different interests and histories: Indonesia, Malaysia, Singapore, Papua New Guinea, East Timor, and Brunei. We can sum up our relationship with these countries in two words: trade and secu-rity. This area, when coupled with Thailand, Vietnam, and the Philippines, is the world's leading rubber exporter. There is also evidence that Indonesia, Malaysia, and Vietnam may be able to serve as alternative sources to China for rare earth minerals, vitally important in the electronics industry. Other industries in the area include tin and petroleum, as well as spices and other tropical agricultural goods.

Several of these countries have large Muslim populations—Indonesia is the largest Muslim country in the world in terms of numbers—so our continued engagement with these nations is vital to our national security. In recent years, Indonesia has been more cooperative in combating terrorism at a time when such incidents are on the rise. Many of the attacks target Western interests, but a significant number are directed against the Indo-nesian government itself or against the Indonesian Christian minority. Since President Obama spent much of his childhood in Indonesia, is popular there, and has been back to visit since leav-ing the presidency, maybe he would be willing to lend a hand in continuing to build our relationship with Indonesia. That appears to be one of his particular strengths. In his farewell address,

Obama vowed that he would not stop serving the American people. Perhaps President Trump could take him up on this and offer him an ambassadorship to Indonesia to see if he was indeed sincere.

While Australia and New Zealand are technically not part of Asia, I will briefly discuss them here. We have had consular relations with both nations for many years but only established full-fledged diplomatic ties around the time of World War II; before that time, America's relations with the Aussies and Kiwis were handled out of London. The first U.S. president to visit the region was Lyndon Johnson—an important visit, since both Australia and New Zealand supported our efforts in the Vietnam War.

Our relationships with these two countries have been close, aided by a common language and a similar culture. This does not mean they have always been rosy. U.S. servicemen clashed with Australian troops in rioting in Brisbane and other cities during World War II, and New Zealand's anti-nuclear policy was a source of contention between that country and the United States during the Cold War. That being said, our ties are probably closer than our ties with any other countries with the possible exceptions of the United Kingdom and Canada. Australian and American troops served side by side not only in World War II, Korea, and Vietnam, but also in Iraq and Afghanistan.

One reason for our warm relations may be our lack of interference in each other's internal affairs. When Australian Prime Minister Malcolm Turnbull visited the United States in February 2018, just after a mass shooting in Florida claimed the lives of seventeen people, reporters tried to get him to sing the praises of

Australia's strict gun control policy as a model for the United States. He refused to take the bait, saying, "We certainly don't presume to provide, you know, policy or political advice on that matter here. I will focus on our own political arguments and debates and wish you wise deliberation in your own." In other words, Australia First.

This does not mean that we don't occasionally benefit from each other's experience. President Trump has suggested Australia's points-based immigration system, adopted in 2016, as a possible model for U.S. immigration reform. Under the Australian system, potential immigrants are assigned points based on their "skills or outstanding abilities that will contribute to the Australian economy." In addition, they are required to have at least a minimal ability to speak English. On the flip side, Prime Minister Turnbull has expressed his admiration for Trump's tax plan. "We have been inspired by your success in securing the passage of the tax reforms through the Congress. The economic stimulus that your reforms have delivered here in the United States is one of the most powerful arguments that we are deploying to persuade our legislature to support reducing business tax." These statements highlight how countries can influence each other for good—not through coercion or preaching, but by adopting policies that make life better for their own citizens and thus serving as an inspiration to other governments wishing to do the same. We tend to forget, but for much of our early history much of what we would call the "Third World" today looked with admiration on the American experiment precisely because we sought to lead by example and not by coercion.

We have overall good trade relationships, with a free trade agreement signed with Australia several years ago, and one pending for New Zealand. In the case of Australia, our free trade agreement has actually been to our benefit; since it was signed we have run moderate trade surpluses with that nation. We run a small deficit with New Zealand, but it's just a blip on the screen in the context of our overall trade.

Both countries' citizens are eligible for our Visa Waiver Program, and large numbers visit the U.S. each year, especially from the land down under; Australians spend some nine billion dollars each year in America. Our relationship with New Zealand and Australia is a good example of how to do things right. We should continue to cooperate in areas of mutual interest and promote both tourism and trade. In light of the success of our free trade agreement with Australia, we might choose to follow up and negotiate one with New Zealand, although this is certainly not our highest priority. As three nations that take in immigrants from all over the world, we should also maintain the excellent law enforcement ties our countries have in order to thwart the attempts of international criminals and transnational terrorists to move across our respective borders.

TEN

THE MIDDLE EAST

THIS IS WHAT HAPPENS WHEN YOU
DON'T HAVE A SENSE OF HUMOR

I begin this chapter on the Middle East with a sense of trepidation. So much ink has been spilled on this subject, and it would be easy to get carried away and let it dominate the book. If I did that, I would be doing nothing different from what U.S. policymakers have been doing for the last fifty years, which is to say letting the Middle East assume a role far beyond its real importance to our overall national interest. Don't get me wrong; we do have clearly identifiable national interests in the area, but in recent years we have failed to distinguish between the dramatic—that is, the events and headlines that grab our attention and that we can't help having a visceral emotional reaction to—and the essential—that is, what happens in the region that really does affect American national interests. We have lost our way.

What countries make up the Middle East? There are many different definitions of this region of the world, and mine would be broader than most. It includes the Levant—that area of the eastern Mediterranean that includes Israel, Lebanon, and Syria—but also the entirety of North Africa, plus the countries of the Arabian Peninsula and Iraq. I throw in Turkey as well, though many commentators like to pretend that Turkey is a European country. While 5 percent of Turkey's territory is on the European continent, the nation's Ottoman past and Islamicizing present make it part of the Middle East. Finally, I include the majority-Muslim states of Iran, Pakistan, and Afghanistan.

For all the importance we assign to the Middle East, one would think that we have been engaged with that region since the beginning of our Republic. While we did have to intervene there during the Barbary Wars, other than that the Middle East did not figure into our foreign policy until well into the twentieth century. For example, even though we were involved in the fight against Germany in World War I, we never officially declared war against the Ottoman Empire, Germany's ally and the dominant power in the Middle East at the time. This vastly underdeveloped area was considered peripheral to U.S. interests and really did not feature in our foreign policy.

That changed at the end of World War II. As we have already discussed, the Cold War saw the United States engaged in a defensive struggle against an aggressive Soviet Empire, and the entire world was the battleground, including the Middle East. In addition, the discovery of massive deposits of fossil fuels in that region—the lifeblood of the modern world economy—magnified its importance. Securing those strategic assets was necessary to guarantee the viability of the American economy. Next, the emergence of the modern state of Israel right on the heels of the Holocaust added an emotional (and sometimes theological) component to U.S. policy that would not have otherwise existed. Finally, the emergence of transnational radical Islamic terrorism in more recent times has forced us to keep our eyes on what was going on over there.

As we have already seen, our contest with the Soviet Union led to alliances that persist to this day. But that's far from a complete explanation of our relationships with the nations of the Middle East. Israel, of course, is our first and foremost ally in the region, and Israel, especially in her early days, was by far the most socialistic of all the countries of the area. Saudi Arabia is another long-term partner and former ally against the Soviet Union, but our interests would likely have coincided in any case because of Saudi Arabia's huge oil reserves. What the Cold War did was to make allies of countries with which we share some interests but that are otherwise not vital to the United States. The rise of radical Islamic terrorism has further complicated the situation.

The Middle East is a passionate place—and a place that Americans are passionately divided about. Questions of religion, ethnicity, and ideology make it difficult to get an objective view of what our interests there are. Otherwise sane people who can agree to disagree on, say, China policy, will froth at the mouth and accuse each other of bad faith when it comes to discussing the Middle East. And of course, the people who actually live in the region are not known for even attempting to be reasonable. We have to take the emotions out of our analysis of this part of the world. Only then can we come up with any kind of coherent policy for furthering America's national interests.

Let's start by looking dispassionately at the issue of oil. The only reason we even began to notice a country like Saudi Arabia was because it sits on huge deposits of petroleum. Our country was dependent on Middle Eastern oil for many years, and the oil embargo of 1973 showed that concerted action by the producers in the region could wreak havoc on our economy. But in recent years that has changed. Of the top five countries exporting petroleum products to the United States (accounting for nearly 70 percent of all imports), only Saudi Arabia is located in the Middle East, and that country, once our largest importer, has slipped to number two.[1] In case you were wondering, our top source of oil is Canada, and the others in the top five are Venezuela, Mexico, and Colombia. The only other Middle Eastern countries with significant exports to the U.S. in recent years are Iraq, Kuwait, and Algeria, each of which imported less petroleum products to the United States in 2016 than did Russia. Even better, a surge in domestic U.S. production—assisted by the "fracking" boom—has led to an overall decline in oil imports as a share of domestic consumption, not to mention relative stability in prices at the pump. Adjusted for inflation, the amount we pay per gallon for gas today is equivalent to the price we paid in the late 1920s and early 1930s.[2]

Still, oil led to our initial involvement in the Middle East, and it continues to play a role in our policy. Even if the majority of our fuel no longer comes from the region, a disruption of those supplies could spike oil prices globally, not to mention causing devastation to economies with greater dependence on petroleum from that part of the world, such as Japan. It is therefore in our interests to ensure the free flow of oil from the producers in the Middle East.

Contrary to popular liberal belief, this does not mean "seizing" oilfields for the United States. For one, we don't train our soldiers to run oil wells, and the State Department's Foreign Service Institute will not be offering a course entitled "Diplomats to Derrickhands" anytime soon. For another, it is unnecessary. Oil without a market is a rather worthless commodity. You can't drink it. The only way any oil-rich nation can use oil to acquire other goods is to sell it. And in a world market with many sources of petroleum, including America's own significant domestic sources, a country that refuses to sell to one of the world's largest consumers of oil is only hurting itself. They need us more than we need them. So all of us, conservative and liberal alike, can join hands and chant "No War for Oil!" all day long, because a war solely designed to steal oil is not going to happen anyway.

What should happen, if we are looking out for our national interests, is that we will act where necessary to prevent anyone from disrupting the supply of oil, including from the Middle East. This ties in with our traditional defense of the rights of free navigation. In the nineteenth century we may have been keeping the sea-lanes open for whale oil rather than crude oil, but the principle is the same. Absent a state of war, we will trade with whomever we please, and woe be to those who seek to disrupt that trade. Thus, it is entirely appropriate for our Navy to patrol the Straits of Hormuz and other areas crucial to the transport of goods, including petroleum products. It is also appropriate for us to cooperate with oil suppliers, offering advice and technology to help defend oil fields from both domestic and transnational terrorist or insurgent forces. What is not in our interest is to be drawn in to local quagmires where we have nothing at stake. After all, if one source of oil dries up there are others to choose

from. The key is guaranteeing the flow of oil from the region as
a whole, not necessarily the flow from every source in the region.

What are the biggest threats to Middle Eastern oil supplies?
The biggest one, ironically, is something we actually helped to
create when we got distracted from defending our national interests. That threat is chaos. Societies that break down into anarchy
do not have the wherewithal to function as normal exporters of
goods and services.

War is the biggest threat to many of the nations in the region,
and yet our policies in recent years have led to almost continuous
war. I am not talking just about the war in Iraq. Our support for
the "Arab Spring," which was supposed to bring democracy, love,
brotherhood, flowers, and grooviness to an arid and oppressive
part of the globe, was also counter-productive. Instead of improving the Middle Easterners' lot, it has led to chaotic conditions in
once stable countries such as Libya, Syria, and Iraq. True, each
of these countries was governed by a brutal dictator. I am no
apologist for the likes of genuinely evil figures such as Muammar
Qaddafi or Saddam Hussein. But the United States has lived
alongside other truly evil rulers throughout the course of our
national existence without lifting a finger to overthrow them.
Some see this as a moral failing on our part, but given the devastation and death that have resulted from our decision to work
for the overthrow of these strongmen, maybe, just maybe, our
traditional policy of non-interference in the internal affairs of
foreign nations could have some merit. We have replaced dictators that oppressed certain segments of their own societies but
posed no threat to us with weak governments that have allowed
the rise of groups that persecute other segments of their societies

and—this is where our interests lie—pose a direct threat to the United States. The region lost Saddam Hussein and Muammar Qaddafi and gained Al-Qaeda and ISIS. The persecution of radical Muslim groups was replaced with the persecution of Christian groups. We got rid of regimes that annoyed us and created the conditions for the rise of terrorists who actually threaten us.

This book highlights many quotations of U.S. presidents and other prominent figures from American history articulating the America First principles that guided our foreign policy from the beginning of the Republic and should guide it again. At this point let me offer a very different quotation from a president with very different principles. This is what Barack Obama had to say on May 19, 2011, about what he saw as America's opportunity, and our duty, to reshape the Middle East in our image—or at least in the image of the America that our liberal elites believe ought to be: "After decades of accepting the world as it is in the region, we have a chance to pursue the world as it should be."

The incredible arrogance that Obama was expressing is symptomatic of what has gone wrong with our Middle Eastern foreign policy in recent years. The fact is that we as a nation cannot even come to an agreement as to what *America* should be, let alone the world. If we continue to divert our attention from what our interests in the region truly are, we are doomed to repeat the failures of our over-ambitious policy there.

Who sits on the throne, presidential dais, or portable leadership chair in Baghdad, Riyadh, Damascus, or Tripoli, is really none of our concern. We should work with any parties that want to work with us in pursuit of our mutual interests and remain agnostic about how they should run things at home.

Even if we entirely give up on our counter-productive efforts to promote pushes for human rights, democratic reform, and regime change in the Middle East, there is plenty to keep us involved in the region. We can't afford to cut and run anytime soon. The destabilization of this part of the world means that a U.S. presence there will be required for the foreseeable future, or for at least as long as oil helps to fuel our economy. But we need not be involved in the way we have been for the past two decades, during which time our actions have served to actively harm our national interest. American advisors—military, economic, and technological—have a role. But their presence should not be the thin end of the wedge, or—as they say in the Middle East—the camel's nose under the tent. (After all, America's involvement in the Vietnam War began when we sent military advisors there.) A vigorous naval presence combined with a rapid action force ready to confront any security threats to Americans abroad should suffice. We must avoid the temptation to place any other forces there on a permanent basis. Leaving matches lying about only increases the chance of fire.

Neither oil nor the fantasy of making the world what it ought to be is our only reason for being involved in the Middle East. Any discussion of U.S. foreign policy in that region would be incomplete without mentioning Israel. The United States writes out checks to Israel—touted by many as "America's clos-est ally," and "the only democracy in the Middle East"—for over three billion dollars a year. The blind hatred many Arabs feel for the Jewish state has historically bled over to the United

States, so that street demonstrators who burn Israeli flags will usually have an American flag handy to burn as well. Many Americans have family ties to Israel: the Israeli policy of *aliyah* allows any person with at least one Jewish grandparent to move to Israel and become an Israeli citizen, and thousands of Americans have done just that over the years. Attacks on the U.S. by radical Islamic terrorists have made many Americans sympathetic to the plight of Israelis who for years have suffered at the hands of terrorists seeking Israel's destruction. Finally, some American evangelicals are convinced that in supporting Israel we are supporting the cause of God Himself—even though the secular modern state of Israel is a far cry from the Israel of the Pentateuch.

America did not always automatically support Israel. While we were the first to recognize the Jewish State, Stalin's Soviet Union was the second, and both Cold War adversaries initially saw Israel as a potential ally. Eventually the Soviet Union changed course and began to push the "Zionism is racism" line that was popular at the United Nations for many years. While the United States eventually became Israel's greatest champion, we actually sided against Israel in its dispute with Egypt during the 1956 Suez crisis, and even as late as the Six-Day War in 1967, U.S. support for Israel was ambivalent. It was during that war that the USS *Liberty* was attacked by Israeli jets, killing thirty-four Americans on board. The Israeli government claims it was an accident, but the circumstances surrounding the attack have made it a source of controversy ever since.

By the early 1970s, however, our support for Israel was assured. As many of the other powers in the region drifted toward Soviet friendship, Israel was seen as a vital forward outpost in the struggle against Communist domination of the region. Our foreign aid to Israel grew by leaps and bounds. The end of the Cold War, which should have led us to reassess our foreign ties, changed little: our political and financial support for Israel didn't waiver. There was a large and vocal lobby in the United States—made up not only of American Jews who support the Zionist ideal but also of Christian evangelicals convinced they are doing the Lord's work in standing up for Israel—devoted to maintaining that support. Among the most extreme members of this lobby is a belief that it is the duty of the United States to stand by Israel no matter what the issue, even when it is not in our national interest to do so. "America stands by its friends," they say, and "Israel is our greatest friend."

Having worked in Israel, I can say that the Israelis do not see things that way. Yes, they appreciate the vast sums of money that come their way each year, and they are happy to be able to count on U.S. support. But the Israelis see our relationship as an alliance in their interests, not a friendship that can never be questioned. Israel is primarily concerned about Israel. Over the years Israelis have spied on the US both at home and abroad; in fact, the theft of sensitive technologies by Israeli agents is a continuing concern. Our diplomats stationed in Israel are sometimes subject to petty insults designed to let them know who is in charge. While I was assigned to our embassy in Tel Aviv, getting an answer to diplomatic notes regarding alleged mistreatment of American citizens could sometimes be an exercise in futility. It is not that the Israelis are hostile to us, it is simply that they are looking out for themselves. We should do the same.

The fight against radical Islamic terrorism has made that a bit more complicated than it would have been pre-9/11. Since we now face many of the same threats the Israelis have faced for years, there is a tendency to see Israel as the only "safe" ally for Americans in the region. There is a certain amount of truth in that, and the Israelis definitely see it that way. I was working in Israel on 9/11, and the reaction I got from Israelis—as soon as they had expressed their sorrow for our losses—was "but now you know how we feel."

But we should not let common experiences and similar adversaries cloud our judgment. U.S. foreign policy should always be determined in Washington, not in Jerusalem. This does not mean becoming hostile to Israel by any means, but it does mean working for our own national interests, just as Israel works for her own.

One thing we need to re-examine is the three billion dollars of aid we provide Israel each year. The Israelis have the strongest military in the region, with nuclear capability. They can look out for themselves. They also have a very well-developed First World economy that in 2015 ranked nineteen on the UN's Human Development Index (just ahead of Luxembourg and just behind South Korea). There is no American interest served by providing this level of aid; it only serves to free up monies in Israel so that they can afford things like universal health care for all Israeli citizens, including free abortions for most women.[3] We should respect Israel's sovereignty by cutting the cords that make it appear to be an American client state.

Of course, I realize that this is probably politically impossible. The Israel lobby is very generous in rewarding its backers with campaign funds—and quite vindictive in targeting for defeat those politicians who disagree with its goals. But if we are to have a foreign policy that puts America first, that includes putting America ahead of Israel. We should obviously continue to work together where our interests coincide. In the security realm there is plenty of room for the sharing of intelligence on potential threats—so long as we can verify the sources for those threats Israel gives us intelligence on. We never want to be in a position where we allow ourselves to simply do the bidding of Israel—or any other nation. In Ronald Reagan's famous phrase, we should trust, but verify.

Lest you get the wrong idea, I actually think that Israel is the best country in the Middle East when it comes to human rights—a point that some Palestinians will agree with, at least in private. I once spoke with an Arab religious leader who lived in the Palestinian territories and had been able to travel back and forth between them and Israel proper. He had been harassed on a number of occasions by Israeli officials, but he admitted that given the chance he would gladly relocate his family to Israel, because even with the petty harassment, Israel was much better for an Arab Christian family than the Palestinian territories—and this was when Yassir Arafat and his relatively moderate faction were still in power, before the Palestinians voted in Hamas. He said that his children were constantly subjected to Islamic propaganda in the schools, even in subjects like mathematics ("If there are two mosques in neighborhood A and three mosques in neighborhood B, how many mosques are there in total?"), and that there was a general suspicion of Christians, as if they were not quite fully Palestinians, but rather aligned with the "Crusaders" of the West. My point is not that Israel is some sort of rogue state, nor that "Zionism is racism," nor that a Jewish conspiracy exists to (fill in the blank with any crackpot anti-Semitic theory you can think of). It is simply that we should go back to thinking of Israel as a *foreign* country. We can love the United Kingdom; we can love Canada; we can love Australia; and yes, we can love Israel. But we should love America above all other nations and support her interests first and foremost.

I will only say a few things about Israel's policy in Gaza and the West Bank—the Palestinian territories. This is another area that has occupied far too much of our time and resources, probably because of our inordinate solicitude for Israel in formulating foreign policy goals. As world peace is certainly preferable to world war, we do have an interest is seeing that people live together in harmony rather than in conflict. But our options are very limited when it comes to resolving conflicts to which we are not a party. We can be available for mediation, should both sides agree, as Theodore Roosevelt did to help end the Russo-Japanese War. Beyond that, we should be bold enough and humble enough to step aside. In the case of the Israeli-Palestinian conflict, the parties that need to make an agreement are the Israelis and the Palestinians. Whether that agreement is in the form of a two-state solution, or a federal state, or some other arrangement is really not any of our concern. Israel has a thriving economy and potent military capability on its side, but the Palestinians have demographics on theirs. The strengths and weaknesses of each party will eventually cause one or the other to cave in on key demands that have thus far made a lasting agreement impossible. And only the two parties involved can make the agreement last.

In the meantime, it is not in our interest to continue to fund communities who actively thumb their noses at us. The United States provides some 30 percent of the budget of the United Nations Relief and Works Agency (UNRWA), the body responsible for providing aid to Palestinian refugees in the Middle East. At least in part because of Palestinian recalcitrance in making peace with Israel, in January 2018 the Trump administration announced it would withhold payment of around half of the $125 million we had pledged to UNRWA. Of course the liberal media promptly predicted disaster.[4] Leaving aside the whole question of what constitutes a "refugee" (many of the Palestinians classified this way are now in their third generation of living outside the borders of modern Israel), it is not clear why it is a U.S. responsibility to bankroll a population some 76 percent of which—higher than that of any other people in the region—according to recent polls, views the United States as an enemy.[5] Why this has not been the responsibility of those nations in the neighborhood who have long trumpeted the Palestinian cause is anyone's guess, but the U.S. has for far too long been willing to play the patsy by writing checks to those who would spit in our face. If paying the parties in the region to make peace is folly, then subsidizing those who refuse to do so is the height of insanity. This is not to say that the Israeli side is without blame. One area of conflict is with continued Jewish settlement in the West Bank. I personally think that Israel hurts her own cause by continuing to build such settlements, but just as I do not want Israel to dictate to the United States what is in our interest, I do not think we should be telling the Israelis what is in theirs. Our policy on new Israeli settlements should be agnostic, as it does not directly concern a vital U.S. interest. This is consistent with what I have asserted concerning our policy in other parts of the world. Whether we are talking about Jerusalem and Hebron or Crimea or Abkhazia, the parties on the ground have to resolve these issues, and we should stand aside and let them do just that.

An aside here is necessary to discuss President Trump's recognition of Jerusalem as the capital of Israel in December 2017. I will admit that if it were up to me I would not have issued this declaration, seeing it as an unnecessary provocation, likely to stir up hostility in the region. But I will admit that I would have been wrong. Of course, the measure met with widespread hostility among all the usual actors, but the world has not ended as a result. Israel has long maintained that Jerusalem is its capital, and it is not likely to move it so long as the Jewish state continues to exist. President Trump, acting again against the conventional wisdom, went with his gut and decided that we would acknowledge that a country with whom we maintain diplomatic relations actually is able to call the shots when it comes to telling the world where it decides to put its capital city. While some might see this as a further alignment of our own interests with those of Israel, it is nothing of the sort. Traditional American policy has been to recognize the de facto government, at least eventually, as the

PUTTING AMERICA FIRST
Donald Trump
Edition

"Respect has to be shown to the U.S. or we're just not doing any further.... That money is on the table, and that money is not going to [the Palestinian Authority] unless they sit down and negotiate peace. Why should we do that as a country if they're doing nothing for us?"

—**DONALD TRUMP** at a meeting with Israeli Prime Minister Benjamin Netanyahu on Thursday, January 25, 2018, in Davos, Switzerland

authority over a particular territory. If we are to recognize Israel as a legitimate country, it only seems logical that we would also acknowledge the capital that that country calls its own. What is more, since our recognition of Jerusalem, Guatemala has followed our lead, and other nations are said to be considering such a move as well.[6]

From Israel, let's fly out of the traditional Middle East and reach the periphery of the region with an examination of Afghanistan, another country whose effect on U.S. policy has been way out of proportion to its importance. Before the 1960s Afghanistan was barely a blip on our diplomatic radar, but fears of Soviet expansion led to increased U.S. involvement. A revolution in 1978 brought a Communist government to power, and instability in the country led to the murder of our ambassador, Adolph Dubs, in 1979. That same year, the Soviet Union invaded Afghanistan in order to reshuffle and stabilize the shaky Communist leadership there. Afghanistan then became part of the front lines of the Cold War for the next ten years, with U.S. assistance provided to various Muslim mujahideen forces fighting the Soviet Union.

Following the withdrawal of Soviet forces in 1989, Afghanistan descended into a period of civil war that was to last into the new century and beyond. One of the mujahideen groups, the fundamentalist Sunni Muslim Taliban that had originated in Pakistan, came to rule much of Afghanistan, including the capital Kabul. Before 9/11, the Taliban was largely known in the West for their destruction of the ancient Buddhist statues at Bamiyan, monuments they considered offensive to Islam. This erasure of Afghanistan's history was often cited as an example of the barbarity and backwardness of the Taliban regime. (This episode is not brought up much anymore, now that American liberals have decided that destroying "offensive" historical statues is actually rather progressive.)

During the Taliban's fight with rivals for control of Afghanistan, they found an ally in the equally rigid and puritanical Islamic group known as Al-Qaeda, led by a Saudi national by the name of Osama bin Laden, whose family had grown wealthy in the construction business. While the Taliban primarily directed their enmity towards Soviets and fellow Afghans, Al-Qaeda was more open-minded in their hatred, not limiting it to actors in their part of the globe but extending it to much of the non-Islamic world. The United States held the prime position as the country most worthy of Al-Qaeda's ire. Osama bin Laden never forgave the United States for deploying troops in Saudi Arabia during the first Gulf War, thereby "profaning" the sacred soil of that country—home to the Muslim holy cities of Mecca and Medina—with "infidels." The belief that certain human beings can pollute the area for others by their very presence provides a valuable insight into the mindset of the radical Islamic terrorist. In an Afghanistan controlled by a Taliban actively eradicating traces of previous "unclean" people in Afghanistan, bin Laden found a comfortable environment from which to plan his attacks.

When the United States was brutally attacked on September 11, 2001, and the Taliban government of Afghanistan continued to harbor the Al-Qaeda leadership within its borders, the United States launched an assault on that country with the dual objective of destroying Al-Qaeda and driving the Taliban from power. It was a completely justified response by the United States that served to safeguard Americans from further terrorist action as well as send a message to any other potential bad actors out there that the U.S. would retaliate for attacks on American soil.

That the U.S. was justified in taking that action can be seen in the world-wide condemnation of the 9/11 attacks and support for our response to it. The United States never enjoyed such widespread support at any time in the post–World War II era. Over fifty nations either participated in or offered support to the U.S.-led effort in Afghanistan, ranging from use of airspace over Oman to the deployment of several thousand troops in the case of the United Kingdom. In addition, Americans were united, as has not happened since. The only vote in Congress against the use of force in Afghanistan came from Barbara Lee (D-Calif.), whose former affiliation with the Black Panthers may explain her stand—apparently, she supports violence only to promote socialist revolution.

But the unity would not last. Forces within the White House and beyond saw an opportunity to launch a campaign to bring universal peace and stability through our exercise of "global unilateralism," a phrase attributed to former Trotskyite and later neoconservative thinker Irving Kristol. The idea was that we could start from Afghanistan and remake not only that country but every other retrograde nation in the region, including Iraq. Two other neoconservatives, David Frum and Richard Perle, even published a book titled *An End to Evil*—a foreign policy goal that's significantly more ambitious than looking out for U.S. interests, to say the least. In a short time, we lost sight of those interests, lost our path, and found ourselves involved in a war that, seventeen years after it all began, appears to have no end in sight. That the people who pushed for our expanded military role in the region were sincere in their belief that they could change the world for the better is beyond question. But that many of the architects of our policy from that time period still defend the course we took shows the triumph of ideology over reality. In any case, our involvement in Afghanistan is a good example of how a foreign policy guided by national interest—as it was in the initial phases of our response—can mutate into grandiose dreams of creating an earthly utopia. National interests can and have been successfully defended over the course of human history. Utopias do not have as good a track record.

At this point the pertinent question is, what do we do now that we are in Afghanistan? We can lament the fact that we did not follow through on our original objectives for being there back in the 2001–2003 period and instead got distracted by an irrelevant war in Iraq. Yes, after taking out the Taliban we should have concentrated on Al-Qaeda, and then maybe Osama bin Laden would not have enjoyed another decade of life. But we did not do that, and no amount of Monday-morning quarterbacking is going to change that. We have to take the situation we're in now and figure a way out with honor.

PUTTING AMERICA FIRST
Donald Trump
Edition

"The American people are weary of war without victory. Nowhere is this more evident than with the war in Afghanistan, the longest war in American history—17 years. I share the American people's frustration. I also share their frustration over a foreign policy that has spent too much time, energy, money, and most importantly lives, trying to rebuild countries in our own image, instead of pursuing our security interests above all other considerations."

—**DONALD TRUMP**, remarks on the Strategy in Afghanistan and South Asia, Fort Myer, Virginia, August 21, 2017

The good news is that Americans who are tired of endless bouts of pointless nation-building for people who neither desire nor value our input appear to have a champion in Donald Trump. President Trump outlined his new Afghanistan strategy in August of 2017, and it appears to be spot on. His goal is to end American involvement in that troubled part of the world, but he does not want to leave it in a worse state than when we arrived. This is not because of altruism or a desire to "pursue the world as it should be," as President Obama wanted to do, but rather to safeguard America's foremost national interest: the security of Americans at home and abroad.

In the recent past, a Taliban-controlled Afghanistan played host to Al-Qaeda and others whose *raison d'etre* was to inflict pain on the West, particularly the United States. There is no reason to doubt that a future Taliban state in Afghanistan would do the same. President Trump, therefore, has dropped the artificial restraints that the Obama administration had imposed in our war effort there and pledged to do what we should have done before we got distracted by Iraq.[7]

Specifically, the president has declared that our military strategy will no longer be governed by a timetable but by conditions on the ground—and that we will not announce ahead of time to our enemies what we are planning to do, whether that involves withdrawing or increasing troop levels. Trump has also announced that "we will not dictate to the Afghan people how to live, or how to govern their own complex society. We are not nation-building again. We are killing terrorists." In other words, we are focusing on America First, and seeking to neutralize any enemies posing a threat to our American homeland and using

Afghanistan as a refuge, as Al-Qaeda did in the lead-up to 9/11. While the press has not spent much time analyzing this new policy, since it has too much substance to make a snappy headline, those who are closely following our involvement in Afghanistan have expressed cautious optimism, with even *Foreign Affairs*, hardly a Trump organ, declaring that the president's policy "could actually work."[8] As of this writing, the optimism expressed by *Foreign Affairs* appears to be warranted. According to a December 2017 interview with Brigadier General Lance Bunch, on the ground with U.S. troops in Kabul, the new policy of "taking the gloves off" is severely disrupting Taliban networks and revenue sources. "The Taliban strategy is moving backwards. As they are unable to conduct offensive combat operations, they have transitioned back to high-profile attacks, assassinations and kidnapping for ransom, all of which indiscriminately target the Afghan people," thus undermining their popular support.[9]

Whether this strategy prevails in the long term is still an open question; after all, we are seventeen years into this war. The tragedy of President Trump's new policy is that it was not implemented back in 2001. Had it been put in place at that time, we would not be talking about Afghanistan today. We need to use our troops to target those forces that wish us harm and destroy them utterly, and, when we have finished that job, come home. Afghanistan has been the graveyard of overambitious peoples, dating back to Alexander the Great. We don't need to join that list.

Incidentally, in the same speech in which he announced his new Afghanistan strategy, President Trump shared some

observations about what being an American is all about: "Loyalty to our nation demands loyalty to one another. Love for
America requires love for all of its people. When we open our
hearts to patriotism, there is no room for prejudice, no place for
bigotry, and no tolerance for hate." I guess this is just another
example that illustrates why many on the Left loudly proclaim
that there can be "no debate"" that Donald Trump is a racist.[10]

Another major change in policy that President Trump
announced in the Afghanistan speech concerns Pakistan, so let's
take a moment to discuss our interests in that country. Pakistan
was born in the struggle for Indian independence after the end of
World War II. Predominantly Muslim, it separated from the
majority Hindu Indian subcontinent, taking East Pakistan (which
later became Bangladesh) along with it. The tensions that led to
this separation continue to exist between the two countries, which
have fought several wars against each other in the latter part of
the twentieth century. Both Pakistan and India possess nuclear
weapons, so any conflict between the two always sees the specter
of mutual nuclear annihilation lurking in the shadows.

During the Cold War, as we have seen, we paid particular
attention to Pakistan, regarding it as a useful buffer against Soviet
expansion in that part of the world, especially as India had
declared herself "non-aligned." As a result, Pakistan benefited
heavily from U.S. aid.

Things got murkier after the end of the Cold War. After 9/11,
Pakistan was seen as a potentially valuable partner in the War
on Terror, but Pakistani actions vis-à-vis the extremists were
contradictory at best. Some of the worst Islamic radicals found
a comfortable home in Pakistan—a state of affairs that seemed

to suggest Pakistani officials were playing a double game, pledging fealty to their American sugar daddy while whoring it up with Islamic terrorists on the side. After all, Osama bin Laden was killed not in a cave in a remote corner of Afghanistan but living in a large compound less than a mile from Pakistan's main military academy. Either Pakistani military officials were complicit in his presence in their country or their incompetence was on a scale rarely seen in the annals of history. It would be as if bin Laden had booked a room at the Fairbridge Inn and Suites in West Point, New York, just down the road from the U.S. Military Academy, ordering the occasional pizza from Domino's, and no one noticed he was there.

Whatever our interest was in Pakistan during the Cold War, times have changed, and President Trump, unique among American presidents since that time, seems to understand this. Without directly threatening Pakistan, he has made it clear that the days of America turning a blind eye to Pakistani double-dealing are over. The Pakistanis are no longer untouchable because their alienation from the U.S. might thwart some long-term ambition to reform and redevelop the Muslim world. Rather, they will be held accountable when their actions threaten American lives and well-being.

One of the first measures the Trump administration has undertaken is a suspension of some $2 billion in security aid to Islamabad until Pakistan does more to attack terrorist sanctuaries in their country. Thus far, Pakistani officials have held back on decisive action, with some threatening through proxies that maybe they will just have to get friendly with China or Russia instead—an attempt to revive the old Cold War game of playing one side off the other.[11] While that may have worked back then, today we can afford to insist that the Pakistanis cooperate with us. As President Trump remarked in the same speech to which I have previously alluded, "No partnership can survive a country's harboring of militants and terrorists who target U.S. service members and officials. It is time for Pakistan to demonstrate its commitment to civilization, order, and to peace." The provision of security aid to any country should be directly tied to our own national interests. If the country is helping to provide us security, then aid may be appropriate in some cases. But if the "aid" is really just a form of extortion—*give me money, or I will be really bad*—we should simply walk away.

We have alluded often to Iraq, so we might as well address that country now. Despite the fight against ISIS, that country largely dropped out of the headlines, partly because of events elsewhere in the world—but also because the media is now focusing on more important things, like menacing, century-old Confederate statues and racist NFL teams that won't sign on second-rate players who insist on making offensive gestures during the national anthem. But, despite the media's lack of interest, Iraq still costs us a lot of money, and our attention to that nation is *way* out of proportion to its importance. Our embassy there is the largest in the world—some ten times the size of our embassy in Beijing, to name a country that just might have a greater impact on our national interests. If we could just expand the embassy by about six acres, it would be larger than one entire country: Vatican City.

Iraq has not always played such an important role in U.S. foreign policy. It is largely an artificial country cobbled together from three Ottoman provinces (*vilayets*) that correspond to the divisions still evident in Iraq today. These are Mosul and the north, home to the large Kurdish minority; Baghdad and central Iraq, home to much of the Sunni Muslim Arab population; and Basra and the south, largely Shi'a Muslim and also Arab. While we recognized the sovereignty of Iraq early on, our involvement there was insignificant until after World War II. Britain remained the dominant power in the region and even invaded Iraq in 1941 after a pro-Axis coup took control of the government in Baghdad.

The Cold War shaped our relations with Iraq, especially after the overthrow of the restored monarchy in 1958 by the socialist Ba'athist movement, of which Saddam Hussein was a member. Iraq's perceived orientation towards the Soviet Union left us suspicious of Baghdad during this period, which was marked by several coups. Saddam Hussein consolidated power in the late 1960s and early 1970s.

The Iran-Iraq War, starting in 1980, changed the way we viewed Iraq. At this time the new revolutionary Islamic Republic of Iran was holding our Tehran-based diplomatic staff hostage, so Saddam Hussein's declaration of war on Iran was seen as a good thing. Perhaps Iraq could take down the rogue regime in Tehran and bring our people home, since we did not seem able to do it on our own (this was during the administration of Jimmy Carter).

The Iranian government eventually released the hostages on the day Ronald Reagan became president, perhaps sensing that they would have a harder time with the new sheriff in town. While our relationship with Iraq was strained at times, we did resume diplomatic relations with Baghdad during the 1980s, and Iraq remained an important counterbalance to potential Iranian expansionism. So we largely turned a blind eye to Saddam Hussein's actions against opponents of his regime—actions later cited as justifications for going to war against Baghdad.

All this changed in 1990. Iraq, citing thin territorial claims to the wealthy Kingdom of Kuwait, invaded and annexed that country. This action was condemned by the United Nations. The United States, then in the presidency of George H. W. Bush, led the response, even though we had no defense treaty with Kuwait. The invasion of Kuwait, while reprehensible, was not part of any larger movement intended to threaten the United States or even U.S. interests. And yet we went to war. As in World War I (our effort to "make the world safe for democracy") we sent American troops in harm's way for an abstract principle, in President George H. W. Bush's words, the creation of a "new world order." In so doing, we would tie American foreign policy to a spot on the globe with no direct bearing on American interests and create the circumstances that would lead to an even more costly war, both in terms of the numbers of lives lost and the amount drained from our national treasury. These are the dangers of a foreign policy that does not put America first. The first President Bush's September 11, 1990 (note the date) remarks before a joint session of Congress on the "new world order" he hoped to create sum up the utopian ideology that has too often obscured America's national interests in recent years: "Out of these troubled times, our fifth objective—a new world order—can emerge: a new era—freer from the threat of terror, stronger in the pursuit of justice, and more secure in the quest for peace. An era in which the nations of the world, East and West, North and South, can prosper and live in harmony. A hundred generations have searched for this elusive path to peace, while a thousand wars raged across the span of human endeavor. Today that new world is struggling to be born, a world quite different from the one we've known."

In military terms, the first Gulf War was a resounding success. We liberated Kuwait and utterly defeated the Iraqi Army. But since Saddam Hussein remained in power, adherents of the "new world order" were still champing at the bit for an opportunity to bring him down.

Barely had the first planes taken off for Afghanistan in 2001 when neoconservatives began plotting how to divert our efforts to settle scores with Saddam. There was no question that the leader of Iraq was a world-class thug, but most Americans would not have been keen to go to war just on that basis—especially when we were already involved in one war against people who had actually attacked us. So those angling for war suggested, contrary to all factual evidence, that Iraq was really involved in 9/11, and resurrected claims about Iraq's development of weapons of mass destruction. The inference was that if we did not go to war *now*, it was just a matter of time before Cheyenne, Wyoming, or Kansas City, Missouri, was nothing but glowing embers of nuclear waste.

In time, many Americans began to believe this version of events, and U.S.

> **PUTTING AMERICA FIRST**
> George W. Bush
> Edition*
>
> "I just don't think it's the role of the United States to walk into a country and say, we do it this way, so should you."
>
> —**GEORGE W. BUSH**, Presidential Debate of October 11, 2000
>
> *He appears to have changed his mind later.

forces invaded Iraq in 2003, diverting resources from our war in Afghanistan and helping to ensure that our efforts there would have to continue for years to come. While we defeated Iraq's conventional forces in short order, as we had in the Gulf War back in 1991, the fall of the Saddam regime lifted the lid on all manner of groups whose aspirations he had suppressed: Kurds, Shi'as, fundamentalist Sunnis, and others. Many of these people hated us even more than they hated Saddam, and our forces soon became targets for an insurgency that would last years.

I won't recount the history of the Iraq War. I will just point out that we have very little to show for the thousands of lives and millions of dollars that were spent in it. The crucial role of Iraq as a counterbalance against Iranian power has largely been negated as the new Shi'a-dominated government we helped bring to power has drawn closer to Tehran in recent years. Iraq's fragile government faced an ISIS-led insurgency that would likely not have arisen under a Saddam Hussein dictatorship. While the Iraqi Army, with effective U.S. assistance thanks in large part to President Trump's administration, has made dramatic gains against ISIS, effectively nullifying their new Islamic Caliphate, the situation in Iraq is far from stable. ISIS is no longer the threat it was just a year ago, but the tenuous nature of the regime in Baghdad leaves space for other groups to arise. Saddam was evil, but between a gangster-like dictator who only eliminated those he sees as a threat to his power, and terrorists whose ideology requires they eliminate everyone who does not subscribe to their narrow vision of Islam—Christians, Yazidis, secularists, and other Muslims, especially Shi'a—I will take Saddam every time.

Our biggest mistake in Iraq was that we acted where our national interests were not at stake. Even the architects of our policy there must have realized this, since they spent so much time coming up with national security reasons to provide a fig leaf for an invasion that was primarily designed to promote a new vision of America as the Universal Arbiter of Right and Wrong. In their estimation, taking out Saddam and remaking Iraq into a Middle Eastern version of Switzerland would be a "cakewalk."[12] Any residual doubts about our new global imperial role would vanish as we went on to transform Iran and Syria and Libya and anywhere else in the world where people dared to think differently than we did. Needless to say, it did not quite work out that way, and our war effort in Iraq officially ended on December 18, 2011.

What are our current interests in Iraq? Frankly, they are very few. We have an interest in not seeing Iraq become a base for an ISIS or similar organizations that could lash out at the West, so our cooperation with Iraqi military forces, providing resources and training, is useful. We want to ensure that radical Islamists are tied down fighting in Iraq rather than planting bombs in America. But we should resist any temptation to re-introduce large numbers of U.S. troops into Iraq. Then once again we will become the issue—those who may be otherwise uncomfortable with the radical version of Islam will be driven over to the extremists as the one force capable of expelling the "infidel." We need to re-think what is truly important to us in the region. We have a long-stated commitment, for example, to the territorial integrity of Iraq, but that is really none of our concern. Iran, too, is very committed to Iraqi territorial integrity, given its friendliness toward the current Iraqi government, and Turkey is committed to Iraqi territorial integrity, given its hatred of the Kurds. Those two countries have clear national interests at stake in maintaining Iraq as a single entity. We do not. Iraq may continue as a nation-state for the foreseeable future, but should it break up into a Kurdistan in the north, a Sunni-dominated belt in the center led out of Baghdad, and a Shi'a state centered on Basra, it would not be the end of the world. In fact, under the Ottoman Empire, just one hundred years ago, that was pretty much the set-up. In either case, we should work to ensure good relations with the de facto government of the moment and assure them that the United States no longer has any designs on the territory of Iraq or any successor states, but also that we will not stand idly by if forces seeking to do harm to American interests are sheltered by any regimes that may take power in the area.

Since our long-term interest in Iraq is only peripheral, we need to scale back our diplomatic presence there. Baghdad no longer needs to be the largest embassy ever built by man. We should look into downsizing there and also re-examine the viability of our consulate in Basra. During the Iraq War, our Provincial Reconstruction Team (PRT) in Basra did a lot of good work (full disclosure: I served for a year and a half at PRT Basra). But it is not clear whether the maintenance of this facility—located miles from the city of Basra itself—is really worth the cost. Even the United Kingdom, which has historic ties with Basra and which maintained a consulate general near our PRT when I was in Iraq, decided to close that facility in 2012 as a cost-saving measure. On the other hand, we should keep our consulate in Erbil open because of its location in the autonomous Kurdish region, to maintain channels of communication with the leadership of Kurdistan, especially should they opt for even greater autonomy, or independence.

Next door to Iraq is Iran, which, unlike most of the countries of the region, is one of great antiquity. The ancient Persian people, whose Zoroastrian religion still exists in Iran, were running one of the largest empires in the world centuries before Rome came on the scene as a world power. Iran was Islamicized in the seventh and eighth centuries A.D., but her language and ancient culture still distinguish her from her Arab neighbors. The fact that the minority Shi'a form of Islam predominates in Iran also marks her as different from her neighbors, most of whom adhere to the Sunni Muslim faith.

While European powers, particularly Russia, carved away at portions of Iran in the modern era and British forces called the shots there in the early twentieth century, Iran, unlike most of the rest of the Muslim world, was never a colony. And Iranian national identity runs deep.

The United States initially became involved in Iran after Mohammad Mosaddegh came to power in 1951. Mosaddegh's nationalization of Iran's petroleum industry severely perturbed Great Britain, which was heavily invested in it. British officials convinced the Eisenhower administration of the potential for the socialist-leaning Mosaddegh and Communist elements within his government to flip Iran—and potentially the entire Middle East, with its vital oil supplies—over to the Soviet Union's side in the Cold War. Reacting to this perceived threat, covert operations, sponsored in part by the Central Intelligence Agency, overthrew Mosaddegh in a 1953 coup d'état.[13]

Over the next two decades, while Iran did maintain a parliamentary form of government, Shah Mohammad Reza Pahlavi
became progressively more autocratic, taking on greater and
greater power and losing popular support. The United States
continued to back the Shah, not only as a bulwark against Communism but because Iran under his rule was one of the rare
Muslim nations to have good relations with Israel. By the late
1970s, street protests against the Shah began to spread, orches-
trated by a wide variety of groups representing Islamist, nationalist, and even Communist constituencies. The situation on the
ground deteriorated, the Shah fled Iran, and the Islamists gained
the upper hand with the formation of a new government led by
the formerly exiled cleric Ayatollah Ruhollah Khomeini. Iran
eventually became an Islamic republic that suppressed non-
Islamic influences across all levels of society. Relations with
Israel were broken (even though unofficial channels were maintained—the Israelis were Tehran's silent partners during the
Iran-Iraq War, seeing the Islamic Republic as a necessary counterbalance to Saddam Hussein's Iraq). Secular parties were
purged, and while Iran's historic minority religious communities—Christians, Jews, and Zoroastrians—were left largely
untouched, members of the Baha'i faith, seen by the ayatollahs
as a Muslim heresy, were severely persecuted, with untold numbers executed.

The United States was singled out for special hate, with the
Iranian leadership labeling America the "Great Satan." Iranian
"students" stormed the U.S. Embassy in Tehran in 1979, taking
most of the staff there hostage. Against every tenet of international law, the Iranian government refused to act against the

"students," and the hostage crisis left the United States paralyzed for over a year, with a failed rescue attempt only adding to the "malaise" that afflicted the American body politic under President Jimmy Carter. As we have seen, the hostage crisis finally ended when Iran was faced with a new American president, Ronald Reagan, who did not subscribe to the Carter Hand-Wringing School of International Relations. Our diplomats were on their way home as Reagan took the oath of office.

Since that time, our relationship with Iran has been quite complex. Iranian support of Hezbollah and other groups inspired by the Iranian Revolution led us to fear that Tehran would do all it could do to destabilize the Middle East—hence our leaning towards Baghdad when Iraqi and Iranian armies went to war. Neither American support for anti-government Iranian insurgent groups nor the downing of an Iranian airliner by U.S. forces in 1988 did anything to warm relations. Then came news that Iran was seeking nuclear capability and U.S.-backed economic sanctions against Iran seemed to nail the coffin shut on any hope of normalized relations between our two countries.

President Obama appeared keen to reverse this downward trend in our relationship, but the way he went about it led to one of the most lop-sided arrangements in the relationship of our two countries. Obama seemed desperate to be remembered as the chief executive who reined in Iran's nuclear program, and an agreement was reached, that, according to Obama sources, would be "the cornerstone of a safer, more secure world."[14] In return for the lessening of certain U.S. sanctions, Iran would halt key aspects of its nuclear program and allow their actions to be verified. At the end of the day the agreement would bring peace and harmony to the Middle East and the world as a whole. If any of that were true, I would be the first to applaud President Obama for his efforts, but it appears that there was more to this deal than first met the eye. According to the liberal journal *Politico*, President Obama secretly released from custody several figures who had been actively involved in attempts to acquire critically important materials for Iran's nuclear and missile program.[15] In addition, Obama administration officials put an end to operations to thwart Iranian-backed terrorist organization Hezbollah's vast network of money laundering and drug trafficking, believing that they would undermine the chances of getting a deal before President Obama left office. Thus, we undid actions that actually contributed to our safety in return for a deal largely based on trust in the Tehran regime. President Trump has criticized this deal—although not the concept of making some kind of agreement—and said that he would refrain from granting relief from U.S. sanctions unless flaws in the arrangement can be fixed.[16]

I will give credit to the Obama administration for staying out of the 2009 "Green Revolution" in Iran, in which thousands of Iranians took to the streets to protest hardline president Mahmoud Ahmadinejad. These protests have led to a reform movement, the "Green Path of Hope," an opposition group working against hardline elements within the Iranian government. Active American support of this movement would have tainted it as a tool of outside interests. Sometimes, good things can happen in the world independent of our all-knowing and benevolent interference. If only the Obama administration had been equally reticent in its support of the so-called "Arab Spring."

Despite our differences with Iran, our countries have occasionally shared common goals. Many of our most dangerous enemies in the Middle East since 9/11—Al-Qaeda, ISIS, and the Taliban—are Sunni Muslim fundamentalists who hate the Iranian government with the same intensity that they hate the United States. It is in Iran's interest that none of these groups achieve a foothold in the area, as they threaten both Iran's security and the well-being of other Shi'a Muslims across the region—of whom Iran sees herself as a special protector. In addition, while we may lament the growing Iranian influence in Iraq, the majority Shi'a government in Baghdad is fighting ISIS and similar extremist groups on a daily basis, thus eliminating any perceived need to re-introduce large numbers of U.S. troops in that country.

Still, too much bad blood and mistrust between our two nations over the last couple of generations make it unlikely that we will establish anything approaching normalized relations anytime soon. There is no question that Iran represents a threat to United States interests. The real question is identifying the specifics of that threat and how to respond to it.

Contrary to what many neocons would have us believe, the greatest threat that Iran poses to the United States is the possibility of America being drawn into a war in Iran itself. Iran, with some eighty million inhabitants and a much stronger sense of identity than most countries in the region, would likely bog down U.S. forces for an indefinite period of time unless the United States resorted to overwhelming force on a level not seen since the Second World War—something the American people would likely not have a stomach for, absent an unprovoked attack by Iran on American soil. One would hope that those who wish for an American invasion of Iran are patriotic and sensible enough not to conjure up yet another sketchy scenario just to get their way.

The good news is that a U.S.-Iran war is something the Iranian leadership would not like to see. Unlike the nihilists of Al-Qaeda, the theocrats in Tehran, while radical, have not shown themselves to be suicidal. They actually enjoy the power they have accumulated and wish to hold on to it. As bad as a war in Iran would be for the United States, it would be far worse for the Iranians, and they know it.

The bad news is that wars often arise out of causes other than careful planning and the rational consideration of alternatives. Because of the hatred on both sides, it is entirely possible that the United States and Iran could blunder into war. We must not let this happen. Besides the appalling human cost and the massive amount of funding that would be necessary to pursue it, there would be a heavy political price to pay. Donald Trump was elected in part because of his pledge to give Americans a more realistic, America First foreign policy. Should his administration lead our country into yet another Middle Eastern "cakewalk," no Republican will ever have credibility as a candidate who can keep the peace.

This does not mean we have to roll over for the Iranians or do their bidding. It simply means that we have to identify what our interests in the region are, and not engage in overreach.

Iran's progress toward nuclear capability is worrying. Given our druthers, we would prefer that no other nation join the nuclear club. After all, one more atom bomb in the world is one more potential atomic explosion. That being said, short of establishing an international anti-nuclear task force that is willing to go to war against any country that appears to be attempting to develop nuclear weapons—a sort of permanent war for permanent peace entity—there is little we can do to prevent a country that has its heart set on this type of weaponry. We can—and should—seek to deny technology to countries we fear are seeking this capability and let them know that our bilateral relations are jeopardized by their efforts. But in the case of nations with whom we have strained relations anyway, our influence will be minimal. In fact, some countries may feel that acquiring nuclear weaponry is the one tool they have to protect them from a potential U.S. invasion.

In the case of Iran, the development of a nuclear weapon does not directly affect American security because of the distance between our nations. Even should Iran develop efficient delivery systems, our nuclear advantage means that an attack by Iran against the United States would likely leave Iran a smoking rubble. An objection could be made that Iran would not have to use nuclear weapons directly. They have not shied away from sponsoring terrorist organizations, such as Hezbollah, when they felt it served their broader interests. But for the Iranian government to allow sophisticated nuclear weapons or technology to fall into the hands of non-state actors or rogue regimes would undermine the deterrent capability that seems to be Tehran's motivation for acquiring nukes in the first place—as any kind of Iranian connection to a nuclear attack would result in the same smoking rubble on the portion of the map once denominated "Iran" as was mentioned above. It would be difficult if not impossible for the Iranians to plausibly deny their handiwork should groups even remotely linked to them acquire nuclear capability.

This does not mean that Iranian acquisition of nuclear weapons poses no danger to anyone. The main threat of Iranian nukes is against Israel, and it is certainly in Israel's interest to see that Iran does not join the nuclear club. The United States would not like to see Tel Aviv—or any other city, for that matter—leveled by an atomic blast. But we have to remember that Israel is also a nuclear power. The Israelis have shown that they have the capability of defending themselves. We should certainly share intelligence with Israeli authorities on Iranian capabilities, hoping they will do the same with us on Iranian and other threats in the region. But we do not need to hold a war guarantee on Israel's behalf against any power she sees as a threat. The best way to keep Iranian aggression toward Israel in check is to let Tehran know that we will not rein in the Israelis should Iran even *appear* to violate international non-proliferation norms. The Israelis have struck before—in 1981 in Iraq and in 2007 in Syria—to block a perceived nuclear threat. They are fully capable of striking again, and Tehran knows this.

According to press reports, the Obama administration thwarted a planned Israeli attack on Iranian nuclear facilities in 2012, apparently worried about the effect such an attack would have on U.S. elections.[17] Whether or not that is true, we should make it clear—to both Israel and Iran—that we no longer have objections to the Israelis defending themselves against any perceived nuclear threat. It is not in our interest to rein other countries' actions in their own national defense; doing so only gives the impression of an obligation on our part to resolve the threat on our own, thus dragging us into conflicts that do not directly affect our people. Just as we should not "go abroad in search of monsters to destroy," we should not go abroad to keep others from destroying those monsters.

The conventional wisdom is that Iranian attempts to gain hegemony in the region are a bad thing. The Saudis, who see the Iranians as heretics or worse, would certainly have us believe that. But from the standpoint of American interests, this is not the case at all. I am not saying that increased Iranian influence is a good thing—rather, that from the standpoint of the American national interest, it is simply not a thing at all. Our vital interests in the Middle East are in protecting ourselves from potential threats to American lives and seeing that the flow of fossil fuels continues. Even if pro-Iranian regimes popped up all over the Arabian Peninsula—a very unlikely prospect—they would still have to sell their oil to someone, and, as we have seen, oil from this part of the world now constitutes only a small portion of our energy resources. In terms of protecting American lives, increased Iranian influence might actually have a positive effect. Groups like ISIS and Al-Qaeda would not be tolerated where Iranian-backed Shi'as have the upper hand. The wild card, of course, is whether continued U.S.-Iranian tensions would give rise to new Iranian-backed international terrorist groups, but that is unlikely if we signal that we are now in the business of protecting our own interests—not seeking our own hegemony in the region.

We should remain vigilant in our relationship with Iran. We should make it clear to the Iranians that any attack on America

or Americans will be met with stunning levels of force. We should
let them know that we are happy to let the Israelis defend themselves, should they feel threatened. Finally, we should also make
it clear that we are willing to work with them—either overtly or
covertly—in areas of mutual interest. Such cooperation will not
lead to peace and brotherhood overnight, but it could help defuse
some of the tensions in the region and keep us from ending up in
a war that neither side desires.

Syria is a country in the area that also would seem to boast
an ancient pedigree—its capital Damascus is one of the oldest
cities in the world—but it is largely a modern creation with an
ancient name. Traditionally, much of the Levant was referred to
by the name "Syria": a nineteenth-century observer would likely
have called someone from Lebanon, Jordan, or even Israel a Syrian. The present state of Syria, like Iraq, is a country that owes
its existence to the collapse of the Ottoman Empire after World
War I. French forces occupied the area and shaped the borders
of Syria that we know and love today. Interestingly enough, during World War II, Vichy France controlled Syria, so when British
and Australian forces invaded they faced stiff resistance from
French troops, not those of Germany or Italy.

Syria joined the ranks of independent countries in 1946 and
was quickly recognized by the United States. Our relationship
has been a problematic one ever since. Syria's adoption of closer
ties with the Soviet Union during the Cold War was a source of
irritation for the United States, and diplomatic relations between
the U.S. and Syria were dissolved following the Six-Day War in
1967, only to be resumed in the 1970s. We looked with suspicion
on Hafez-al-Assad's Ba'athist regime all through the 1980s,

largely because of its support of terrorism against Israel and its intervention in the Lebanese Civil War, but Syria made common cause with the US during the first Gulf War, contributing several thousand troops to the effort against fellow Ba'athist, Saddam Hussein. Syria did not assist us in the 2003 war, though; in fact, there were accusations that Damascus allowed foreign fighters to cross its territory on the way to fight American troops in Iraq.

Despite the ups and downs of our relationship with Syria, there were no calls for actual war with that country until the administration of Barack Obama. By this time, Hafez-al-Assad, a bloodthirsty tyrant who was Saddam Hussein's equal in ruthlessness, had passed away and been replaced by his son Bashar al-Assad. The younger Assad had been educated in the West, and it was assumed he would be a kinder, gentler version of his father.

To a degree, these predictions were correct. But in the wake of the Arab Spring, protests against the Assad regime broke out all over Syria. I remember these well, as I was then in neighboring Iraq when similar protests erupted (but soon fizzled out). What started as peaceful protests became increasingly violent as Syrian security forces opened fire on protesters in a number of cities. Syria soon plunged into civil war. The United States, pursuing its new dogma of remaking the Middle East into a collection of middle class Western-style suburban democracies, failed to see what was at stake here and instinctively sided with those seeking to overthrow Assad. That the anti-Assad forces contained Western-oriented, non-Islamist groups is beyond question—although I find it interesting that the Communist parties in both Syria and Iraq were considered by Americans working in the region as positive forces for change—O tempora, o mores!

But these are not the only groups seeking to overthrow the Assad regime. A sizeable portion of the Syrian opposition is composed of hard-core Islamists, including ISIS, and because of the fractured nature of the rest of the opposition these groups would be the most likely beneficiaries of the collapse of the government of Bashar al-Assad.

Who would clearly *not* benefit from such a collapse? Syria's religious minorities. Assad himself is an Alawite, a secretive sect that split off from mainstream Islam and believes in, among other things, reincarnation. One can rest assured that the Alawite population, associated as they are with the Assad regime, would have ample opportunity to test the veracity of their belief in reincarnation if fundamentalist Muslims took power in Damascus.

Also threatened would be Syria's large population of Christians, which dates back to the preaching of the Apostle Paul and is one of the biggest in the Islamic world in terms of the percentage of the overall population. The Syrian Civil War has already caused thousands of Christians to abandon their homeland, just as the Iraqi Civil War decimated the ancient Christian population in that country. We have largely ignored the negative effects of our policies on Christians in the Middle East, and this is shameful, not just because they are Christians and thus—all liberal naysaying to the contrary—share common values with us, but also because if they were a more exotic minority, the bicoastal opinion makers would be outspoken in their demands that we "do something." In this regard, it is too bad that Middle Eastern Christians did not have the foresight to dress up as baby seals.

There is no question that Assad has been brutal in his suppression of the revolt against his regime. This is certainly not excusable, though it is understandable. The use of chemical weapons, however, especially against civilian populations, can never be justified. I can understand President Trump's decision to strike back at the Assad regime after he saw photos of the broken bodies of children. But—and this may sound callous, so bear with me—we cannot base our foreign policy on emotionalism; we must have the courage to tie it to the rational defense of national interest. Foreign policy, particularly involving the use of force that is not in pursuit of a clearly thought through outcome, runs the risk of unintended consequences that may be worse than the atrocities that moved us to act out of emotion in the first place. We can all agree that the Assad regime is bad, but based on the recent history of this region what is likely to replace it will be far worse. If Islamists take over Syria, there will be far *more* broken bodies of children—only this time there will be no photographers to snap the shots, since the ones who don't pack their bags and go home will have been beheaded. Whether Syria has a democratic government, a monarch, or a continuation of Ba'athist rule under the Assad family really does not affect vital U.S. interests. An ISIS or ISIS-type regime, dedicated to nihilistic attacks on all things American, would. Fortunately, we do not have to put U.S. forces at risk to stop such a regime from coming to power in Syria. In addition to facing Syrian government troops, radical Islamic terrorist forces in Syria also face Russian military might. John McCain and others of his ilk may see this as some sort of vast conspiracy for Russia to re-establish a greater Soviet Empire, because, you know, "K-G-B." The fact is that Russian efforts to destroy ISIS support our interests. If the country involved were France rather than Russia, I am certain we would see things differently. And I do not think Russia has any intention of creating a protectorate in Syria—they have problems enough of their own—but even if they did, what vital U.S. interests would be at stake? Who rules in Damascus, provided they desire normal relations with the United States, should not even be an issue for our foreign policy. Naturally, in a perfect world we would love to see every government in the Middle East commit to a policy of peace and understanding, with hugs replacing guns and every dispute solved by town hall meetings enthusiastically supported by the entire populace with smiling faces and no ill will towards those with whom they disagree. We do not live in a perfect world. And in the imperfect world we do live in, the very fact that we support a particular faction within a country often leads others there to oppose that faction. At this point in time, given the chaotic situation on the ground in Syria, our only national interest in that country is to ensure that it does not become a base for radical Islamic terrorists. Whoever is willing to help prevent that outcome should not face opposition from the United States.

So it was a wise move when in 2017 President Trump ended our covert program of support for anti-Assad rebels, which had been put in place by President Obama four years earlier.[18] But what about the gassing of opposition forces by the Assad regime? Does this mean we turn a blind eye to Syrian use of chemical weapons? On the contrary, we and the rest of the international community should make it clear that we find such usage unacceptable. But we should rely on those with closer ties to the Syrian regime—such as the Russians—or those more likely to be threatened by Syrian capabilities—such as the Israelis—to make this point. After all, we pretty much turned a blind eye to Saddam Hussein's use of chemical weapons during the Iran-Iraq War, since we considered the Tehran government as the worse of two evils and were worried about Iranian expansion in the Middle East.[19] The nations of the region can therefore be excused for thinking that an attack on Syrian chemical capability by U.S. forces is not a sheerly disinterested humanitarian action.

The same principle holds for our relations with other countries across the Middle East. We should adopt a policy of non-interference in their internal affairs and work with them to ensure that forces hostile to the United States do not take root within their borders. For those that produce significant amounts of fossil fuels, we can assure them of our national interest in keeping the sea lanes open. Nations that prosper through trade are less likely to engage in hostile acts that might jeopardize that prosperity, all other things being equal. We should also reconsider our foreign aid to this part of the world. There is already a push in the U.S. Congress to slash our aid to Egypt,[20] one of the largest Middle Eastern recipients of such aid after Israel. We have already seen how, early on in our history, we decided against a policy of paying tribute to avoid conflict, as was demanded by the Barbary States, the first nation in this part of the world with which we had significant dealings. Our aid to Egypt has always struck me as just that—a kind of tribute in return for keeping the peace, except in this case, the peace is with Israel and not necessarily with us. Egypt has not done so well in prior conflicts with the Jewish State. I don't think they need our money to convince them that they are better off living in peace with their neighbors.

Turkey is a special case. A little over one hundred years ago, the Ottoman Empire was the dominant power in the Middle East. The Turks were the official overlords of this entire region, even if over the years bits of the empire had been detached or were functioning autonomously. At that point in history, in some respects the Ottoman Empire *was* the Middle East. The religious foundation for the empire's government and the late Ottoman policy of pan-Islamism would have put Turkey squarely in the tradition of what we today call fundamentalist Islam.

But after the collapse of the Ottoman Empire following the First World War, the new secular state of Turkey moved away from its Islamic roots. Kemal Atatürk, the founder of modern Turkey, sought to create an ethnically Turkish state similar to the new ethnic states, such as Czechoslovakia and Yugoslavia that were arising in Europe after the fall of the Austro-Hungarian Empire.

And U.S. policy mostly ignored Turkey before the period of the Cold War—with perfect safety. We did not establish diplomatic relations until the late 1920s, and Turkey, which was neutral during World War II, did not figure in our plans during that conflict either.

Our confrontation with the Soviet Empire changed all of that. Turkey had long been a traditional adversary of Russia, and while the Bolshevik government was quick to recognize the secular Turkish state under Atatürk, tensions continued. The United States was hopeful that Turkey—located right on the borders of the Warsaw Pact—could be helpful in resisting Soviet aggression. Turkish leaders, seeking a more Western orientation for their country, were happy to comply. Turkey became a member of

NATO in 1952 and was an effective ally in the struggle to contain Communist expansion, sending troops to Korea during the conflict on that peninsula and allowing the U.S. to build bases on Turkish soil that remain to this day. As a reward for the Turks' assistance, several U.S. administrations have lent their support to Turkey's efforts to join the European Union.

But even during the Cold War, there were tensions in our relationship. Turkey's invasion of Northern Cyprus in 1974 led to an embargo against Ankara that lasted several years. Incidentally, it was during the unrest sparked by this invasion that our ambassador to Cyprus, Rodger Davies, was killed by an unidentified sniper. Turkish failure to acknowledge any responsibility for the 1915 massacres of Armenians in the former Ottoman Empire has rankled many Americans, including a number of U.S. Congressmen.

Despite these tensions, our relationship with Turkey remained strong even after the end of the Cold War. For example, U.S. forces flew missions out of Turkey during the first Gulf War. But in the meantime, new tensions have developed. Over the last thirty years, the secular consensus that dominated Turkish politics has eroded significantly. The chances of Turkey becoming a part of the European Union have diminished, and the Turks are quietly but surely returning to their Middle Eastern roots. Our war in Iraq, and particularly our support for Kurdish forces there—and in Syria—have greatly annoyed Turkish authorities, who see the Kurds as a threat to Turkish territorial integrity. Recently there have been clashes between Turkish and Kurdish forces in the area. While the United States remains popular with members of the military and diplomatic class, things are different on the street, where some 80 percent of Turks view the United States unfavorably.[21]

There is no question that both the United States and Turkey have benefited from the close relationship that developed out of the Cold War. A Soviet-dominated Turkey would have posed tremendous strategic difficulties for Western forces, not to mention causing untold hardships on the Turkish people. Both countries had a common interest in protecting Turkish soil from the Soviet foe.

And we should continue to cooperate with Turkey in matters of mutual national interest, but our view of Turkey as an ally is most assuredly obsolete. As the Turks move away from the West, our interests will likely conflict as much as they intersect. This does not mean that we should consider Turkey an adversary any more than any other nation in that region. It just means that we should not cling to the naïve assumption that Turkey will be forever "on our side." In fact, we should re-think the NATO alliance provisions that commit us to going to war on Turkey's behalf.

Even as American presidents loudly proclaim our friendship and alliance with Turkey, serious tensions have arisen out of differences in our Middle Eastern policies. For example, when it comes to Syria, the U.S. supports an anti-Assad coalition that includes Kurdish forces that Ankara considers a threat to her own security. Rather than pretending that such differences do not exist, we should acknowledge that we and the Turks will both work for our own interests in the region, and that those interest may not always coincide.

Our current policy puts us in a bit of a quandary. We have U.S. troops on the ground advising those same Kurdish forces that Ankara considers a threat to her own national security. The presence of U.S. troops in the region where Turkish and Kurdish forces have come to blows has led some to speculate that we may see the unthinkable scenario of two NATO allies (the U.S. and Turkey) actually doing battle with each other.[22]

This would be a classic example of a war that serves no one's interests, and we should do all we can do to prevent it. The quickest way to do that is to withdraw our forces from the region. This is not "turning our back on an ally," since the Kurds are not fighting as our proxies but rather for their own interests as a people (leaving aside the additional nuance of whether we can accurately describe as an "ally" forces that do not represent a sovereign state). In fact, technically speaking, it is the government of Turkey that is our ally via NATO—which shows the difficulties created by entangling alliances that last well past their expiration date. Ironically, the same voices that loudly proclaim eternal friendship with Turkey have also advocated for a U.S. policy in Syria that is inimical to Turkish interests.[23] Since Americans have no true interest in who rules Damascus provided that it is not a regime that directly threatens American security and well-being, we can actually improve our standing in Turkey by adopting a policy of non-interference in the internal affairs of Syria. This would certainly not be the primary purpose of adopting such a policy, but it's another example of the principle that, more often than not, when we stay out of areas where our national interests are not at stake, we create goodwill in those countries that do have such interests at stake.

Likewise, we have no interest in whether or not Turkey becomes a part of the European Union. This is strictly a matter between Brussels and Ankara, and telling the EU that we think they should open up to Turkey is akin to the EU insisting that Puerto Rico be made a U.S. State (or be granted its independence, for that matter). Let me point out again that the United States does not have to have a position on *everything*—just on those things that directly affect our national interest.

Another area that should not be a matter for U.S. policy is the genocide of the Armenian people in the Ottoman Empire during the First World War. There is no doubt that atrocities were committed by agents of the Ottoman Empire, not only against Armenians but also against other national minorities, like the Greeks and Assyrians. Hundreds of thousands of innocent people—if not more—were subjected to sometimes horrific methods of execution by Turkish officials. There can be no justification for this. That being said, this is now history, as all of the parties involved have been dead for more than a generation. The Armenian Genocide is obviously a sore point with modern Turkish officialdom, who see any admission of their grandfathers' guilt as tainting their struggle to create a Turkish state. It is also obviously a sore point for the descendants of those Armenians (and Greeks and Assyrians) who were brutally persecuted during that time and wish for an official Turkish apology as a means of closure (or, perhaps to discredit the Turkish state). At any rate, it is a dispute best left up to the historians and the descendants of the people involved; it should not be a part of U.S. policy in any manner whatsoever. Armenian Genocide resolutions before Congress often have little to do with the events of 1915, in any case, but are merely sparring matches between opposing Turkish and

Armenian lobbies and highlight some of what is wrong with American politics in general.

We have an interest in maintaining good relations with Turkey, just as we have an interest in maintaining good relations with any country. We no longer, however, have any interest in being yoked to that country in any kind of permanent alliance. We should be bold enough to recognize that our interests change as times change. Agreements made in the past to address events that are in the past should not be allowed to keep a stranglehold on us in the present.

ELEVEN

AFRICA

THE CONTINENT WE FORGOT ABOUT

With the exception of Europe, no continent has had a greater impact on the United States than Africa. The first recorded Africans to arrive in British North America came over as indentured servants from Angola in 1619, although there were Africans in Spanish areas of what is now the United States well before that date. As indentured servitude evolved into chattel slavery, Africans and their descendants were responsible for a large percentage of the growth of the American economy, and Africans' cultural mores influenced their European and Native American neighbors. Despite being relegated to an inferior status for much of their history, the sons of Africa in the New World had an indelible effect on American language, culture, cuisine, and music.

But this influence was a result of people from Africa being brought to a new land and forced to adapt, rather than of an exchange of ideas between sovereign entities. One reason for this is that until very recently there were very few nation-states on the African continent—and the ones that did exist, such as Ethiopia, had little or no contact with the United States. Most of the African continent not subject to tribal rule was under the governance of European colonizers. The exception to that rule was North Africa, whose states were then under the theoretical domination of the Ottoman Empire, but culturally, linguistically, religiously, and politically, they belonged to the Middle East. In this chapter we will address Sub-Saharan Africa.

The United States played an important role in the gradual development of nation-states across the African continent. The American Colonization Society, believing that freed slaves would be at a disadvantage if left in North America, worked for the creation of an African homeland for the descendants of those who had been brought over to America in chains. Their efforts led to the creation of the nation of Liberia in 1847, the first republic on the African continent. The leadership of that colony would remain in the hands of former American slaves and their descendants, the Americo-Liberians, until a bloody coup in 1980 ended their rule and that of their political organization, the True Whig Party. The neighboring country of Sierra Leone was originally created for the similar purpose of resettling former British slaves, but it remained a colony until 1961.

With the exception of the efforts to create Liberia—which were spearheaded by private individuals, rather than the U.S. government—the United States remained largely aloof from Africa for all of the nineteenth and much of the twentieth centuries. Interaction with Sub-Saharan Africa was largely the province of American sailors, both merchantmen and U.S. Navy ships on patrol to suppress the African slave trade. (While the question of slavery itself inspired violent disputes—not to mention actual warfare—in the nineteenth century, the international slave trade was almost universally condemned. It was banned by 1808 in the U.S. Constitution—and outlawed in the Constitution of the Confederate States of America as well.)

Even the First and Second World Wars had little effect on U.S. policy toward Africa. Only with the emergence of independence movements on the African continent and the simultaneous development of the Cold War did America begin to take notice. Lefty professors blame American racism for our historical lack of interest in Africa, but that is far too simplistic an appraisal. We did not conduct diplomacy with the countries of Africa before the post-World War II period because, by and large, they did not exist. If we were concerned about affairs in Nigeria or Niger, we contacted London or Paris, respectively, as that is where the decisions were made.

In addition, once the United States abolished slavery in the 1860s, the only countries or territories in the Western Hemisphere with chattel slavery were Brazil and Cuba, and they gradually phased it out by the end of the 1880s. Because of this, the international slave trade was no longer an issue—at least for us—and we had no real national interests that would cause us much interaction with Africa on any level. Incidentally, slavery, including race-based slavery, continued to be legal in Africa for decades. The last holdout was the Islamic Republic of Mauritania, which only abolished chattel slavery—typically the holding of Black Mauritanians by Arab Mauritanians—in 1981 and did not criminalize it until 2007! And despite abolition, the practice

of slavery continues underground there.[1] Navel-gazing culturally
Marxist millennials beating their breasts over how evil those of
European descent are because their ancestors held slaves a century and a half ago seem unperturbed about present-day slave-
holding by non-Europeans.

The end of World War II triggered wars of national independence in a number of colonial dependencies across the globe. By
and large, the European powers soon realized that the maintenance of colonies, particularly where those colonies craved sovereignty, would be far more expensive than it was worth. Thus,
the vast majority of the African continent was divided into independent countries in the 1950s and '60s. The transition was a
peaceful one in many cases, but not always. Kenya was plagued
by a low-scale insurgency for much of the 1950s, and the Portu-
guese did not give up any of their colonies—Angola, Mozam-
bique, and Guinea-Bissau—without a fight. In addition, South
Africa and Rhodesia, countries that had declared independence
under minority white governments, faced long-term insurgencies
of increasing brutality on both sides, and those conflicts got tied
into the narrative of the Cold War. This was particularly the case
in South Africa, which was seen as a bulwark of anti-Commu-
nism, especially as the main insurgent party, the African National
Congress (ANC), was openly allied with the South African Communist Party.

Incidentally, while more moderate elements of the ANC
predominated in the years immediately following the end of
apartheid in South Africa, in recent times the leadership of that
country appears to be taking a more Marxist direction, as its
parliament voted at the end of February 2018 to expropriate the

lands of white South African farmers *without compensation*. This has already been done in neighboring Zimbabwe, with catastrophic results for all of its inhabitants, black and white. But left-wing ideologues are quite uncompromising in their measures to support The People, even when real live human beings suffer as a result.

Once democratic rule was put in place, it often did not last. Coups, civil wars, and guerrilla operations plague the African continent to the present day. One of the factors that contributes to this instability is the artificial nature of most African countries. Their national borders correspond to lines drawn in colonial times, often having little relationship to tribe, religion, or ethnicity, unlike the borders between European and Asian countries. Unfortunately, as many of these wars lasted for years and even decades, they became self-perpetuating, as an entire class of people have become accustomed to making their way through life by means of banditry and oppression of neighboring groups.

It behooves the United States to steer clear of taking sides in most conflicts in Africa. Instead we should concentrate on engagement with all sides to ensure that forces actively hostile to U.S. interests, such as Al-Qaeda and Boko Haram, do not gain a strong foothold on the continent. We can do that by providing intelligence, training, and weaponry to those engaged in the fight against Islamic extremists in Africa, but resisting any temptation to introduce U.S. troops. As in the Middle East, American troops on the ground would make the conflict more about us than about local disputes. Our presence could even serve as a valuable recruiting tool to the jihadists, who are trying to convince potential followers that the true goal of the United States is to invade and occupy all of the *ummat al-Islamiyah* (Muslim world). We don't need to assist them in their propaganda, especially when local forces can contain radical Islamic expansion. For this reason, we should disband AFRICOM, the United States Africa Command. Dividing the globe into military districts is a relic of the Cold War (or an echo of the Roman Empire). We can provide assistance where our interests coincide with those of African countries without providing the optic of a United States seeking world domination. Those who believe that AFRICOM is somehow vital to U.S. national security should remember that this command has only existed since 2007. Somehow, we managed to survive without it for the first 231 years of our history. And those who say that it represents a vital military foothold on the African continent should remember that, despite its name, AFRICOM is based in Germany.

We do have national interests in Africa. Long-term poverty, largely caused by mismanagement, embezzlement, and war, has put millions of Africans at risk of contracting contagious diseases. We cannot solve the crisis of good government in Africa, as this is something only the Africans themselves can do. But we can provide assistance in combating disease. It is in our interest to do so, not just out of a humanitarian impulse on our part but because stopping these diseases in Africa will ultimately save American lives as well in a world where international travel is ever increasing.

One of the diseases we have to be concerned about is HIV/AIDS, which, according to the World Health Organization, affects nearly forty million Africans.[2] We have made a political decision to treat HIV/AIDS sufferers differently from the bearers of other dangerous contagious diseases and freely admit them into our country without any determination as to whether or not they are a threat to public health. I won't get into the wisdom of that policy or lack thereof in this narrative, but suffice it to say that it is in our interest to keep this disease under control overseas. The good news is that we have made great strides in helping to contain HIV, mostly thanks to President George W. Bush's administration's efforts in this area. PEPFAR (the President's Emergency Plan for AIDS Relief) was established during Bush's first term in office and was supported by the current vice president, Mike Pence. For a government-sponsored program, it has received high marks for effectiveness. Nearly twelve million African men, women, and children receive anti-retroviral treatment as a result of PEPFAR—treatment without which they would perish. In addition, some two million babies who would have contracted HIV through their mothers have been born disease-free.[3] Obviously, programs like PEPFAR need to be continuously monitored for their effectiveness and to ensure that taxpayer funds are actually being used for the purposes for which they were appropriated, but this particular program is a good example of one that protects American lives by helping people overseas.

Unfortunately, we sometimes undermine our own efforts with contradictory policies. During the Obama administration, heavy emphasis was given to the promotion of so-called LGBT rights across the globe—but especially in Africa, where an attachment to traditional marriage and sexual norms prevails. As a part of this push, abstinence programs that were a part of our anti-AIDS activities in Africa were eliminated as we sent the message that while health is important, unrestrained sex is the American way.

Homosexual activity remains a crime in many African nations, as it did in many American jurisdictions until at least the 1980s, when such legislation was upheld in the U.S. Supreme Court case of *Bowers v. Hardwick* (subsequently overturned less than twenty years later by a one-vote court majority in *Lawrence v. Texas*, reminding us that what is constitutional in the United States is whatever five justices in Washington say it is).

Despite our own history on this matter, Obama-era diplomats were instructed to push their recalcitrant interlocutors on LGBT rights, threatening the cutoff of aid or worse for those who held firm to beliefs common in the Western world from the beginning of time until less than a generation ago. So committed were we to promoting this ideology that at one point we even cancelled joint military exercises with Uganda over the issue—military exercises designed to enable Uganda to fight Islamic extremism. That fight took a backseat to Washington's promotion of the gay agenda. This ideological imperialism, which sought to undermine the very foundations of traditional society, ranks right up there with the worst of Soviet imperialism.

We have no business telling African nations what constitutes a legitimate marriage. Last I heard, we did not threaten Saudi Arabia because of their support for polygamy, a practice that (for now) remains illegal in the United States. Likewise, we should not punish nations for adhering to the traditional sexual norms that the world's great religions and philosophers have always held to be right and just. It is symptomatic of the arrogance of our political class—an arrogance to which Ronald Reagan alluded in a different context—that we believe that we are entitled to lecture the rest of the world on "norms" that we ourselves have only recently discovered.

Meanwhile, as our diplomats wagged their fingers at benighted African leaders, Chinese companies made major inroads into Africa by providing aid without the strings that we often attach. This has given the Chinese a quiet advantage when it comes to bidding on development projects in Africa, thus helping to grow the Chinese economy. We need to emulate the Chinese example and allow African nations to develop in whatever political fashion they desire while working with them to forward our mutual national interests. As I have said repeatedly, it should be a matter of supreme indifference what type of government a foreign nation has, so long as that nation does not pose a threat to our security and well-being. By treating African nations with the respect they are due as sovereign nations, rather than serving as some sort of latter day Great White Father who knows what is best for his savage children, we can avoid being sucked into controversies that are none of our concern and work to safeguard American lives and well-being as we defend our interests across the African continent.

> **PUTTING AMERICA FIRST**
> ### Ronald Reagan Edition
>
> "It would be an act of arrogance to insist that uniquely American ideas and institutions, rooted in our own history and traditions, be transplanted to South African soil. Solutions to South Africa's political crisis must come from South Africans themselves."
>
> —**RONALD REAGAN**, Remarks to Members of the World Affairs Council and the Foreign Policy Association, July 22, 1986

TWELVE

CANADA AND MEXICO

THE FOLKS NEXT DOOR

By virtue of geography, what happens in Canada and Mexico will always play a greater role in the day-to-day foreign policy of the United States than what happens in any other countries—assuming California does not secede from the Union. Even should we adopt a completely insular foreign policy, it would be impossible to ignore the two countries with whom the United States shares vast land borders. Our relationships with Canada and Mexico must necessarily be different from our relationships with the rest of the world.

We'll start with Canada. Many Americans don't think of our neighbor to the north when considering foreign policy because except for Quebec, Canada doesn't really seem that *foreign*. As President Franklin Roosevelt said on the occasion of his state visit to Canada in 1936, "I read in a newspaper that I was to be received with all the honors customarily rendered to a foreign ruler. I am grateful for the honors; but something within me rebelled at that word 'foreign.' I say this because when I have been in Canada, I have never heard a Canadian refer to an American as a 'foreigner.' He is just an 'American.' And, in the same way, in the United States, Canadians are not 'foreigners,' they are 'Canadians.' That simple little distinction illustrates to me better than anything else the relationship between our two countries."

Our border with Canada has been open for much of our history, and culturally speaking an outsider would find it difficult to tell a resident of International Falls, Minnesota, apart from one of Fort Frances, Ontario. That confusion annoys Canadians to no end. One easy way to distinguish American from Canadian backpackers in Europe is that the Canadians all seem to be sporting their national flag somewhere—just to let everyone know that they are *not* from the United States. They seem to have a chip on their shoulders when it come to the country that Canadian prime minister Lester Pearson, in a 1953 speech, called "our big, our overwhelming partner." As Pearson explained, Canadians "claim the special privilege, as a close neighbor and a candid friend, of grousing...and of complaining at some of the less attractive manifestations of her way of life. It makes our own junior status seem relatively superior and helps us forget some of our own problems and mistakes."

Setting the Canadian inferiority complex aside, the United States and Canada enjoy a very close relationship. Many countries vie for the title of "special relationship" with the United States, but that prize is definitely Canada's. We share the world's longest land border—over 5,000 miles in length. We mostly speak the same language. Canada is officially bilingual with a large Francophone population, and we have ever increasing pockets of Spanish speakers; but otherwise, we all speak English. Both countries derive most of our political and cultural heritage from Great Britain, although that link has traditionally been stronger in Canada (Queen Elizabeth is still technically the head of state there). In addition, it is far easier for our people to travel, live, study, and work in each other's countries than it is for any other nationals not linked by special confederation, such as the European Union. For example, while citizens of many nations, under the Visa Waiver Program, do not require visas to visit the United States for tourism or business for up to ninety days, Canadians do not need visas at all except for a few limited categories of travel.[1] Finally, American and Canadian troops have stood shoulder to shoulder in such conflicts as World Wars One and Two, Korea, the Gulf War, and Afghanistan.

But our relationship has not always been so rosy. The whole reason that there is a separate country called Canada is that American troops failed to take the northern colonies during our own War of Independence. After that war, thousands of loyalists fled the new United States, and many of them ended up in what is now Canada. Just as there is a Sons of the American Revolution in the United States, there is a United Empire Loyalists' Association in Canada. The War of 1812 saw renewed fighting between Americans and Canadians, and tensions along the northern border continued for much of the nineteenth century. During the American Civil War, when two Confederate diplomats were illegally seized off of a British ship by a U.S. man-of-war, the United Kingdom sent several thousand troops to Canada in preparation for a possible intervention on the side of the South (Lincoln apologized and ended this particular crisis). After the

Civil War, the Fenians, Irish Republicans based in the United States, launched several attacks on targets across the northern border, and some Canadians accused the United States of not doing enough to prevent these attacks.

By the twentieth century, however, things had settled down on the U.S.-Canadian border. While some Canadian politicians still feared American domination, Canada was no longer a top priority for American policymakers. We behaved as friendly neighbors who waved across their respective picket fences and occasionally dropped in for a cup of tea but otherwise minded our own business.

Our shared experience in the World Wars and especially the Cold War, brought us much closer. U.S. and Canadian forces worked closely together to secure the Arctic from Soviet encroachment. The most northern reaches of Canada are actually closer to Moscow than they are to Paris, Washington, DC, or even some other parts of Canada itself. Still Canada did not agree with every aspect of U.S. Cold War strategy; differences arose, particularly regarding the Vietnam War, which Canada did not support. Tens of thousands of young American draft dodgers took refuge in Canada during that period, and many of them stayed there, eventually becoming Canadian citizens. Times have changed, though, and even though Canada differed with the U.S. over the Iraq War, our northern neighbors have taken a dimmer view of the handful of U.S. soldiers who fled to Canada to avoid service in the Middle East.

Canada is our largest export market and our third largest supplier of imports. American goods sold in Canada make up nearly one-fifth of our total exports and include vehicles, machinery, electrical machinery, agricultural products, mineral fuels, and plastics. Canadian imports to the U.S. include vehicles, mineral fuels, agricultural products, and machinery. In addition, U.S. direct foreign investment in Canada tops $350 billion per year, while Canadians invest nearly $270 billion in the United States.[2] With all the focus on the Middle East, a lot of people don't realize that Canada is our greatest supplier of imported oil.

Because of the North American Free Trade Agreement (NAFTA), there are very few trade barriers between the United States and Canada. Criticism of NAFTA by President Trump and others has centered on our trade relationship with Mexico since wage scales and safety standards in the U.S. and Canada tend to be similar—so that neither side has an unfair advantage in that respect. But points of tension do exist. Lumber was specifically excluded from NAFTA because of Canadian government subsidies of that industry. The Trump administration has slapped duties on Canadian wood products, a move that has bipartisan support, with former president Jimmy Carter writing an editorial in favor of this action.[3] Canadian government interference in the dairy market is also a source of contention, as dairy products *do* come under NAFTA and American dairy farmers have complained that they are facing unfair competition. The United States runs a significant trade deficit with Canada, so tweaks to our free trade agreement with our northern neighbor might be in order.

Our trade in aviation has been a particular source of tension. In May of 2017, Boeing filed a complaint with the International Trade Commission (ITC) against Canadian aircraft manufacturer Bombardier, claiming that Canadian subsidies to that company constituted unfair trade practices.[4] The ITC found in favor of Boeing, and Bombardier could be slapped with tariffs of over 200 percent, reflecting the level of government subsidy that offsets the real price of the product.[5] Naturally, Canadian Prime Minister Justin Trudeau, taking a break from correcting the politically incorrect grammar of women he views as less feminist than himself,[6] has vowed to retaliate against Boeing—apparently not so much on the basis of the rule of law, but as a form of grandstanding.[7] So free trade disciples are warning of an impending trade war, as they always do when countries fail to abide by the strict tenets of their ideology.[8] But that is rather unlikely. Even though the American consumer could be made to feel some pain, Canada, with a vastly smaller population and industrial base, would be the ultimate loser in any tit-for-tat trade squabble. In the long run, President Trump's decision to focus on those areas of our mutual trade relationship where the United States has been getting the short end of the stick should lead to a fairer commercial relationship with our Canadian cousins.

While much attention has been paid to our southern border in recent years, and rightly so, our largely undefended border with Canada is not often discussed. One reason for this is that we have a great deal of confidence in the integrity and professionalism of the Canadian police forces. The bad actors who could target the United States are also a threat to Canada, and it is in both of our interests to see that they are prevented free movement. In addition, the relatively open border works both ways. Since Trump became president, there has been an uptick in illegal aliens from Mexico and other Latin American countries crossing the border from the U.S. to ask for asylum in Canada, which has more lenient immigration policies.[9] Some reports suggest that the Canadian border could be a point of vulnerability in our fight against terrorism, with jihadis trying to enter the United States.[10] It is neither feasible nor desirable to build a wall on our Canadian border. But we must ensure that our border is secure. During my days of adjudicating visas for the U.S. Department of State, I can remember dozens of stories of foreign nationals who had applied for Canadian visas rather than U.S. ones in the belief that it would be easier to visit Canada because of higher refusal rates for those applying at the American Embassy. Many of them hoped that once they were in Canada they could easily walk across the border into the U.S. While these cases tended to be economic migrants, they do highlight the fact that our northern border is a potential source of weakness. Working with the Canadians, we need to examine how that border can be made more secure.

In general, however, our relationship with Canada is a good one, and it is in both of our national interests that it remain so. Canada and the U.S. have made it a point to stay out of each other's internal affairs for a century or more, and we should continue to do so. We can do better on trade and on border security, but the good news is that we have a competent partner with whom to discuss these matters. Canadian public policy may run to the left of the American version, but we share common ideas about civil society and the rule of law. We can't take our relationship for granted, but we should be able to continue to work together for our mutual benefit for the foreseeable future.

Our relationship with Mexico is far more complex. Even with the exponential growth of the Hispanic population in the

United States, our two countries do not share a common history or language, and our political traditions are as different as those of any two republics can be. The economic disparity between our two nations, compounded by massive government corruption in Mexico, especially under the long-dominant Institutional Revolutionary Party (PRI), means that millions of Mexicans have abandoned their homeland to seek their fortune in the United States. The growth of the power of the drug cartels in Mexico means that our southern border is a major gateway for illicit substances and crime as well.

Our relationship with Mexico has always been problematic. As Mexican president Porfirio Diaz is reported to have said, "Poor Mexico! So far from God and so close to the United States!" Mexico's long war of independence against Spain (1810–1821) was followed by a period of instability. In the first two years after independence our southern neighbor went from a monarchy under Emperor Agustin I to a republic under President Guadalupe Victoria, with different factions competing for power to shape what kind of republic Mexico would be. Nine different individuals would hold the office of presidency in the first ten years of the Mexican Republic. This level of instability would continue well into the latter half of the nineteenth century.

Meanwhile the United States was growing in power and influence, with American settlers moving into untamed lands within her borders—and beyond. A number of these settled in what is now Texas while it was still under Spanish control, and the numbers only increased after Mexican independence. Many Mexican officials welcomed the American pioneers as means of settling the northern frontier of Mexico, bringing prosperity to that region, and protecting Mexicans against attack by Native American tribes such as the Comanches.

When politician and strongman Antonio Lopez de Santa Anna assumed the presidency of Mexico, he sought to consolidate his power by abolishing the Mexican Constitution of 1824. Santa Anna was a slippery character who over the course of his career had served nearly every cause possible in Mexico, from Spanish loyalism to Mexican royalism to republicanism. His primary allegiance was to himself. Santa Anna's suspension of the Constitution weakened the power of the Mexican States and concentrated power in Mexico City. One of the parts of Mexico that strongly objected to this attempt at centralization was Texas, which declared separation from Mexico and after a decisive victory against Mexican forces gained that independence in the Treaties of Velasco—later repudiated by the Mexican government.

Texas was an independent republic for nine years, recognized by several European countries not to mention the United States and the short-lived Republic of Yucatan, which had also revolted against the central government in Mexico. In 1845, Sam Houston and other Texans advocating union with the United States triumphed, and the Lone Star Republic became the Lone Star State.

The admission of Texas into the Union led to immediate conflict between Mexico and the United States. The United States recognized the southern boundary of Texas as being at the Rio Grande, as the Republic of Texas claimed. When U.S. troops came under attack by Mexican forces north of that river, the United States and Mexico went to war.

Liberal mythology portrays the Mexican War as being an unequal struggle between a lumbering North American bully and a weak and innocent Mexican victim. But in fact, it was by no means certain that the United States would win an all-out war with Mexico. Santa Anna was back in power, and he considered himself to be the spiritual heir of Napoleon, outfitting his army accordingly. The Mexican Army had years of experience, both in internal fighting against rebellious political factions and Indian uprisings and in a short war with France in 1839 (the so-called "Pastry War"). The American Army, on the other hand, had a small core of regulars with frontier experience, but mainly was composed of volunteers who had never seen action.

Despite this apparent inequality, American forces triumphed. Unlike in later wars in which American troops were held back from "finishing the job," our soldiers took the fight to Mexico itself, launching one of the first successful amphibious assaults in U.S. history at Veracruz and marching to take the Mexican capital. A thoroughly defeated Mexico then agreed to sell the United States vast areas of its sparsely-settled northern territory, which would become the American Southwest, plus California.

In recent years it has become fashionable to be ashamed of the U.S. effort in the Mexican War, but we have nothing to be ashamed about. Our forces were attacked, and we responded. In Santa Anna we were confronted by a two-faced dictator who represented a threat to our security, particularly in the border areas. The decisive victory of American arms ensured that Mexico would never again represent an existential challenge to the United States, and the lands gained in that conflict would create untold wealth for the American nation.

While the United States was tied up in its own Civil War, Mexico was engaged in yet another of its internal conflicts and had defaulted on its foreign loans. European powers intervened in Mexico to secure debts owed by the government. While most quickly pulled out, the French, then led by Napoleon III, the nephew of the original Napoleon, saw an opportunity for expansion. The president of Mexico at the time was Benito Juarez, a fiercely anti-clerical liberal who sought to strip the Catholic Church of its influence on Mexican society. His forces had recently vanquished those of the pro-Catholic conservatives, but large portions of the population remained restless. French troops soon occupied large parts of Mexico, and, with the support of Mexican conservatives, established a monarchy, with Austrian Hapsburg prince Maximilian I named Emperor of Mexico.

The new monarchy did not last long, even though Maximilian appeared to genuinely desire to improve the lot of Mexico's people. The French were soon facing problems of their own closer to home, and the end of the American Civil War meant that U.S. troops were less likely to look kindly on a European intervention so close to home. Without French backing and with conservatives demoralized, Maximilian was overthrown in 1867 and executed along with his wife, the Empress Carlota. Incidentally, Maximilian's older brother, Franz Josef, was Emperor of the Austro-Hungarian Empire at the time—and would remain so until 1916. Some twenty years after his brother Maximilian was executed, Franz Josef's oldest son and heir to the Austro-Hungarian Empire, Rudolf, killed himself in a murder-suicide pact with his mistress. This made Franz Josef's nephew, Franz Ferdinand, heir to the throne, which he would not inherit, as he and his wife were assassinated in Sarajevo in 1914—the spark that touched off World War I. Franz Josef's successor would end up being another nephew, Karl, a religiously observant leader who sought assiduously but unsuccessfully to bring an end to World War I and ended up losing the empire. While Karl failed in his earthly quest, his reputation for holiness led to his beatification by the Catholic Church in 2004—not a fate that likely awaits many of our present political class.

In the late nineteenth century Mexico would stabilize and actually become a wealthy nation, something for which President Porfirio Diaz—who cracked down on corruption, brought in a group of technocrats to run the government more efficiently, and reconciled conservatives by reaching out to the Church—was largely responsible. His long reign provided much needed stability to a country that had never enjoyed much of that commodity. This new prosperity and peace also led to immigration to Mexico from Europe and Asia, but also from the United States, with colonies of American Mormons settling in the north. These Americans included the great-grandfather of former Massachusetts governor, Mitt Romney (the family moved back to the United States in the early twentieth century).

By the early twentieth century, elements of Mexico's population were beginning to agitate for change: democrats who objected to the long rule of Diaz and his suppression of some civil liberties, radical anti-clericalists who wanted to destroy any vestige of Christian influence on Mexican society, Communists and agrarian reformers who sought redistribution of land wealth, and assorted opportunists who saw the chance for individual profit in an unstable society. Beginning in 1910, Mexico would see nearly twenty years of revolution, civil war, and instability. Diaz was driven from power and free elections brought to the presidency Francisco I. Madero, a devoted spiritualist who often obtained political guidance through séances. He was assassinated two years later, and the new leader of Mexico was Victoriano Huerta. It is unclear how involved the United States was in Huerta's rise, but at least initially American business interests were far more comfortable with Huerta than they had been with the unpredictable Madero. Whatever the circumstances of Huerta's assumption of the presidency, it was not long before Washington and Mexico City were at odds. U.S. troops occupied the port of Veracruz in 1914 after Mexican officials arrested several U.S. sailors and then refused Washington's terms for rectifying the offense.

Huerta was also subsequently overthrown, and the Mexican government was largely stabilized under Venustiano Carranza, even if unrest continued throughout the country, with agrarian rebels in the south fighting under Emiliano Zapata and bandits in the north under former Carranza ally Francisco "Pancho" Villa. Villa would draw the U.S. back across the Rio Grande when his forces went over the border into Columbus, New Mexico, in 1916 and launched an unprovoked, criminal attack. The United States responded by sending troops into northern Mexico under General Pershing, but American involvement in World War I brought an end to this last intervention. (Allowing ourselves to be distracted from real security threats because of wars that are none of our concern is not something that started with Iraq and Afghanistan.) We kept a wary eye on events in Mexico, though, especially after the Zimmermann Telegram revealed that

Germany had offered U.S. territory to Mexico if she would join the Central Powers. After U.S. and Mexican forces traded fire at the border in Nogales, Arizona, in 1918, our history of direct involvement in Mexican affairs came to an end.

But we had no way of knowing that at the time. Mexico remained unstable—Villa, Zapata, and Carranza all met violent ends—and, in the wake of the Bolshevik Revolution in Russia, Mexican government moves toward a socialist economy sparked much concern in Washington. Mexico's turn to the left was accompanied by massive persecution of Catholics, leading to the Cristero War in the late twenties. Interestingly enough, according to French-Mexican author Jean Meyer, the fiercely anti-Catholic Ku Klux Klan, which was at its zenith in the 1920s, supported the Mexican government's efforts to crush the Catholic Church in that country, offering financial assistance to support those measures.[11] While anti-clerical laws remained on the books for years (some to this day), enforcement slacked off. The Catholic Church was soon able to function relatively freely in Mexican society, and the Cristero War ended. Any perceived need for U.S. intervention fell by the wayside. Our bilateral relations were strengthened, and Mexico even entered World War II on the Allied side, sending a squadron of fighter plane pilots to combat the Japanese. The tensions that had arisen out of Mexico's revolutionary period began to fade away.

What did not fade away was the new party that had arisen out of the ideals of the Revolution: the Institutional Revolutionary Party (PRI), which held a virtual monopoly on political office until 2000. A socialist-oriented party with anti-clerical elements, the PRI brought political stability to Mexico while squandering the wealth of what should have been one of Latin America's richest countries. As a result, millions of Mexicans have sought their fortunes elsewhere, particularly in the United States, through legal and illegal immigration. Mexico's one-party state came to an end in 2000 with the unprecedented victory of the center-right Party of National Action (PAN), a result made possible by a left-wing split from PRI. While the election of an opposition party brought hope for change in Mexico, it did not bring an end to Mexico's problems. The rise of drug gangs has further weakened the Mexican state since that time. In addition, the PRI remains powerful, with current president Enrique Peña Nieto returning that party to the presidency in 2012.

In light of Mexico's tortured history, high levels of corruption, and economic difficulties, why did anyone think a free trade deal would be in the best interests of the United States? In fact, the results of our NAFTA agreement with Mexico have been abysmal for the U.S. According to statistics kept by the United States Trade Representative, the trade deficit with Mexico amounted to over $63 billion in 2016.[12] NAFTA is definitely a win for Mexico, as it creates Mexican jobs. It is a win for multinational corporations, who can move factories south of the border where U.S. wage and safety laws don't get in the way of profits. And consumers see some benefit in terms of short-term lower prices on certain goods. But in the long-term it hurts the U.S. by further eroding our manufacturing base. These days it is considered oh so sophisticated not to give a damn about lowly American manufacturing jobs ("jobs Americans won't do"). But the kinds of jobs that factories in the United States created in the

---

---

past are precisely the kinds of jobs that give working class families hope for a better future. Not everyone is cut out to be stockbrokers and college professors, and Americans who aren't should have options beyond the checkout line at Wal-Mart. Of course, many of these people are the Donald Trump voters that Hillary Clinton called "deplorables." These people are obvious racists, so why should the bicoastal elite care whether or not they can get decent jobs? Isn't that why we have welfare?

Blue-collar jobs are not the only ones at stake. NAFTA has created a whole new category of people eligible to enter the United States to work in high-paying jobs that might otherwise be filled by Americans. The Code of Federal Regulations at 8 CFR § 214.6 provides for a special visa category for Canadian and Mexican citizens seeking work in the United States under the provisions of NAFTA. These are for people seeking "temporary entry as a business person to engage in business activities at a professional level." Lest you think that these are workers with special or unusual skills we can't find in the United States, the list of professions eligible for this type of visa includes accountants, computer systems analysts, landscape architects, hotel managers, social workers, dieticians, dentists, and librarians, among others. U.S. Embassies and Consulates issue several thousand of these visas each year to Mexican nationals (Canadians qualifying for this status do not require a visa), and the initial validity of the visa is three years, although it can be extended indefinitely as long as the visa holder stays with the same employer. This visa, like most work visas, enables the recipient to bring in his dependents; there are even provisions for allowing boyfriends and girlfriends to come in as well. A comprehensive study needs to be done on this visa category to determine if it really fulfills a need or is merely a short cut for employers who prefer not to hire Americans. Do we really not have enough people in the United States willing to work as hotel managers?

This does not mean that we should stop trading with Mexico, our second largest trading partner for both imports and exports. Mexico is behind only Canada, Saudi Arabia, and Venezuela in the amount of petroleum it exports to the United States (Mexicans are also major consumers of U.S. petroleum products). Mexico is our largest supplier of agricultural imports (read the labels next time you visit the produce section), and that includes over three billion dollars in wine and beer (mostly beer—think Corona, Pacifico, Tecate, and Dos Equis). Even bigger than that, however, are vehicle imports—some $75 billion worth. On the flip side, American agricultural products, particularly corn, soybeans, and pork, are very popular in Mexico, and we still send a lot of machinery south of the border.[13] Prohibitive trade barriers are not the answer, but we need to negotiate a better trade agreement, perhaps on a bilateral basis, rather than linking it to Canada, whose economy and political system are vastly different from those of Mexico.

The most visible issue in our current relationship with Mexico is our porous southern border. According to the Pew Research Center, there are nearly six million undocumented immigrants (a.k.a. illegal aliens) in the United States from Mexico.[14] Beyond a doubt, many of these people are hard-working folks who just want to earn money for their families. But the fact of the matter is that these people cut in line to do so. Also, according to Pew, we have nearly the same number of *legal* Mexican immigrants. These are people who fit into one of our established immigrant visa categories and patiently waited their turn. They were screened to ensure they did not represent a threat to our security or well-being. Those who entered *illegally* did not face such screening, nor did they have to wait their turn. It is true that many of these Mexican illegal aliens would not have qualified for an immigrant visa based on lack of family ties or special employment expertise, but our Congress has seen fit to limit immigration to certain specific categories of people. Those who cross the border illegally thwart the will of the American people and contribute to a disregard for law itself. In addition, the fact that illegal aliens face no screening means that drug dealers, rapists, murderers, thieves, and pedophiles are among their number—not to mention carriers of infectious diseases. While some may argue that malefactors and

---

PUTTING AMERICA FIRST
Patrick J. Buchanan
Edition

"Mexico is moving north. Ethnically, linguistically, and culturally, the verdict of 1848 is being overturned. Will this Mexican nation within a nation advance the goals of the Constitution—to 'insure domestic tranquility' and 'make us a more perfect union'? Or has our passivity in the face of this invasion imperiled our union?"

—**PATRICK J. BUCHANAN**, *Suicide of a Superpower: Will America Survive to 2025*, Thomas Dunne Books, 2011

threats to our security and our public health represent a minority of illegals in the U.S., how do we know? No one who enters illegally is screened for anything. Liberals often obfuscate this fact by acting as if the argument against illegal immigration were against immigration in general—suggesting that those who think we should do something about illegal aliens are somehow "anti-immigrant." But if a nation allows anyone, willy-nilly, to enter the country without regard for whether that person is a criminal, a terrorist, or a human trafficker, that nation has ceased one of the most basic functions of governance: providing security for its people. We can argue all day long about how many or how few legal immigrants we should have, but that we should blithely accommodate people whose first act in entering the U.S. is to break the law, is absurd.

Our open southern border is not simply a gateway for Mexicans. When I worked in El Salvador, I heard many stories from local Salvadorans about their relatives who were living illegally in the United States. In nearly all cases, entering the U.S. was easy: just a walk across the southern border. In fact, a number of them said it was harder to cross Mexico's *southern* border than its northern one. If a villager in a remote corner of El Salvador knows it is easy to get into the United States, how much more informed would be a member of ISIS or Al-Qaeda?

If we are serious about stopping illegal immigration—and the drugs and crime that come with it—we need to construct a wall on our border with

NOT PUTTING AMERICA FIRST
Hillary Clinton Edition

"I voted for border security; there are some limited places where that was appropriate."

—**HILLARY CLINTON**, presidential debate, October 19, 2016

Mexico. Democratic politicians seem to like the idea of fortifying symbolic areas of our southern border, as if illegal aliens and drug runners would only try to cross where it is most difficult to do so. Contrary to Hillary Clinton's assertions, border security is appropriate *anywhere* our country faces a threat. It is true that we also face a vulnerability on our northern border with Canada. But illegal immigration from Mexico is a vastly larger problem. And fortunately, our border with Mexico is less than half the length of the Canadian one. There is no point in deliberately leaving the front door ajar just because you find out the lock on the back door doesn't work. True, an enterprising criminal may get in anyway, if he goes around to check all the doors, but that does not mean you should make it easier on him. The locked front door is not fool-proof, but it serves as a deterrent.

I particularly applaud President Trump's pledge to make Mexico pay for any border wall. I do not know how he will do it, but the costs should at a minimum be borne by both countries, rather than the United States alone. Perhaps we can introduce some sort of nominal border-crossing fee for Mexican citizens or put a tariff on selected Mexican goods until the wall is paid for. It is certainly something we need to explore, since Mexico benefits from illegal aliens crossing into the U.S. It drains off the unemployed, thus lessening pressure on the Mexican government to improve the lives of its people within Mexico. It provides a handy way to get rid of criminals by allowing them to become our problem. It also keeps Central and South American migrants from remaining in Mexico and putting a strain on the Mexican social fabric. Just direct them to "El Norte," and all problems are solved. Not only that, but it provides a livelihood for Mexican alien-smuggling "coyotes," who then spend their ill-gotten gains in the Mexican economy. As long as this process is cost-free for Mexico, the Mexican government has no incentive to assist the United States in upholding the rule of law.

In the meantime, however, the United States will certainly have to bear the costs. As of this writing, there is no final agreement on funding for the border wall, but testing of prototypes is underway, and reports indicate that, if constructed, most of them would significantly reduce the flow of illegal immigration across our southern border.[15] Of course, this has not stopped liberals from opposing the border wall as somehow "immoral," even though most of them were remarkably silent when previous presidents fortified selected portions of the U.S.-Mexican border, and presumably many of them lock the doors to their own homes when they go to bed at night. The ultimate irony was when the San Diego City Council went on record in September 2017 opposing a border wall[16]—this in a city that is already separated from Tijuana, Mexico, by a wall that goes back to 1989. But this is different because, well, Trump.

The United States and Mexico have a strained relationship. Pretending that differences don't exist will not make things better; it will only compound the problem. Resolving our trade disputes and securing our common border is necessary to removing the major sources of tension between our two nations. Maybe then we can look forward to enjoying a normal and balanced relationship with our neighbor to the south.

THIRTEEN

CUBA

AN OBSESSION WHOSE
TIME HAS PASSED

I remember walking through the streets of Havana. With the old cars, the crumbling buildings, the Revolutionary slogans where advertising should be, and the people who knew little of the world beyond their island's shores, I felt like I had traveled to the end of the Earth. The old colonial city is full of tourists, mostly Europeans, Canadians, and Latin Americans, and it has been extensively restored, thanks in part to European Union funding. But beyond the tourist hotspots, Havana feels like a once-great city that is at the end of a long decline. Names of long-dead businesses still adorn the broken-up sidewalks, and crumbling fancy plaster cornices speak of a time when Cuba was one of the wealthiest nations in Latin America. I was reminded of Eastern European stagnation, in the last years of the Warsaw Pact, when even totalitarian governments seemed to just be going through the motions. Maybe it is akin to Rome of the late Empire, when lip service was paid to the old gods, but except for a few simple people no one actually believed in the Olympian pantheon anymore. The pictures of Fidel and the red flags and Marxist slogans seem designed as much to strengthen the weakening faith of the true believers as to convince the many who have long doubted.

Cubans are naturally friendly and curious, and a foreigner will often be asked where he comes from. Unlike in some countries, this is not used as an opening to request a hand-out or to get you to buy something; it is merely a way of connecting with someone who comes from Outside. At first, I was hesitant to let on that I was an American, but I soon learned that I had nothing to fear. In nearly every case, the average Cuban would tell me how much he loved the United States. One fellow even said that his whole life he had heard from his government how evil the U.S. is but that he had never believed it. The political distance between our countries made me as exotic to them as they were to me.

It wasn't always this way. For much of our nation's history, Cuba was seen as our closest foreign neighbor. Cuba was quite accessible, and in the years before the American Civil War it was frequently visited by Americans. Regular sailings left out of New Orleans, Mobile, and New York, and there were even hotels that catered to American tourists. One of them, the Hotel Cubano, was owned by a woman from Tennessee and served as a sort of headquarters for Southerners on holiday, including Jefferson Davis (the building still stands at #9 Teniente Rey in Havana and now houses the Old Aquarium).

In fact, Cuba was so close to the United States that a number of Americans looked at the fertile island with covetous eyes. In the 1850s, some thought it could be the newest frontier territory and make four or five excellent American states. (It is nearly eight hundred miles long, after all.) The fact that a lot of Cubans seemed anxious to shake off Spanish rule was a strong argument for American intervention. The United States stayed out of Cuba, though, even if individual Americans sometimes conspired with Cuban rebels and "filibusters." These included such luminaries as Democratic Governor John Quitman and Whig Senator John Henderson, both of Mississippi. Our Civil War effectively put an end to the idea of adding Cuba as one or more stars on our flag.

But Americans did not stop going to Cuba. If anything, it was a more popular destination after the Civil War than before. Some former Confederates took up residence there in the immediate aftermath of the war, including C.S.A. Secretary of State Judah P. Benjamin (who would later move to England) and General Jubal Early (who would move back to Virginia after a year or so). These were followed by Americans from every stratum of every level of society, from businessmen taking advantage of Cuba's prosperity to wealthy vacationers taking advantage of Cuba's climate and charm. To this day, there is a plot in the Colón Cemetery in Havana, founded in 1876, that features the insignia of the major U.S. veterans' organizations of the late nineteenth and early twentieth centuries: The Grand Army of the Republic, the United Confederate Veterans, and the United Spanish-American War Veterans.

Events at the end of the 1800s would open Cuba up to even more American influence. Back in the 1890s, the "fake news" of the day was known as the "yellow press." William Randolph Hearst's *New York Journal* was nearly as sensational and shallow as today's CNN. The purveyors of yellow journalism adopted the cause of Cuban independence early on and began to fill their pages with wildly exaggerated and even invented tales of Spanish brutality on the island. Over time, many Americans began to believe the worst of the Spanish, so when an American warship, the USS *Maine*, exploded under suspicious circumstances in Havana Harbor in 1898, killing over two hundred sailors, most Americans were convinced that this deed had been planned in Madrid with malice aforethought (as many of their descendants would believe that Iraq was responsible for 9/11).

No one knows what actually happened to the *Maine*, but the most likely explanation is a boiler explosion. The *least* likely explanation is that the Spanish were behind it. Spain had nothing to gain from antagonizing the United States, as the war that followed would prove. If anyone had an interest in setting off a bomb on an American ship, it would be the Cuban insurgents, who realized that any hostile act would likely be blamed on the Spanish and help draw American support for the insurgents' cause. (Interestingly, even today there is a large monument in Havana in memory of the sailors who died on the *Maine*. With all the tensions between the U.S. and Cuba over the last fifty years, no one has thought to remove it for being "offensive" or "racist." It is hard to believe that, at least on this one issue, the Communists in Cuba have more sense than our own homegrown leftists.)

In the Spanish-American War, the United States decisively defeated Spain in less than one year and with this victory acquired not only Cuba but Puerto Rico, Guam, and the Philippines. Cuba was granted its independence in 1902, but under terms that allowed the United States a tutelary role as Cuba established its democracy. Today we would call that "nation-building." Following a breakdown in order in 1906, the U.S. would temporarily take control again, but Cuban sovereignty was resumed a couple of years later.

Over the next four decades, Cuban politics would seesaw between authoritarian leaders, military coups, and general instability, in the fashion popular in many Latin American republics of the time. Despite these problems, Cuban prosperity grew. Cuba's sugar dominated the American market, and products such as rum (derived from sugar), tobacco (cigars), and coffee also provided wealth. Tourism was a major aspect of Cuba's economy, and the nightlife in Havana rivaled anything North America had to offer, especially in the 1920s, during Prohibition in the United States. Cuba was a land of immigrants as well, with nearly one million Spaniards coming to Cuba in the first half of the twentieth century. While I cannot speak for the veracity of the story, one source in Cuba told me that before the Revolution the wait list for immigrant visas at the Cuban Embassy in Rome was one year. By the 1950s, Cuba was one of the richest countries in the Americas, with a large middle class and a standard of living that equaled several U.S. states and rivaled some nations in Western Europe.[1]

Not all of this wealth was evenly distributed, however, and high levels of government corruption led to discontent on the margins of society. An insurgency led by former gang leader Fidel Castro and assisted by an asthmatic Argentinian psychopath by the name of Ernesto "Che" Guevara came to dominate the forces opposed to then–Cuban strongman Fulgencio Batista. In 1959 Batista fled the country, and Castro took power. What appeared to be yet another Latin American coup, with the exchange of one leader for another, revealed itself as something very different when Castro announced his intention to transform Cuba into a Marxist-Leninist State.

What is rarely discussed about this turn of events is that Castro, in overthrowing the Batista regime, was putting an end to the presidency of Cuba's first—and only—chief executive of African descent. Ever since Castro assumed control, the upper echelons of Cuban power have remained lily white. I suppose liberals give Castro a pass on this though, what with him being a Communist and all, and therefore "on the right side of history."

Coming in the midst of the coldest years of the Cold War, the establishment of a Soviet client state ninety miles from the Florida coast was a matter of utmost concern to Washington. Ham-fisted efforts to overthrow the Castro regime led nowhere, and the United States soon faced the specter of Soviet nuclear missiles just off our southern shores. The Cuban Missile Crisis of 1962, considered by many to have been the closest the U.S. and the Soviet Union came to all-out war, was resolved with a compromise agreement that took some American missiles out of areas closer to the USSR in exchange for the removal of Soviet missiles from Cuba. It also ended U.S. attempts to directly overthrow the government of Fidel Castro.

Instead of military action, our policy towards Cuba was one of isolation and embargo. The idea was that if Cuba suffered enough from a lack of goods and services, the Cuban people themselves would remove Castro from power and return Cuba to the ranks of non-Communist nations. Unfortunately, this approach did not contend with the brutal crushing of any kind of dissent in Cuba, especially in the early years, and the massive subsidies provided to Cuba from the Soviet Union. These Soviet funds allowed Cuba to move forward with a number of state-sponsored projects that brought some changes to Cuba, even some positive ones. While Cuba's middle class suffered greatly (and many left the country), there were improvements in the lives of the very poor. Access to health care was expanded, and a universal literacy program was quite successful. But these improvements came with a price. Opposition political activity was not tolerated, religious practice was demonized and occasionally suppressed, and equality was enforced not by bringing everyone up to comfort but by bringing everyone down to comparable levels of misery. This enforced equality did not apply, of course, to Party members, who, in *Animal Farm* fashion, were more equal than the others.

The fall of the Soviet Union brought an end to subsidies for Cuba and led to a time of austerity known as "the special period." However, the opening up of new sources of trade—the United States is virtually alone in maintaining sanctions on Cuba—and a limited liberalization of Cuba's state-controlled economy allowed the Communist government of Cuba to survive.

Today, except for carefully cultivated Potemkin village tourist areas, Cuba is a sort of open-air Museum of Socialist Failure. While there is a growing class of entrepreneurs that the Cuban government allows to exist to cater to the tourist trade, most Cubans with any ambition dream of leaving the island. For the most part they are no longer prevented from doing so by official government policy, but rather by the reluctance of many countries to grant Cubans visas, knowing that they are unlikely to return to their homeland. Because of historic Spanish immigration to Cuba, thousands of Cubans have obtained EU passports, which they use either to work in Europe or to try to enter the United States.

Unfortunately, our policy toward Cuba also resembles something one might find in a museum. It is a product of the Cold War, and, even if it made sense then it no longer does today. Cuba is far from the only country in the world with an oppressive regime. It does not pose an existential threat to the United States and is certainly in no position to affect our economic interests. Our policy since the days of our Founding Fathers has been one of trade with any country who wishes to do so, without such commerce being seen as an endorsement of the internal workings of that country.

Besides being a departure from long-standing principles of American policy in support of our national interests, the Cuba embargo is also counter-productive. Those who believe that just a few more years of sanctions will be the magic that serves to bring down Communism in Cuba have not paid attention to what has happened over the last fifty years. Rather than bringing down Fidel, sanctions ensured that he remained the embodiment of the Cuban state until his death—in bed, of old age. U.S. sanctions helped to strengthen the reign of the Castro brothers, Fidel and Raul, as it gave them a convenient excuse to explain why the Revolution never brought utopia to Cuba. It is all the fault of the United States, you see, Cubans are continuously reminded. When President Obama traveled to Havana he had to pass by billboards showing the island of Cuba with a noose around it and proclaiming the U.S. embargo "the worst genocide in the history of the world." The accuracy of that claim would likely be contested by Jews, Armenians, and Cambodians, to name a few but, then, as Fidel's hero Lenin said, "People have always been the foolish victims of deception."[2]

But keeping Cuba isolated, especially when we are the only ones doing so, just provides an excuse for the economic failures of Cuba's Communist government and keeps American companies from getting a share of the now liberalizing Cuban market. Increased exposure to Americans and American ideals on a person-to-person level would be far more effective at eroding Castroite control than a regime of sanctions that was originally devised during the week when Americans drove their Chevy Corvairs to the malt shop while listening on the radio to Gene Chandler's top hit, "Duke of Earl." We have no compelling national interest in keeping the Cuban embargo alive. American tourism would strengthen Cuba's infant private sector, giving more Cubans a reason to want to stay and try to effectuate change in their own country. Investment in Cuba by American companies means that money that would otherwise go to Europe or China comes to us instead. Because of our geographic proximity to Cuba, we have a natural trade advantage with which no nation can compete. Unleashing the power of American business on Cuba will create a free market firestorm that even the mummified Marxist mannequins in charge of Cuban state planning will have a hard time putting out.

Thus, President Trump's recent rollback of some of the Obama-era loosening of trade and travel restrictions is a cause for concern, especially as it seems to go against his overall America First policy. These changes, which prohibit American firms

from doing business with entities linked to the Cuban military—
which controls nearly 60 percent of the island's economy—and
that prevent Americans from individual travel to the island,
appear to put Americans at a competitive disadvantage in doing
business in Cuba, not to hurt the Cuban regime.[3] It may be that
President Trump has information unavailable to the public that
demonstrates a concrete need to limit this kind of investment and
contact, but if that is not the case, we should continue our overhaul of our Cold War-era sanctions regime. We have a unique
opportunity with the substitution of Miguel Díaz-Canel for the
aging Raul Castro as president of Cuba. While Díaz-Canel is no
outsider—he has long served as a Communist Party leader—he
does represent a change in Cuban government leadership. He is
the first president since the Castros came to power not to be part
of the revolutionary generation. Trump should seize this opportunity to re-set our relationship with the island nation.

Our policy toward Cuban visas also needs an overhaul. I am
not much in the habit of praising former President Barack Obama,
but I give him full credit for bringing an end to a policy that was
long overdue for elimination: the so-called "wet foot, dry foot"
policy. Under its terms, any Cuban national could gain eventual
permanent status in the United States and a path to citizenship
merely by getting to U.S. soil or presenting himself at a U.S.
border crossing (the "dry foot"), while those intercepted at sea
would be sent back to Cuba ("wet foot"). This was itself a mod-
ification of our original policy, which had allowed those taken
at sea to come to the United States as well. Both of these schemes
were legacies of the Cold War, during which we took in anyone
who had managed to escape a Communist regime on the

assumption that the few who did get out were at risk of persecution if they were forced to return.

But as with the embargo, the reasons behind this policy no longer exist. Cubans can now travel outside their country relatively freely, provided they have the funds to do so and can get a visa. While Cubans fleeing in the 1960s may have been primarily political refugees, Cubans fleeing today are economic refugees, no different from a Mexican, Salvadoran, or Dominican trying to find opportunity in the U.S. One U.S. immigration officer told me that Cubans claiming asylum under the "wet foot, dry foot" rule were unlike any other seekers of political asylum; the first question they asked after being granted asylum was when they could go back to Cuba to visit family. That doesn't sound like a person with a well-founded fear of persecution in his home country. And many Cubans who might be persecuted at home have other options than immigration to the United States—there have been many cases of Cubans *with Spanish passports* entering the U.S. from a third country and then claiming asylum. Since our immigration policy is primarily designed to support our own national interests, there is no reason why we should grant Cubans rights that no other people have.

In addition, the "wet foot, dry foot" policy was actually detrimental to our stated goals. By allowing clandestine Cuban immigrants to remain in the U.S., we were creating a valve that released pressure on the Cuban regime. Not only that, but U.S. residents or citizens with family in Cuba were not subject to many of the restrictions that bound other Americans in regard to travel to the island nation. Anyone who ever took a charter flight from Miami to Havana can attest that nearly every Cuban-American on board carried a whole host of consumer goods to share with his relatives still living in Cuba—subsidizing that Communist regime with the fruits of American capitalism, and again releasing pressure on the Castro regime. Treating Cubans like any other foreign people in regard to admission to the U.S. was a necessary first step in adapting our Cuba policy to the modern age. This does not rule out political asylum claims, but it simply means that any such claims will be evaluated on a case-by-case basis, rather than with a blanket assumption of veracity each and every time.

The ending of "wet foot, dry foot" is a good start, but more work needs to be done. United States Citizenship and Immigration Services (USCIS) still runs the Cuban Family Reunification Parole Program, which is administered out of our embassy in Havana using State Department resources, since the USCIS presence in Cuba is quite small. This absurd program gives Cuban relatives of American citizens and certain permanent residents a shortcut to immigration that no other relatives of Americans enjoy. Rather than waiting some twenty years, as is the case with most siblings of American citizens, Cuban siblings can come to the U.S. in one-tenth the time. As a result, the incentive for committing fraud is very high: pretending you have an American relative is a lot easier than swimming to Key West. Created to promote "family reunification," it can actually separate families by allowing an avenue for immigration for someone who might leave his family behind to do so. This program should be ended immediately; Cubans should have no better nor worse chance than any other people to immigrate to the U.S.

Another issue in our relationship with Cuba is our naval base at Guantanamo Bay. Our original 1903 lease with the Cuban government was not exactly an agreement between two parties on an equal footing—given that Cuba had only gained independence the year before, and that we still maintained the right to intervene unilaterally in her affairs. Of course, had it not been for the United States, there would not have been an independent Cuba, at least not in 1903, and allowing the United States to maintain a base on one small, remote part of the island of Cuba must have seemed a small price to pay. In any case the base provided jobs and other economic benefits to the Cubans. Since the Cuban Revolution, however, the base has been isolated from the rest of the country—or the rest of the country has isolated itself from the base, depending on how you look at it. The subject of U.S. rights to Guantanamo only became problematic when Castro came to power, aligned himself with the forces of international Communism, and demanded the return of Guantanamo to Cuban control. Whatever the merits of keeping Guantanamo or returning it to the Cubans, the question should be analyzed from a national interest perspective. If Guantanamo serves a vital national security function, we should continue to maintain it. In any case, resumption of normal, sane relations with the government of Cuba should be a prerequisite to any discussion of a transfer of sovereignty.

A normal, sane relationship with Cuba will start with Cuba returning wanted American criminals to justice in the United States. These include Joanne Chesimard (a.k.a. Assata Shakur), a black nationalist who was convicted in the murder of a New Jersey policeman and later escaped from prison before fleeing to Cuba; Cheri Dalton (a.k.a. Nehanda Abiodun), an activist who is suspected of committing bank robbery and murder to advance "the Republic of New Afrika"; and William Morales, a convicted terrorist with the Puerto Rican group FALN, who also escaped from prison. We should press the Cuban government on these cases at every opportunity. I would not link this issue to ending the embargo, which, as we have seen, is actually in our own interests. But I would insist upon it as a prerequisite for any other concessions, including any potential talks about Guantanamo. Especially in an era when extremists in the United States advocate the killing of law enforcement personnel, we need to send the message that ideology is no excuse for murder, and that the United States will bring you to face justice even after the passage of many years.

The safety of our diplomats in Cuba is another cause for concern. It is the responsibility of the host government to ensure that diplomatic staff are kept safe. Between late 2016 and mid-2017, some twenty-one U.S. government employees assigned to our embassy in Havana reported a number of similar symptoms—ranging from dizziness and headaches to partial hearing loss and, in a few cases, brain damage—usually following exposure to odd or high-pitched sounds from an unknown source. Not only has the source of what appears to have been a deliberate attack not been established, to date, but the medical community remains puzzled about what type of device or procedure could have caused these symptoms.[4] When these attacks occurred, there was immediate speculation that they were some kind of retaliation for the scaling back of Obama-era trade liberalizations by the Trump Administration, but the Cuban government has disclaimed any responsibility. The fact that at least five Canadian diplomats were similarly affected[5] tends to back up the Cuban denials, since Cuba and Canada have long enjoyed warm ties, with nearly half of Cuba's tourists coming from our neighbor to the north.[6] And yet the sophistication of the attacks seems to suggest that they were not carried out by casual third parties engaged in some sort of sick prank, and the nature of Cuba's totalitarian society makes this even more unlikely. Perhaps rogue elements in the Cuban government (who somehow can't distinguish Americans from Canadians) are to blame, or maybe a third country was involved. As of this writing, we simply do not know, but, if 1898 has taught us anything, it is that we should not be quick to jump to conclusions about any attacks that take place in Cuba. That being said, Cuba needs to cooperate openly and transparently with the United States in determining the source of this attack and work to ensure that nothing like it happens again. That is what normal countries do.

Scaling back the consular services at our embassy in Cuba in the wake of the attacks was a proper response—not only signaling our displeasure to the Cuban government in a way that hits them directly (by lessening the flow of visitors from Cuba to the U.S., and thus, also the flow of hard currency from the U.S. to Cuba) but also protecting our diplomatic personnel from potential harm. It also sent the message that improvement in our long-term relationship will largely depend on how this matter is resolved.

In this and all other matters, we should expect Cuba to behave like a normal country—and treat it like one. Assuming the Cuban government was not behind this attack, isolating it because of circumstances from thirty, forty, or fifty years ago does not serve our national interests, nor, for that matter, the interests of the Cuban people. It just contributes to a legacy of mistrust, which helps the Communist regime of Cuba remain in power. Playing David to our Goliath gives the Communists in Cuba a legitimacy they would otherwise not enjoy. But if Cuba is just another Latin American country with a government that regularly fails its own people, then it is not so different from countless other regimes in the region.

FOURTEEN

THE REST OF LATIN AMERICA AND THE CARIBBEAN

THE GOOD NEIGHBOR POLICY

In 1823, when the Monroe Doctrine against Old World interference in the New World was formulated, large parts of the Americas were in the process of establishing their independence. The United States was naturally sympathetic to these movements, but the Monroe Doctrine's clarion call was not ideological. It was realistic—a simultaneous admission of both weakness and resolution. The leader of the young Republic realized that our independence was far from secure. A determined European power, whether it be England, France, or Spain, could put the United States in jeopardy. Therefore, it behooved us to state openly that further European encroachments would not be viewed lightly. A European power that could snuff out the independence of a Mexico or an Argentina could also threaten the United States, so America put the world on notice that we would not stand idly by if attempts were made to recolonize those nations who had broken their European shackles. Even if our military did not

measure up to European standards of the time, we wanted anyone thinking about recolonization to know that we were prepared to make him pay a price if he tried.

Even so, the Monroe Doctrine had little relevance to U.S.
foreign policy for most of the nineteenth century. In the early years
of the United States, we had no force to back up our threats to repel
European powers intervening in the Western Hemisphere. Not to
mention that we were a bit distracted with our own internal difficulties—such as the Civil War—to look much beyond our
national borders. But as we have seen, the end of the Civil War
freed up troops to be deployed to the Rio Grande as Washington
looked with great disfavor on the French intervention in Mexico.
The threat of U.S. intervention may have been one of the factors
that prevented Emperor Maximilian from accepting the services
of former Confederate units who crossed into Mexico in 1865
offering to draw their swords in favor of the Hapsburg monarchy.

Then the Spanish-American War changed everything. We
now possessed an abundance of overseas possessions, including
a couple in Latin America. We had become, said some, a Modern
Nation, and Modern Nations have obligations to those peoples
not as enlightened as themselves. Had not the Modern Nations
of England, France, Germany, Spain, and even Italy, the Netherlands, and Belgium acquired colonies in Africa and Asia, leading
the subject peoples there to enlightenment, modern hygiene, and
the benefits of electricity? So what if the natives did not always
appreciate our efforts on their behalf—we had to take up "the
white man's burden."

As a result of this way of thinking, in the first thirty-odd
years of the twentieth century, the history of our dealings with

Latin America was a story of almost constant intervention. We backed secessionist rebels in Panama fighting against the Colombian government and in return were granted the Panama Canal. We invaded the Dominican Republic in 1916 and occupied the country for eight years. Neighboring Haiti was taken over by U.S. troops for twice as long a period around the same time. American ground forces assumed control of Nicaragua in 1912; they would not leave until FDR's administration. Honduras saw half a dozen interventions by U.S. troops in the 1910s and 1920s. While the Left, particularly the Latin American Left, has pointed to these military actions as evidence of the United States' imperial designs on the region, the truth is far more complex. There were also humanitarian impulses in play. The idea was that the United States, as the most advanced nation in the region, had an obligation to bestow good government on its benighted neighbors. All of the countries mentioned above—Haiti, the Dominican Republic, Nicaragua, and Honduras—suffered from instability, internal violence, and a leadership class that was more intent on lining its own pockets and those of its cronies than of governing countries in a way that benefited the populace. Haiti, for example, had had six presidents in a five-year period, and the countryside was plagued by warlords who would not have felt out of place in twenty-first-century Somalia. American intervention did bring some stability to these regions. But it also fueled anti-American sentiment. That is the key takeaway here. Even given the best intentions in the world, and even if they improve the situation for everyone involved, solutions imposed from above are often unpopular. People generally resent being saved from themselves.

Then, just as now, supporters of America's interventionist foreign policy tried to make the case that we really had no choice. The United States was a world power, and world powers have to behave a certain way. If we didn't do it, who would? But in promoting a policy of soft imperialism, these precursors of the neoconservatives had strayed away from the Founding Fathers' vision of a free America that would not repeat the errors of the Old Continent. Our interventions in Latin America in the early twentieth century made us neither more secure nor more prosperous. Instead, they left a bitter legacy among the peoples of the Americas that endangers our real interests to this day. What's more, by aping our former European colonizers, we betrayed the very foundations of our Republic, as Williams Jennings Bryan pointed out.

We were granted a reprieve when Franklin Roosevelt was elected president. Declaring that the United States wished to be a "Good Neighbor," he brought an end to the ongoing occupations in Latin America, some of which dated the administration of Woodrow Wilson. (Apparently Wilson's much celebrated support for the principle of self-determination only applied to European countries.)

With this change in policy, American troops were no longer bogged down in unwinnable conflicts in our own hemisphere, and much goodwill toward America was restored. Renewed faith in American leadership meant that most of the countries of Latin America followed the lead of the United States in declaring war on the Axis Powers in World War II, even if their support was more symbolic than real. Only Brazil and Mexico contributed troops to the war effort, with the Brazilian Expeditionary Force of some twenty-five thousand men seeing significant action in the Italian Campaign. Our efforts with Latin America were less successful in the Korean War, but Colombia did send a battalion over in 1951, and it engaged in several bloody battles with Chinese forces.

The era of goodwill came to an end with the Cold War. In that conflict Latin America, like the rest of the world, served as a battleground between East and West. Once again, we began taking sides in our neighbors' internal affairs. Unfortunately, more often than not, the fiercest anti-Communists in the region tended to have few scruples about setting up military dictatorships and suppressing human rights. Rebel groups, remembering earlier U.S. interventions in the region, were open to Communist infiltration, and Washington feared the opening of a Marxist front in the Americas. We saw ourselves in a similar position as our ancestors back in the days of the formulation of the Monroe Doctrine, except this time the European power that threatened our independence was Soviet Russia.

PUTTING AMERICA FIRST
Franklin Delano
Roosevelt Edition

"In the field of world policy, I would dedicate this nation to the policy of the good neighbor, the neighbor who resolutely respects himself and, because he does so, respects the rights of others, the neighbor who respects his obligations and respects the sanctity of his agreements in and with a world of neighbors."

—**FRANKLIN DELANO ROOSEVELT**, First Inaugural Address, March 4, 1933

Because we felt threatened, we renewed interventions that had been put on hiatus in the FDR years. U.S. covert operations helped to overthrow the elected left-wing president of Guatemala in 1954 and had a hand in right-wing coups across the region into the 1970s. Lyndon Johnson sent our soldiers back to the Dominican Republic in 1965, and Ronald Reagan sent troops to the island nation of Grenada in 1983. America provided support for government forces fighting Communist rebels in El Salvador and for rebel forces fighting a Communist government in Nicaragua.

An argument can be made that these interventions, unlike those of the early twentieth century, were directly in the American interest: they were a part of the larger struggle against Soviet Communism, and thus an element of the United States policy to protect its people from an existential threat. But the ground had already been contaminated by our earlier interventions, which did not serve such clear purposes. It was no accident that the Marxist Sandinista organization in Nicaragua took its name from a rebel leader, Augusto César Sandino, who had fought against U.S. Marines in the 1930s. Our earlier involvement in Latin America allowed Communists to usurp the higher ground and claim to be acting on behalf of "the people."

I don't mean to imply that our interventions were not justified in light of the struggle against international Communism. The invasion of Grenada, sparked by concerns for the safety of several hundred American college students resident on the island at the time, denied the Soviet Union and Cuba another base in the Caribbean. Support for anti-Communist forces in Central America likely kept the Marxist insurgency contained. If the isthmus of land between Mexico and Colombia had been Cubanized, not only would millions living in those countries have suffered a loss of freedom, but millions more would have voted with their feet and sought refuge in the United States, thus exacerbating our already delicate border control problems.

The other side of the argument is that many of the folks we backed in Latin America had little to recommend them beyond the fact that they were on our side in the struggle against global Communism. (FDR is reputed to have said of one of these allies, the notorious Nicaraguan dictator Anastasio Somoza, that "he may be a son of a bitch, but he is our son of a bitch.") This was a real problem for an America representing herself as the defender of democracy and liberty. The story of the Cold War in Latin America is a tragic one of oppression, murder, rape, kidnapping, and disappearances. That some of our allies, or those acting in their name, inflicted such atrocities on their own people is beyond question. That the Communists opposing these allies also committed similar atrocities is equally true—and all too often ignored. The battle between East and West in Latin America was a dirty one on all sides. It is difficult to say how we could have done things better, in light of the stakes involved. In any case, we cannot do anything about the past except to remember it and learn from it, understanding that our actions—and *the perception of our actions by those in the region*—have an effect on our current relations with those people.

Once again, the end of the Cold War gave us a tremendous opportunity to reset the clock, as we had in the 1930s. No longer would the region serve as a proxy battleground between rival superpowers, with all parties divided by whether they supported "us" or "them." Instead we could focus on more limited national interests and work with the countries of the region when those interests intersected. Unlike in some other parts of the world, we have been largely successful in this changed policy, even if our intentions are still not trusted by some of the governments of the region. This is particularly true as socialist-oriented governments have taken power in a number of South American states in recent years.

Focusing on ways to work with the countries of the region rather than attempting to dictate their path does not mean that we will never intervene again. The Cold War was barely out of the refrigerator when our troops landed in Panama at the end of 1989. Forces under corrupt ruler Manuel Noriega, whose regime was fueled by illicit drug money, had attacked U.S. personnel stationed in the Panama Canal Zone. Our quick and effective intervention removed Noriega from power. He would spend years in prison in the United States for his criminal activities and later be extradited to France to face similar charges before eventually dying back in Panama while awaiting trial there. Not surprisingly, many of the usual suspects on the Left attacked our operations in Panama as part and parcel of the long history of nefarious U.S. activity in the region. That we went to war in Panama in order to protect our national interest is beyond question. And had the United States not already had a history in the region, our actions in Panama would have been soon forgotten. However, because of that history, critics of U.S. Latin American policy lump that intervention under the long list of episodes of "Yankee Imperialism."

The only way to combat this narrative is to continue with our twenty-first-century version of the Good Neighbor Policy. Rather than falling to the temptation for nation-building as we did in the early twentieth century in Latin America (and more recently in the Middle East), we should treat the nations of our hemisphere as sovereign entities free to fall into any error their people and rulers see fit to lead them into—so long as they do not pose a direct threat to American security or well-being. Therefore, when Hugo Chavez and his followers tried to adopt the highly successful (sarcasm alert) Cuban model to Venezuela, thereby destroying the economy of one of the world's wealthiest countries, that should be a cause for concern for the United States, but not a cause for intervention. If Cuba has taught us nothing else, it should be that pressure and vilification of any Latin American regime by the United States will guarantee that regime a level of support it would not otherwise enjoy.

Despite that example, under the Obama administration Congress passed a series of sanctions against the Venezuelan regime in 2014. These sanctions were limited, in that they targeted persons suspected of human rights violations rather than the country of Venezuela as a whole. While like any sanctions they were of questionable utility (and to date do not seem to have modified anyone's behavior), they were at least surgical in precision, going after the interests of particular individuals.[1]

One would have hoped that—consistent with Trump's promised America First foreign policy—the sanctions would have not been expanded with the change of administration in Washington. Unfortunately, they have been. On August 24,

2017, by executive order, President Trump established a new series of sanctions—this time directly targeting the government of Venezuela and its petroleum industry. The new sanctions were imposed, said Trump, "in light of recent actions and policies of the Government of Venezuela, including serious abuses of human rights and fundamental freedoms; responsibility for the deepening humanitarian crisis in Venezuela; establishment of an illegitimate Constituent Assembly, which has usurped the power of the democratically elected National Assembly and other branches of the Government of Venezuela; rampant public corruption; and ongoing repression and persecution of, and violence toward, the political opposition."[2] Of course these are all very serious charges, but at the end of the day, they are really none of our concern, if we wish to have a foreign policy centered on protecting American interests in the world rather than one where the U.S. serves as the "indispensable nation," righting the wrongs committed in every corner of the globe. I do not know why President Trump has taken such a special interest in Venezuela that he appears to have abandoned, in this particular instance, his overall America First foreign policy. One can only hope that events in Venezuela will take care of themselves before the United States gets drawn into a conflict where no direct American interests lie. As things stand today, only about 25 percent of Venezuelans support the regime of President Nicolas Maduro, and the Venezuelan economy is a shambles.[3] By imposing harsher sanctions, we run the risk of providing a legitimacy to Maduro's government that he would not otherwise enjoy by offering an excuse as to why things cannot improve for the Venezuelan people. It would be far better to let him fail on his own, so that his government and its Chavismo ideology can bear full responsibility for destroying a once vibrant and robust economy.

Absent a direct threat, we should not go where we are not wanted. Period. On the other hand, if a country asks for our support, and it is in our national interest to intervene, that is something to consider. For instance, the provision of logistical support, training, and intelligence to Latin American governments fighting narco-criminal gangs would certainly be legitimate. These gangs flood our streets with toxic substances at great profit to themselves. Providing tools to countries willing to fight them saves American lives in the long run. It is akin to our support for countries battling radical Islamic terror in the Middle East and beyond. But providing assistance need not mean doing the heavy lifting ourselves. Ideally, the people most directly affected should be the ones doing the fighting, lest our presence create confusion about the real cause of the conflict—especially in Latin America, where suspicions of "Yanqui imperialism" are never far from the surface.

Our assistance need not be all military in nature. Working with countries to develop alternative sources of income for farmers whose livelihoods have been dependent on coca production, for example, is in our interests since the lion's portion of their processed crop ends up within our borders poisoning our people. This is not providing a foreign aid handout but rather providing for our own national security. Adjusting our tariff schedules, if applicable, to further encourage this crop diversification is also something to consider, as long as it does not hurt our own farmers in the United States.

This is not the place to argue whether or not legalization of recreational drugs is a good or bad idea (I am against it, for the record). But only the blindest ideologue would assert that the use of illicit substances in the United States has had a benign effect on our society. Drying up the sources of these substances will certainly raise the price, and that could generate greater profits, at least in the short-term, for certain drug dealers. Scarcity, though, means that these substances will be less available—they will be *scarce*. Hard-core addicts will do anything they can to get their hands on what they crave, but casual users (who often go on to become addicts themselves) will drop off. Basic economics tells us that more people are likely to use a substance if it is readily available and cheap than if it is hard to find and expensive. We certainly need to do more to stem the demand for addictive and life-destroying drugs—through education, law enforcement, and counseling, as well by as addressing the motivations that lead to people wanting to escape reality in the first place. But we can also address the supply side to make it that much more difficult to acquire these substances as well.

The good news is that, despite economic ups and downs, the future of Latin America is mostly positive. With only a few exceptions like Venezuela, most countries in the region have stable democracies and sustainable economies. Brazil, once wracked by coups and internal conflict, is now a regional power whose economy is just behind that of Italy and ahead of that of Canada.[4] In recent years, the U.S. Department of State has had to allocate additional resources to deal with the demand for U.S. visas from that country—not for people trying to flee Brazil for greener pastures but for regular folks with good jobs at home just seeking to spend a little money on their North American vacation. Even Colombia, once almost an anarchy due to the criminal activities of Pablo Escobar and similar gang leaders, has rejoined the ranks of habitable countries. Not only does it have a stable government and a growing economy, it comes just behind Mexico as one of our top sources of imported petroleum.

In more good news, our trade relationship with Latin America is working. The United States runs a trade surplus with most countries in the region, meaning that we are selling them more goods than they are selling us. Even in the case of a small and poor country like Haiti, the U.S. Department of Commerce estimates that American exports to that country support four thousand jobs in the United States.[5] Our trade with Latin America creates American wealth. This is not something we should take for granted, as China is energetically working to open up Latin American markets to their own goods. We need to build on the successes of the past and maintain an open dialogue with our trading partners so that American products will continue to enjoy the position they have traditionally held.

Despite superficial differences, we have a lot in common with the people of Latin America. We are all the offspring of European Christian civilizations, and the majority of our peoples share a lot of the same values: support for family, faith in God, appreciation of hard work and free enterprise, and a belief in the inherent dignity and value of the individual human being. Our national interests may sometimes conflict, as the interests of neighbors sometimes do, but there is no reason why we cannot continue with this new chapter that began with the ending of the Cold War.

FIFTEEN

WALK SOFTLY AND CARRY A BIG STICK

When Donald Trump ran on the platform "Make America Great Again," many of his opponents recoiled in disgust. To talk about one's country in a *non-inclusive* way—well, wasn't that racist or something? But large numbers of voters knew exactly what he was talking about. Most Americans still believe that the United States is the best nation on Earth, but in recent years there has been a growing suspicion that our best years may be behind us. Our institutions don't inspire the trust they used to, nor do we believe that our children will be better off than we have been. The lack of hope is especially pervasive when it comes to America's relations with the rest of the world. Despite the fact that our soldiers are without equal, we seem to get involved in conflicts that have no rational end and no clear victors. We pick fights with foreign leaders over disputes in lands that most Americans have never heard of, and we tell other nations that they have to support

PUTTING AMERICA FIRST
Ronald Reagan Edition

"Freedom is never more than one generation away from extinction. We didn't pass it to our children in the bloodstream. It must be fought for, protected, and handed on for them to do the same, or one day we will spend our sunset years telling our children and our children's children what it was once like in the United States where men were free."

—**RONALD REAGAN**, Address to the Phoenix Chamber of Commerce, March 30, 1961

policies over which Americans have profound differences. Well-paying blue-collar jobs that used to provide a chance for working class families have been sent overseas.

We have a change of administration every four or eight years, but while some cosmetic adjustments are made to our policies, most stay in place, and the whole mechanism of bureaucracy purrs on as before. Our "public servants" know that the people must bow down before them, as they have made the rules so complex as to require a gnostic initiation to even begin to understand what is going on. Our news channels don't just give us the news—that would be too hard for us, you see—but rather, put on "analysts" and "experts" to tell us what we should think about the three or four stories they choose to cover that day.

Then came 2016. We really stood at the precipice. Ours was the generation that could have seen our freedom become extinct, not in dramatic fashion as in France in 1789 or Moscow in 1917, but by subtle measures in the courts, in the legislatures, and above all in the government bureaucracies. Measures that would limit our freedom of speech, freedom of association, and our freedom of religion would be imposed first upon us and then extended, by virtue of our self-designation as the "indispensable nation," to the world at large.

The election of Donald Trump moved us back from the precipice—for now. Only time will tell how far and for how long. But for the first time in years we have a president who, despite his wealthy upbringing, connects with the hopes and fears of the average American. This is especially true in the area of foreign affairs. President Trump, in a way not seen since Ronald Reagan, appreciates that our ultimate loyalty, after our loyalty to God, should be to our nation.

This is not to say that Americans are better than everyone else. Every human being on the face of the Earth is valuable in the sight of God. We are all children of the same Creator. And each of us, as individuals and as part of the associations that make up our lives—churches, charities, fraternal societies, and so on—should do all we can to make life just a little better for our fellow man.

But we as human beings are also each a part of a particular society in a particular place. Just as we have certain attachments to family and community that we don't share with anyone else, so too will we necessarily have attachments to our nation. This is called patriotism, and—despite liberal protests to the contrary—it is a good thing. It is easy to pledge allegiance to "the Earth," because the Earth does not require anything of you. Pledging allegiance to a nation makes you a part of a concrete society of real human beings that have real hopes, real fears, and real needs.

PUTTING AMERICA FIRST
Donald Trump
Edition

"I was elected not to take power, but to give power to the American people where it belongs."

—**DONALD TRUMP**, Speech to the United Nations, September 19, 2017

But each of these nations must live with all the others on the same globe. Our foreign policy is the means by which we steer the ship of state through competing interests to obtain what is best for us and our fellow citizens. You see, we *can't* do what is best for the whole world. It is hard enough to determine what is best for ourselves, especially in a divided country like the one we have now, let alone what is best for those we really don't know.

So a policy of America First is not one of selfishness; it is one of realistic pragmatism. When we abandon our own country's needs in our foreign affairs, we do not better serve the needs of others; rather, we serve no one. Americans can best determine what is good for Americans, and that is the way it should be. When we orient our foreign policy to help us achieve those goals, we not only make life better for our own citizens but paradoxically make things better for others as well—because we no longer stand in anyone's way for reasons of ideology or paternalism or misplaced altruism.

But how exactly do we pursue our genuine interests? First of all, we need to ensure that we have a military and diplomatic capacity second to none. This does not necessarily mean that we need to have the biggest budgets we have ever had, but we need good people with top-notch tools to do the job. We can best chart an independent course in the world if we do not fear invasion or destruction by foreign foes. We must have armed forces capable of responding to any attack. We also need the best and the brightest diplomats to engage with other nations on the globe—so that we don't come to blows in the first place.

Second, we must correctly identify our national interests abroad. We do that by asking two questions: Does it affect American lives, and does it affect American well-being? If the answer to both questions is no, then the affair does not concern us. A territorial dispute on the opposite side of the world, a coup d'état in a distant land, or a new law in a foreign legislature that goes against what we hold to be common sense or common decency is only our concern if it leads to direct danger to American lives or well-being.

Yes, we should monitor developments even in the most remote corners of the Earth, since, in our interconnected world, threats to our well-being can arise even in the most unlikely places. This is why, as I mentioned above, we need to continue to have a robust diplomatic corps. If there is one area where President Trump can do even better, it is in spending time making sure that our embassies and consulates abroad receive the support they need to do the jobs they are entrusted to do. They really are the front lines of our national defense, both providing analysis of political and economic developments across the globe and actively keeping Americans safe through our consular

> **PUTTING AMERICA FIRST**
> George Washington Edition
>
> "It is our true policy to steer clear of permanent alliances with any portion of the foreign world.... Taking care always to keep ourselves by suitable establishments on a respectable defensive posture, we may safely trust to temporary alliances for extraordinary emergencies."
>
> —**GEORGE WASHINGTON**, Farewell Address, September 19, 1796

officers who evaluate visa applicants wishing to come to our shores and who provide assistance to American citizens in distress or danger overseas. As I have mentioned before, there is a distinct liberal bias in the personal politics of many of our Foreign Service Officers, but we should not let politics get in the way of doing the job that needs to be done. My own experience as a Foreign Service Officer (FSO) has shown me that the vast majority of FSOs take their jobs seriously and will carry out their duties regardless of which administration holds the reins of power. President Trump needs to have faith in his Foreign Service, and most of them will reciprocate the favor. This does not mean that analysis from State should be accepted uncritically, or that perceived biases should be ignored. It simply means an acknowledgment on the part of the executive that this venerable department plays a vital role in Making America Great Again. That being said, it is incumbent upon my former colleagues that they recognize that we now have a president who wishes to take American foreign policy in a different direction than his immediate predecessors—to put America First. Those who cannot in good conscience put the cause of their country before that of globalism should probably seek employment elsewhere.

Taking the information provided to us by our diplomatic corps, by our intelligence services, and by our military analysts, we can then evaluate whether or not developments abroad pose a threat to the folks at home. That should be the criterion under which we operate: a specific threat to our well-being, rather than vague disruptions in the way we think things ought to be. A threat to our nation is one about which we can answer one of the following questions in the affirmative: Are Americans at risk of death or serious harm? Will the threat directly impact our economy, our infrastructure, or our way of life? Will the threat directly erode our freedom or our ability to provide for our well-being?

If we can answer "yes" to one of those questions, then we have an international threat that we should seek to neutralize in the most effective manner possible. But even then, we should take the lowest effective measure possible in response, limiting ourselves to countering the threat and not seizing the moment to "make things better."

On the other hand, if we can answer all those questions in the negative, then it is likely that we are not facing a threat to our nation or our people. The development may be something we don't like or even strongly disapprove of, but if it does not affect us directly, our involvement runs the risk of being open-ended, and it can actually work against our interests by transforming an event that we can afford to ignore into one which affects us directly. For example, we may decide that one of two foreign entities in conflict has the bulk of right and justice on its side. If we intervene on behalf of that entity where American interests are not directly involved, we have created an enemy of the other party where we may not have had an enemy before. Whether "our side" wins or loses, the other side will now be against us for the foreseeable future. That may only mean that they sit and fume at the United States while having drinks with their friends, but it could also mean that they will go out of their way to do us harm as a means of revenge—whether diplomatically, economically, or by engaging in acts of terror. Our leaders are primarily entrusted with the safety of Americans.

If they make Americans less safe, they have failed in their basic duty.

Third, we must treat all nations as sovereign entities—and with extreme indifference. Just as we should have no permanent enemies, we should have no permanent friends. We should, as St. Paul told the Romans, live at peace with all men, as much as it is possible with us. This means that our default will be a friendly relationship, where we trade with and respect each other in the absence of any reason to do otherwise. We should put the world on notice that we will look out for our interests and expect them to do the same. This would add a transparency in our foreign affairs that has been lacking for some time.

PUTTING AMERICA FIRST
Thomas Jefferson Edition

"Peace, commerce, and honest friendship with all nations—entangling alliances with none."
—**THOMAS JEFFERSON**, First Inaugural Address, March 4, 1801

Fourth, in the event that we do have to go to war—which should always be the last resort—we must ever remember that there is no substitute for victory. That means clearly defined goals and the utmost resolve to carry them out. If we lack either the clearly defined goals or the resolve, then perhaps war is not the best or only option in the circumstances.

Finally, our foreign policy leaders, both elected and unelected, need to remember that they serve the American people—not some abstract Marxist entity of "The People," but flesh and blood human beings. Every policy should be measured for its effect on *Americans*, first and foremost. This goes not only for political policies, but also for economic policies, and for visa policies. A foreign policy that seeks to promote an unmeasurable goal or an abstract ideology is not worth one measurable, concrete American life.

Has Donald Trump's foreign policy put America First? I think the answer is a cautious "yes"—with some caveats. There is no question in my mind that President Trump's instincts on foreign policy are generally good and consistent with his campaign promises. Just after the election, *USA Today* ran a list of Trump's top ten foreign policy campaign promises:

1. Building the wall with Mexico
2. Moving the U.S. Embassy from Tel Aviv to Jerusalem
3. Reworking the Iran nuclear deal
4. Reducing U.S. troop strength and expenditures in Asia
5. Pulling out of the Paris climate deal
6. Reconsidering membership in NATO if the other members did not increase their contributions
7. Withdrawing from or restructuring NAFTA
8. Improving relations with Russia, combating the Islamic State
9. Withdrawing support from Syrian rebels fighting the Assad regime in order to concentrate on
10. Defeating ISIS.[1]

If we look back at that list less than two years after Trump took office, we see impressive progress on nearly every item on the agenda—with the notable exception of our relationship with Russia. Considering that many Americans are quite cynical about campaign promises, which we are used to candidates abandoning once they take the oath of office, the fact that Trump is still using the commitments he made during the campaign as guidelines for his foreign policy is refreshing indeed.

Also in keeping with his campaign promises, the president has made fair trade a centerpiece of his foreign policy. Unlike recent presidents from both parties, Donald Trump is not afraid to use protective tariffs when he feels that American industry and workers are getting the short end of the stick—announcing, for example, a plan to impose duties on imported steel and aluminum in March 2018.[2] Of course, this hurts him with the free-trade doctrinaires, but in resorting to this tool, he is merely resurrecting a course of action that was common among Republican presidents all through the nineteenth and early twentieth centuries.

That he chose steel and aluminum is particularly significant. Both of these metals are crucial in producing such things as aircraft, vehicles, and weaponry, and the executive order imposing them specifically does so on national security grounds.[3] The idea is not so much that we can't get the materials to defend ourselves from outside sources; it is that we should not be dependent on foreign countries for materials crucial to our national defense. Free trade ideologues assume that the world is one vast marketplace, where producers are always willing to sell to each and every buyer who will pay them a good price. During times of crisis or national emergency, that is not always the case. If we allow unfair trading practices to destroy so vital an industry, we might not be in a position to revive it should our international sources dry up or be cut off. We must not let industries crucial to our defense wither away because we are afraid that someone could trot out the protectionist label. On the contrary, we should glory in protecting those industries that can Make America Great Again, not only by assuring us a defense second to none but also by providing well-paying, stable jobs to blue-collar workers right here in the good old U.S. of A.

Making sure we have fair trade is a good start, but President Trump can do much more by trusting his America First instincts. This is especially the case in our relationship with Russia. It appears to me that the #NeverTrumpers have all jumped on the anti-Russia bandwagon and continue to try to beat the president with a Putin-shaped club, making it difficult for Trump to reset this very important relationship without looking like he is selling out. In fact, on several occasions he has even felt the need to loudly signal his toughness in standing up to the Russian bear.[4] That is unfortunate, not because Vladimir Putin is the leading candidate for the Nobel Peace Prize, but because there is really no reason for our two countries to descend into another Cold War. As he has in other matters, President Trump should stand up to his critics and accusers and work for accommodation with Russia where our direct interests are not involved. There may come a time when we have to face down Putin over some matter of national security, and President Trump should not hesitate to do so if such a circumstance should arise. But he should refuse to sacrifice the possibility of lasting peace and cooperation with Moscow just because critics who hate him anyway will accuse him of being soft on Putin. Staying out of Russian affairs that do not concern us is not a form of appeasement. It is an America First policy that will protect our interests, including our interest in peace. There is no need for us to go around the world picking fights with the biggest guy on the block just to show that we can kick his tail.

President Trump should also realize that his critics will attack him no matter what he does regarding Russia. When President Obama congratulated Vladimir Putin on his 2012 electoral victory, not a voice was raised in opposition, because that is what presidents do. But when Donald Trump did the same thing in 2018, it was considered a national scandal and disgrace by the mainstream media and their political lackeys in Congress. "An American president does not lead the free world by congratulating dictators on winning sham elections," said Republican Senator John McCain of Arizona, who never seems to miss a chance to criticize anyone in the Republican Party except for himself.[5] The key here is that President Trump will not earn any points with his opponents by watering down his desire for better relations with Russia. He will also not be able to carry out his program of change and reform if he listens to advisors that are keen on a replay of the Cold War. As he did so boldly with the steel and aluminum tariffs, he should ignore both his critics and supposed friends and do what he feels is best for our country and its people by developing a closer—or at least, less antagonistic—relationship with Moscow.

This advice is valid not only for Russia, but for anywhere else where the conventional wisdom (which is often not very wise) tells us that we have a duty to intervene because of our "national greatness." This includes not only the far-flung corners of the Middle East but areas closer to home, such as Venezuela. Make no mistake—if we are ever attacked, we should respond with overwhelming military might and do whatever it takes to neutralize the threat against us. In addition, we should stand up for our rights as a nation, including those economic interests that contribute to our well-being (and thus, give us the means by which we may do good). But we should not intervene in the affairs of other nations around the world in the name of liberty, fraternity, and equality or whatever notion du jour has captured the imagination of those chattering classes who are always so skilled in identifying the problems of *other* people that *we* need to solve.

The appointment of John Bolton as National Security Advisor is a cause for concern. Bolton's previous statements seem to imply that he believes there is no problem anywhere in the world that could not be solved by use of American military might, especially in the Middle East. That being said, he is a very intelligent man with a wealth of experience who could provide valuable insights to the Trump team, provided his views are not allowed to dominate the discussion. Not only that, but his appointment could have the effect of letting our adversaries believe that President Trump is not someone to be trifled with—that military options are never off the table should our interests be threatened. What would not be a positive development is if Bolton's appointment represents a return to the high-octane global interventionist foreign policy of the Bush era. I would frankly be surprised if that were so, as it would represent a repudiation of everything that President Trump has stood for thus far, and the president has been quite consistent in using his campaign platform as a blueprint for what his administration hopes to achieve. Perhaps Trump decided it would be better to have

PUTTING AMERICA FIRST
Donald Trump
Edition

"Together, we will make America strong again. We will make America wealthy again. We will make America proud again. And yes, together, we will make America great again. Thank you. God bless you. And God bless America."

—**DONALD TRUMP**, Inaugural Address, January 20, 2017

someone like Bolton on the inside rather than throwing bombs from without.

The good news is that in Donald Trump we have a president who seems to understand that an American executive is best equipped to handle challenges facing... *America*. In seeking to carry out an America First foreign policy, however, Trump has been called a racist, a xenophobe, and a nativist (and these are the nicer labels).

This is ironic, really, because those with an interventionist foreign policy—whether of the Right or Left—are the real racists out there. Their insistence that America strive ceaselessly to save the world makes sense only on the theory that all the little brown people will never come to enlightenment unless they can follow the lead of their Great White Father in Washington. Thus, we must go abroad to right the world's wrongs—as we see them, which may be quite differently from how the people actually affected understand the situation—and to tell them that they must be just like us in everything they do (except, of course, for those charmingly quaint "diverse" local customs that do not contradict our prevailing secular ideology). While President Trump has not put together a perfect America First foreign policy, he is light years ahead of the chief executives we have had over the last few decades. Under his leadership, there is great hope for the future.

Pursuing an America First foreign policy will not solve all of our problems. Any foreign policy that pretends to do so is automatically suspect. But if we put America first, when we face a challenge or even a defeat, we will have the consolation of knowing we did so in a good cause, the cause of our own people. This will make us all the more determined to go back out and make it work better the next time around.

CHAPTER SIXTEEN

MORE WINNING

The awkward thing about writing a book that deals with current events is that they continue to happen even as the manuscript is laid to rest. Bold predictions and sound analysis can look like so much foolishness when they are overtaken by events. In the case of President Trump, however, the initial promise of his "America First" foreign policy seems to be borne out by the latest developments. Unlike so many politicians, Trump genuinely seems to believe in the promise he ran on: that putting America First will reap benefits not only for our own country but for the world. Thus, I still remain cautiously optimistic that Donald Trump will be recognized as the first president in nearly a century to realign American foreign policy with traditional American principles.

President Trump is boldly seizing opportunities to put those principles into practice. Nowhere have events taken a more dramatic turn than in Korea. While the major military operations in that part of the world ended in 1953 with a ceasefire agreement, a state of war has existed between the two Koreas since 1950, and it was universally accepted that that state of war would continue to exist for the foreseeable future. Presidents Truman, Eisenhower, Kennedy, Johnson, Nixon, Ford, Carter, Reagan, Bush I, Clinton, Bush II, and Obama all governed in a world where Pyongyang and Seoul were enemy capitals. Then in recent years, since at least 2002, North Korea regularly threatened the United States with nuclear war, on the assumption—accurate enough, until Donald Trump was elected president—that the United States could not or would not do anything about it. According to former South Korean president, Kim Young-Sam, speaking in 2009 during the Obama administration, "the North Koreans think they can say whatever they want because no matter what they do, the Americans will never attack them."[1] That changed in January of 2017. President Trump, taking seriously his pledge to put America First by standing up to anyone who would put our people in harm's way, refused to back down in the face of North Korean threats. The media blasted Trump's approach as irresponsible or worse, but the president's actions soon paid dividends. Like the schoolyard bully who suddenly faces a kid who won't back down, North Korea could no longer be certain it could get away with anything it wanted. Things began to change and change rapidly. In April 2018, just over a year into the Trump administration, the Korean War was officially ended when the leaders of North and South Korea signed the Panmunjom Declaration for Peace, Prosperity and Unification of the Korean Peninsula. Let that sink in: twelve American presidents could not bring an end to the conflict between North and

South Korea, but Donald Trump did. Pyongyang came to its senses because, for the first time, the North Koreans faced an American president who refused to take anything off the table when it came to defending American interests. The situation in Korea still has a long way to go, and there could be setbacks, but so far the results of Donald Trump's change in tune have been quite dramatic. Where just over a year ago the media were predicting nuclear war, now the question is what will happen when President Trump and Kim Jong-Un meet face-to-face. Trump's new Secretary of State, Mike Pompeo, has already met the North Korean leader on a couple of occasions, and as a result he released three Americans held in detention for more than a year. In May, North Korea committed itself to eventual denuclearization. While it is premature to say whether or not that will actually happen, it is a stunning first step, and something that pundits as recently as the month before had said would "never happen."[2] So dramatic have developments on the Korean Peninsula been that there is talk of a Nobel Peace Prize for President Trump; even the *New York Times* called that a "possibility."[3] (If awarded, this prize would be for actual contributions toward bringing peace to the globe, rather than just for being perceived as cool and hip, as was the case with at least one prior presidential Nobel recipient.)

Korea is not the only place where there have been dramatic developments. Following through on another campaign promise, President Trump pulled the United States out of the Iran nuclear deal. In doing so, he faced tremendous criticism from the EU partners to that agreement, as well as from much of the media. Surprisingly muted, however, was the reaction from Iran: the

Islamic Republic said it would continue to abide by the terms of the deal.[4] To be honest, I have mixed feelings about scrapping the Iran accord, but it is consistent with President Trump's vow to obtain the best deals possible for the United States, something he felt was not the case with the agreement with Iran, and (as I explained in chapter 10), there were indeed severe flaws in the terms of this accord. Provided that President Trump can resist the siren song of advisors who might push for regime change in Tehran, this could end up being another big win for the administration, as Iran is forced back to the table to come up with an agreement that is more balanced than the one worked out during the Obama administration.

Another big issue is our massive trade imbalance with China. President Trump has not hesitated to threaten to impose tariffs on goods coming out of China—more than fifteen hundred of them. This has opened the door to further talks with the Chinese government, and, for now at least, it seems that not all of the tariffs will be imposed. The key takeaway is that President Trump does not seem to have the same fear his predecessors had of "doing the unthinkable." Even when all of the self-proclaimed foreign policy experts are certain that only doom and gloom will result, his bold moves actually strengthen his hand in negotiations with other countries and allow him to get a better deal for America—because a negotiator who appears open to any course of action has a better bargaining position than one who limits himself to a few predictable responses. I believe that this approach will eventually pay off in trade with China, just as it did on the political side with North Korea.

President Trump has also made great strides in protecting American sovereignty. This is especially true on immigration. There is increased vetting taking place at our embassies and consulates for those seeking to enter the United States, either as temporary visitors or as immigrants. And on international migration policy, the administration determined that it would not be party to the Global Compact on Migration being developed at the United Nations. According to a statement read by UN Ambassador Nikki Haley, the United States is "proud of our immigrant heritage and our long-standing moral leadership in providing support to migrant and refugee populations across the globe, but our decisions on immigration policies must always be made by Americans and Americans alone. We will decide how to best control our borders and who will be allowed to enter our country."[5]

Even in areas where President Trump seems to assume an interventionist foreign policy more typical of American presidents in recent generations, there is a qualitative difference. A good example of this is Syria. My own belief is that any kind of intervention in Syria could end up leading our country into another Middle Eastern war with the same predictable catastrophic results not only for our own interests but for the people of the area. And on the surface President Trump's decision to attack Syria's chemical weapons infrastructure following allegations of continued use of chemical weapons by the Assad regime appears to follow the same old tired pattern of open-ended intervention in a global hotspot with no discernable long-term goal. A closer examination reveals otherwise. For President Trump, unlike President Obama, the use of chemical weapons truly does cross a red line—and there should be consequences for crossing it. That being said, the Trump administration's response has thus far been measured, tailored not to destroy the regime, but to damage its capability to wage war by unacceptable means. As one pundit noted, "when the attack came, it was precise, discriminate and limited."[6] As of this writing, Assad appears to have refrained from using chemical weapons again. So the intervention seems to have been effective, without leading to adverse consequences. That being said, the use of force in that part of the world for whatever reason is a risky business. President Trump has apparently decided that it is in America's interest to discourage the use of chemical weapons anywhere in the world, and while I understand the logic of that position (and can certainly sympathize with the victims of chemical weapons attacks), I do hope that he continues to administer any future deterrent action in the same measured way as he has done thus far in Syria.

Before we can close down operations completely in the Middle East, there is some mopping up to do. The ideal, of course, is a non-interventionist foreign policy in which U.S. military force would only be used in defense of clearly-defined U.S. interests. The problem is that we have not pursued such a policy in a very long time and cannot just snap our fingers to eliminate the consequences of our misguided foreign adventures. This is particularly the case in Iraq. What shape the government of Iraq—or any successor states to Iraq—takes is really none of our concern, provided that the regime or regimes seek to live in peace with the United States. What is of concern are those non-state and para-state actors, such as ISIS and Al-Qaeda, that actively seek to bring violence to our shores. President Trump understands this and has offered effective but limited assistance to the Iraqi government in helping to contain and defuse that threat. And this policy has been massively successful. ISIS, an organization that just over a year ago threatened to create a radical Sunni version of the Kingdom of the Assassins occupying large swaths of Mesopotamia and beyond, has been eliminated as a serious threat to peace in that region. During Trump's first year of office, ISIS lost over 96 percent of its territory—some 21,400 square miles![7] Thanks to Donald Trump, the Islamic State is no longer a "state"; it has been reduced to just another stateless group of terrorists on the defensive against America and our allies, and on the run. Had any president other than Trump accomplished this, the media would be loudly proclaiming victory. Instead, they conduct endless discussions about the private lives of porn stars to distract the public from this administration's real achievements.

The U.S. Embassy has officially moved to Jerusalem—at least symbolically (it will require years of construction and planning to get everyone moved from the massive chancery building in Tel Aviv). As of this writing, Guatemala and now Paraguay have chosen to follow the U.S. lead, and there are rumored to be up to a half dozen others who will do so. The Palestinian response was predictable, with riots breaking out in the Palestinian territories—but no signs of a Third Intifada, at least for now. President Trump promised to move the embassy, and he delivered on his promise. America Firsters with ambivalent feelings about the whole enterprise can take comfort in the fact that unlike most politicians this president actually intends to keep his campaign pledges, one of the biggest of which is his promise to return to a more national interest–centered foreign policy.

Our relationship with Moscow is still a concern. The new Secretary of State, Mike Pompeo, is said to be an advocate of a "tougher line" with Russia.[8] Naturally, where America's vital interests are at stake, we should take the toughest of lines. But most of our political conflicts with Russia in recent years have been over issues that have little or no impact on American lives or well-being. It is important to let Vladimir Putin know that we will stand up for clearly-defined American interests, but that we will no longer be the world's policeman. How Russia gets along with Ukraine, for example, is a matter for those two parties to iron out, without American threats on either side. President Trump has repeatedly signaled a desire to improve the relationship between Washington and Moscow, but his efforts have been compromised by the "Russian collusion" witch hunt that continues to generate headlines, despite a notable lack of substance to the claims of Trump's opponents, who, using the Goebbels playbook, continue to repeat the lie in the hope that the people will eventually come to believe it. President Trump should push for a re-set in our relationship—not because Vladimir Putin is just a misunderstood sweetheart, but because it is in our own national interest to do so.

The key to understanding Donald Trump's foreign policy is his willingness to try new approaches, even if the "experts" predict disaster. Or maybe *especially* if the so-called experts predict disaster, seeing as how these same experts are responsible for some of our biggest foreign policy disasters. One of the most surprising recent developments has been the not-so-covert alliance between Israel and Saudi Arabia fostered by the Trump administration. Cynics may see this as a mere marriage of convenience, since both parties fear Iran more than each other, but whatever lies behind the cooperation between the world's only Zionist state and the custodian of the most sacred shrines of Islam, it is a matter of great astonishment, to say the least. When I was posted in Israel, some fifteen years ago, my uncle was working with the United Nations in Saudi Arabia. It was the closest we were ever assigned to each other during our careers, but in some ways it was as if we were on different planets. Even something as simple as a telephone call was impossible because, as my uncle discovered, if you dialed the country code for Israel in Saudi Arabia, a recording came up saying that the area code selected did not exist. Now we have the heir to the Saudi throne recognizing not only Israel's actual existence—but its right to do so.[9] The Trump administration's willingness to work with any and all states on matters of mutual self-interest continues to pay dividends.

These are just a few of the accomplishments of the Trump administration over the past few months. I am certain that, by the time you read this, there will be many more. The key is that, as the left-wing media continues to focus on every non-story they can think of to undermine the president, Trump continues to get results on both the domestic and foreign policy fronts. And while I would not necessarily ascribe every aspect of President Trump's foreign policy to a doctrinaire reversion to traditional American standards, he has come closer to implementing an America First foreign policy than any president of the last eighty or ninety years.

Of course, much can happen in the remaining time of President Trump's first term in office, but if he holds fast to his instincts and stays the course, we can expect even greater things for the future.

ACKNOWLEDGMENTS

"Seek not the things that are too high for thee, and search not into things above thy ability: but the things that God hath commanded thee, think on them always..." (Sirach 3:22, Douay-Rheims Version)

It is a very humbling thing to think that thousands of people I have never met will soon read the words I have written in order to better understand the history of our dealings with other nations and how the current administration is returning to our collective roots in implementing a national interest-based foreign policy. After all, despite my years of experience in foreign affairs, I can make no special claim to secret knowledge not available to the general public in formulating my arguments (even if I did have such knowledge, I certainly could not share it!) Rather, the present work is largely the result of observations that I have made over the years after having, by the Providence of God, the opportunity to extensively read, travel, and interact with all manner of people over the course of many, many years.

It behooves me to single out some of those individuals—a very daunting task, as I will certainly leave people out! I would first like to thank my wife and children, to whom this book is dedicated, for not only accompanying me on most of my foreign travels during my career as a Foreign Service Officer, but also for being the best family a man could ever have. Serving my country in diplomatic service was certainly a fulfilling job, but, at the end of the day, it was a way of making ends meet. My true vocation was being a husband to my wife, Dana, and a father to my children, Nicolae, Mimmo, Patrick, and Emily.

I would also like to express my appreciation to my parents for their encouragement as I was growing up to do my best in whatever I set out to do in this world. This book would not have come about had I not had that initial push so many years ago. I would also like to thank them for being great neighbors, since, after so many years living far apart, we actually live across the street from each other.

My uncle, Stefan Toma, also had a profound influence on my future career. A globetrotter himself, he not only brought the world to us, he took my brother and me to see some of it at an early age, as we spent some six weeks in Rome when I was only eleven years old, and an equal amount of time in Geneva when I was fourteen, not to mention several trips across Mexico in between. I don't think I would have developed the interest in foreign affairs, and certainly not in foreign languages, had it not been for his influence.

It is one thing to develop the experience, but certainly quite another to write about it. My friend, Howard Bahr, the author of several wonderful novels, as well as a long-time teacher of creative writing, was instrumental in helping me put together the manuscript that eventually led to this work (more on that later). We have known each other for decades, going back to when we worked together in running Rowan Oak, the home of William Faulkner, back in the 1980s. Another friend of mine (and of Howard's), Frank Walker, was a great encouragement in helping me develop some of my arguments, as he was quite patient with me as I pontificated for many years on how I would run things if I were in charge. Of course, it certainly helped that I would occasionally buy him a beer as a reward. A friend from my days in Ireland, Colm Ó Cribin, led me to believe I could actually write when I set my mind to it, after a few of my articles ran in the Dublin-based magazine *The Brandsma Review* a number of years ago (and thanks to Nick Lowry and to Peadar Laighléis for actually running those articles).

I would be completely remiss if I did not mention my editor, Elizabeth Kantor at Regnery Press, because this book *really* would not have happened were it not for her. I have known Jeff and Elizabeth Kantor for many years, from countless coffee hours after the Latin Mass at Old St. Mary's Church in Washington, DC, our parish home during my times in our nation's capital while I was with State. I thought of her when I had written a very different manuscript on a different subject, knowing she was in the "book business," and she very graciously offered to take a look at it. That manuscript was not published, but she apparently saw something in it to believe that I might have it in me to come with something her folks could use. This work is the result of that collaboration.

I would also like to thank my former colleagues at the United States Department of State, with a special shout-out to the good people at the Bureau of Consular Affairs, who not only look out for the interests of our fellow citizens overseas, but who are also in the frontlines of keeping America safe by screening those seeking to visit or immigrate to the United States. No doubt, many of my former State colleagues will not share some of my conclusions on policy, but there is no question in my mind that the vast majority of them work very hard to implement our president's foreign policy initiatives, regardless of the person who sits in the Oval Office.

Finally, I would like to offer a word of appreciation to Patrick J. Buchanan. He kept the flame of "America First" burning during the times when it seemed certain that we would never again have a president who would even pretend to bring back the type of foreign policy that served us so well during most of our first one hundred forty years as a nation. As one of his books is entitled, he truly was *Right from the Beginning*.

NOTES

ONE: A NEW POLICY THAT IS NOT SO NEW AFTER ALL

1. Christopher Hitchens, "Bush's Secularist Triumph," *Slate*, November 9, 2004, http://www.slate.com/articles/news_and_politics/fighting_words/2004/11/bushs_secularist_triumph.html.
2. John Feffer,"Trump's Unprecedented Right-Turn on Foreign Policy," *Counterpunch*, October 17, 2017.
3. David A. Graham, "Donald Trump's Radical Foreign Policy," *The Atlantic*, July 29, 2016.

TWO: IT MAY BE INTERESTING. BUT IS IT IN THE NATIONAL INTEREST?

1. "Chapter Two: The Human Communion," Sections 1883, 1885. *Catechism of the Catholic Church*, 2nd ed. Vatican: Libreria Editrice Vaticana, 2012.
2. William Minter and Elizabeth Schmidt, "When Sanctions Worked: The Case of Rhodesia Reexamined," *African Affairs* 87:347 (April, 1988): 207–237.

3. "Remarks by President Trump to the People of Poland," White House, July 6, 2017, https://www.whitehouse.gov/briefings-statements/remarks-president-trump-people-poland/.

4. "Immigration Reform That Will Make America Great Again: The Three Core Principles of Donald Trump's Immigration Plan," no date, https://assets.donaldjtrump.com/Immigration-Reform-Trump.pdf.

5. Liz Moyer, "Black Unemployment Rate Falls to Record Low," CNBC, January 5, 2018, https://www.cnbc.com/2018/01/05/black-unemployment-rate-falls-to-record-low.html.

THREE: RUSSIA—OUR ETERNAL FOE?

1. Dina Smeltz, Stepan Goncharov, and Lily Wojtowicz, *US and Russia: Insecurity and Mistrust Shape Mutual Perceptions*, Chicago Council on Global Affairs, November 4, 2016, https://www.thechicagocouncil.org/publication/us-and-russia-insecurity-and-mistrust-shape-mutual-perceptions.

2. Ibid.

3. "Memorandum on Security Assurances in Connection with Ukraine's Accession to the Treaty on the Non-Proliferation of Nuclear Weapons," Pir Center, December 5, 1994, http://www.pircenter.org/media/content/files/12/13943175580.pdf.

4. Roman Goncharenko, "Ukraine's Forgotten Security Guarantee: The Budapest Memorandum," DW, May 12, 2014, www.dw.com/en/ukraines-forgotten-security-guarantee-the-budapest-memorandum/a-18111097.

5. John McCain, "Russia Dissidents are our moral equals," *USA Today*, February 13, 2017, https://www.usatoday.com/story/opinion/2017/02/13/trump-gets-it-wrong-on-putin-russia-moral-equals-john-mccain-column/97822770/. See also Philip Rucker, "Hillary Clinton says Putin's actions are like 'what Hitler did back in the '30s,'" *Washington Post*, March 5, 2014.

6. *Arms Freeze: Who is For, Who is Against*, Moscow, Novosti Press Agency Publishing House, 1984.

7. Kaitlan Collins, Jeremy Herb, and Daniella Diaz, "Trump Signs Bill Approving New Sanctions against Russia," CNN, August 3, 2017, https://www.cnn.com/2017/08/02/politics/donald-trump-russia-sanctions-bill/index.html.

8. Chris Miller, "The Surprising Success of Putinomics," *Foreign Affairs*, February 7, 2018.

9. Oliver Carroll, "US-Russia Relations Fail to Improve in Trump's First Year and They Are Likely to Get Worse," *Independent*, January 19, 2018, http://www.independent.co.uk/news/world/americas/donald-trump-first-year-inauguration-anniversary-russia-vladimir-putin-relations-moscow-a8168801.html.

FOUR: EUROPE—THE ORIGINAL ENTANGLING ALLIANCE

1. U.S. Census Bureau, Census 2000 special tabulation.

2. Thomas Jefferson letter to Tench Coxe, June 1, 1795.

3. Alexander Hamilton, Philadelphia, 1794 (Alexander Hamilton Papers at the Library of Congress, Container 25, Reel 22).

4. "The League of Nations: Esperanto Snubbed," *Time*, August 13, 1923.

5. Marc Trachtenberg, *A Constructed Peace: The Making of the European Settlement, 1945—1963* (Princeton University Press, 1999), 148.

6. "U.S. Military Presence in Europe, 1945—2016," U.S. European Comand Communication and Engagement Directorate Media Operations Division, May 26, 2016.

7. Allen Cone, "More Nations on Track to Meet NATO'S 2% Spending Goal," UPI, February 13, 2018, https://www.upi.com/More-nations-on-track-to-meet-NATOs-2-spending-goal/3581518541366/.

8. Pamela Engel, "'It Will Be Like Christmas in the Kremlin': Hillary Clinton Blasts Donald Trump over NATO Comments," *Business Insider*, March 23, 2016, http://www.businessinsider.com/hillary-clinton-donald-trump-nato-russia-2016-3.

9. Associated Press, "Brussels the New Moscow? Once in Soviet Sphere, 7 Countries Weigh Pros, Cons of Decade in EU," Fox News, May 1, 2014, http://www.foxnews.com/world/2014/05/01/brussels-new-moscow-once-in-soviet-sphere-7-countries-weigh-pros-cons-decade-in.html.

FIVE: THE UNITED KINGDOM—MATER SI, MAGISTER NO

1. Miles S. Pendleton, "'There Will be Blood': The British Recapture the Falklands," *Moments in U.S. Diplomatic History*, Association for Diplomatic Studies and Training.

2. "Britain's Visitor Economy Facts," Visit Britain, https://www.visitbritain.org/visitor-economy-facts.

3. "Table 28. Nonimmigrant Admission (I-94 Only) by Selected Category of Admission and Region and Country of Citizenship: Fiscal Year 2015," U.S. Department of Homeland Security, June 27, 2017, https://www.dhs.gov/immigration-statistics/yearbook/2015/table28#.

4. Pat Buchanan, "Ideology Was Bush's Undoing," Pat Buchanan, November 27, 2007, http://buchanan.org/blog/pjb-ideology-was-bushs-undoing-888.

SIX: CHINA—THE SLEEPING GIANT

1. "GDP—Current US$," World Bank, 2016.

2. Tom Phillips, "China on Course to Become 'World's Most Christian Nation' within 15 Years," *Telegraph*, April 19, 2014.

3. "Trade in Goods with China," United States Census Bureau, https://www.census.gov/foreign-trade/balance/c5700.html#2012.

4. Eleanor Albert, "China in Africa," Council on Foreign Relations, July 12, 2017.

5. "Excerpts from Trump's Interview with the Times," *New York Times*, December 28, 2017, https://www.nytimes.com/2017/12/28/us/politics/trump-interview-excerpts.html.

SEVEN: JAPAN AND KOREA—NICE PEOPLE, COOL CARS, TRENDY CUISINE. ANYTHING ELSE?

1. "Negative Views of Russia on the Rise: Global Poll," BBC World Service Poll. June 3, 2014.

2. "I-94 Program: 2016 Monthly Arrivals Data," National Travel & Tourism Office, http://travel.trade.gov/view/m-2016-I-001/index.asp.

3. Binyamin Appelbaum, "Textile Makers Fight to Be Heard on South Korea Trade Pact," *New York Times*, October 11, 2011.

4. Robert E. Scott, "Trade Policy and Job Loss: U.S. Trade Deals with Colombia and Korea Will be Costly," *Economic Policy Institute*, February 25, 2010.

5. "George W. Bush Expresses Support for NAFTA, Says 'Anger Shouldn't Drive Policy,'" *Week*, November 15, 2016, http://theweek.com/speedreads/662166/george-w-bush-expresses-support-nafta-says-anger-shouldnt-drive-policy.

6. "Japan Country Commercial Guide: Japan—Trade Barriers," export.gov: Helping US Companies Export, https://www.export.gov/article?id=Japan-Trade-Barriers.

7. See Fred Kaplan, "Sorry, Trump, but Talking to North Korea Has Worked: The President's Claim That Negotiations Are a Waste of Time Ignores History," *Slate*, October 10, 2017, http://www.slate.com/articles/news_and_politics/war_stories/2017/10/it_is_possible_to_negotiate_with_north_korea_bill_clinton_did_it.html.

8. Ross Douthat, "Can North Korea Trust Us?," *New York Times*, March 10, 2018, https://www.nytimes.com/2018/03/10/opinion/sunday/trump-north-korea-negotiations.html.

9. Jon Swaine, "Trump under Pressure over Chaotic Approach to North Korea Nuclear Talks," *Guardian*, March 11, 2018, https://www.theguardian.com/world/2018/mar/11/trump-north-korea-kim-jong-un-denuclearisation-pompeo-shah.

10. "President Donald J. Trump Is Promoting Free, Fair, and Reciprocal Trade," White House, January 30, 2108, https:/www.whitehouse.gov/briefings-statements/president-donald-j-trump-promoting-free-fair-reciprocal-trade/?utm_source=ods&utm_medium=email&utm_campaign=1600d.

EIGHT: INDIA—THE BIGGEST COUNTRY IN THE WORLD THAT WE NEVER TALK ABOUT. I'M OKAY WITH THAT.

1. Ashok Malik, "The Best American President India's Ever Had," *Forbes*, November 2, 2009

2. "H.R.170—Protect and Grow America Jobs Act," Congress, 2017–18, https://www.congress.gov/bill/115th-congress/house-bill/170/text?q=%7B%22search%22%3A%5B%22Protect+and+grow%22%5D%7D&r=2#.

3. Ana Campoy, "Request for Evidence: Trump Is Quietly Swamping Visa Applicants in Extra Paperwork," *Quartz*, January 11, 2018, https://qz.com/1176576/h1b-visa-under-trump-is-already-harder-to-get/.

NINE: THE REST OF ASIA—TWO AND A HALF BILLION PEOPLE, BUT WE REALLY NEED ONLY ONE CHAPTER

1. Robyn Ironside, "America Is on the Hunt for More Australian Tourists As Dollar Dampens Travel Lust" *Courier-Mail* (Brisbane), May 12, 2017.

TEN: THE MIDDLE EAST—THIS IS WHAT HAPPENS WHEN YOU DON'T HAVE A SENSE OF HUMOR

1. "Top Sources and Amounts of U.S. Petroleum Imports (Percent Share of Total), Respective Exports, and Net Imports, 2016," United States Energy Information Administration, April 4, 2017.

2. "Fact #915: Average Historical Annual Gasoline Pump Price, 1929–2015," Office of Energy Efficiency and Renewable Energy, United States Department of Energy, March 7, 2016.

3. Debra Kamin, "Israel's Abortion Law Now among World's Most Liberal," *Times of Israel*, January 6, 2014.

4. Sara Roy, "Trump's Move to Slash Aid for Palestinian Refugees Will Lead to Tragedy," *Nation*, January 24, 2018, https://www.thenation.com/article/trumps-move-to-slash-aid-for-palestinian-refugees-will-lead-to-tragedy/.

5. https://www.algemeiner.com/2014/02/24/pew-survey-palestinian-arabs-dislike-america-more-than-any-other-group/pew-enemy.

6. Noa Landau, "Israel in Talks with 'More than 10 Countries' on Jerusalem Recognition, Officials Say,'"*Haaretz*, December 25, 2017, https://www.haaretz.com/israel-news/israel-talking-to-10-countries-on-jerusalem-recognition-officials-say-1.5629620.

7. "Remarks by President Trump on the Strategy in Afghanistan and South Asia," White House, August 21, 2017, https://www.whitehouse.gov/briefings-statements/remarks-president-trump-strategy-afghanistan-south-asia/.

8. John Hannah, "Trump's Afghanistan Strategy Could Actually Work," *Foreign Affairs*, September 1, 2017.

9. Jamie McIntyre, "US General on Trump's Afghanistan Strategy: 'This Will Be a Very Long Winter for the Taliban,'" *Washington Examiner*, December 12, 2017, http://www.

washingtonexaminer.com/us-general-on-trumps-afghanistan-strategy-this-will-be-a-very-long-winter-for-the-taliban/article/2643252.

10. "Ilhan Omar: No Debate on 'Whether Trump Is a Racist,'" *Al Jazeera*, February 10, 2018, http://www.aljazeera.com/programmes/upfront/2018/02/ilhan-omar-debate-trump-racist-180209162142703.html.

11. Touquir Hussain, "Why Trump's Troubling Pakistan Policy Dooms Afghanistan Peace: The Administration's Approach to Islamabad Undermines Potential Solutions in Afghanistan," *Diplomat*, February 15, 2018,"https://thediplomat.com/2018/02/why-trumps-troubling-pakistan-policy-dooms-afghanistan-peace/.

12. Kenneth Adelman, "Cakewalk in Iraq," *Washington Post*, February 13, 2002.

13. Malcolm Byrne, ed., "CIA Confirms Role in 1953 Iran Coup," in *National Security Archive Electronic Briefing Book No. 435.* The National Security Archive, The George Washington University.

14. "The Iran Deal," Medium, n.d., https://medium.com/@ObamaWhiteHouse/introduction-fcb13560dfb9.

15. Josh Meyer, "Obama's Hidden Iran Deal Giveaway: By Dropping Charges against Major Arms Targets, the Administration Infuriated Justice Department Officials—and Undermined Its Own Counterproliferation Task Forces," *Politico*, April 24, 2017, https://www.politico.com/story/2017/04/24/obama-iran-nuclear-deal-prisoner-release-236966.

16. Eli Lake, "Obama's Alternative Facts on the Iran Nuclear Deal: We're Getting a Glimpse of What the U.S. Gave Away in Order to Win Tehran's Pledge of Cooperation," *Bloomberg*, December 18, 2017, http://www.telegraph.co.uk/news/2018/02/22/

iran-may-quit-nuclear-deal-donald-trump-sabotages-benefits-sanctions/.

17. Adiv Sterman and Mitch Ginsburg, "'US Pressure Nixed Israeli Strike on Iran Last Year': Former National Security Council Head: Netanyahu 'Seriously Considered' Attack on Islamic Republic's Nuclear Facilities," *Times of Israel*, September 3, 2013.

18. Greg Jaffe and Adam Entous, "Trump Ends Covert CIA Program to Arm Anti-Assad Rebels in Syria, a Move Sought by Moscow," *Washington Post*, July 19, 2107, https://www.washingtonpost.com/world/national-security/trump-ends-covert-cia-program-to-arm-anti-assad-rebels-in-syria-a-move-sought-by-moscow/2017/07/19/b6821a62-6beb-11e7-96ab-5f38140b38cc_story.html?utm_term=.65cabd5c49ef.

19. Shane Harris and Matthew M. Aid, "CIA Files Prove America Helped Saddam as He Gassed Iran," *Foreign Policy*, August 26, 2013.

20. Associated Press, "Senate Panel Slashes Military Aid to Egypt: Frustrated Appropriators Vote to Cut Military Assistance to Cairo by $300 Million," *U.S. News & World Report*, September 7, 2017, https://www.usnews.com/news/world/articles/2017-09-07/senate-panel-slashes-military-aid-to-egypt.

21. Richard Wike et al., "The Tarnished American Brand," Pew Research Center: Global Attitudes and Trends, June 26, 2017.

22. Rod Nordland, "On Northern Syria Front Line, U.S. and Turkey Head into Tense Face-Off," *New York Times*, February 7, 2018, https://www.nytimes.com/2018/02/07/world/middleeast/us-turkey-manbij-kurds.html?smid=tw-nytimes&smtyp=cur&mtrref=t.co.

23. For example, Republican Senator Lindsey Graham of South Carolina, a senior member of the Congressional Turkey Caucus, was one of the earliest supporters of U.S. military assistance to

the anti-Assad rebels. See "Senior U.S. Senator Calls for Arming Syrian Rebels," Reuters, March 4, 2012, https://www.reuters.com/article/us-syria-usa-senators/senior-u-s-senator-calls-for-arming-syria-rebels-idUSTRE8230LZ20120304.

ELEVEN: AFRICA—THE CONTINENT WE FORGOT ABOUT

1. "How Many People Are in Modern Slavery in Mauritania?," Global Slavery Index, 2016, https://www.globalslaveryindex.org/country/mauritania/.
2. "HIV/AIDS Factsheet," World Health Organization Regional Office for Africa, 2017.
3. PEPFAR *Annual Report to Congress 2017*, U.S. Department of State Office of the U.S. Global AIDS Coordinator and Health Diplomacy, February 2017.

TWELVE: CANADA AND MEXICO—THE FOLKS NEXT DOOR

1. For more information, see the State Department's travel website at https://travel.state.gov/content/travel/en.html.
2. "Canada," Office of the United States Trade Representative, https://ustr.gov/countries-regions/americas/canada.
3. Jimmy Carter, "Trump Is Right. Canada's Lumber Trade Practices Are Unfair," *Washington Post*, May 9, 2017.
4. "Boeing Says Trade Complaint against Bombardier Designed to Prevent Larger CSeries," CBC News, http://www.cbc.ca/news/business/boeing-bombardier-cseries-dispute-1.4136436.
5. "Fact Sheet: Commerce Preliminarily Finds Countervailable Subsidization of Imports of 100- to 150-Seat Large Civil Aircraft from Canada," International Trade Administration, n.d., https://enforcement.trade.gov/download/factsheets/factsheet-canada-large-civil-aircraft-cvd-prelim-092617.pdf.

6. Anna Livsey, "Justin Trudeau Tells Woman to Say 'Peoplekind' Not 'Mankind': Canadian Prime Minister Draws Ridicule for Being Too Politically Correct, Though It May Have Been Lighthearted Sarcasm," *Guardian*, February 7, 2018, https://www.theguardian.com/world/2018/feb/07/justin-trudeau-tells-woman-to-say-peoplekind-not-mankind.

7. Mark Milke, "Trudeau's Banana Republic Approach to Bombardier and Boeing: Trudeau's Threat to Ban Boeing from Federal Contracts Unless It Drops a Trade Complaint against Bombardier Was like Something Out of Venezuela," *MacLean's*, September 21, 2017, http://www.macleans.ca/opinion/trudeaus-banana-republic-approach-to-bombardier-and-boeing/.

8. See Jeffrey Kusik, "Trump's Trade War Begins, *Foreign Affairs*, October 10, 2017, https://www.foreignaffairs.com/articles/united-states/2017-10-10/trumps-trade-war-begins.

9. Allen Woods, "Illegal Border Crossings into Canada Continue to Rise," *Star* (Toronto), April 19, 2017.

10. Jana Winter, "FBI Reports Show Terror Suspects Coming From Canada While Trump Stares at Mexico," *Daily Beast*, February 7, 2017.

11. Jean Meyer, *La Cristiada: The Mexican People's War for Religious Liberty* (Square One Publishers, 2013).

12. "Mexico," Office of the United States Trade Representative, https://ustr.gov/countries-regions/americas/mexico.

13. Ibid.

14. Ana Gonzalez-Barrera and Jens Manuel Kronstad, "What We Know About Illegal Immigration from Mexico," FactTank, News in the Numbers, Pew Research Center, March 2, 2017.

15. William La Jeunesse, "Trump's Border Wall Prototypes Virtually Impassable, Pass Rigorous Testing," Fox News, January 30, 2018, http://www.foxnews.com/us/2018/01/30/

trump-s-border-wall-prototypes-virtually-impassable-pass-rigorous-testing.html.

16. David Garrick, "San Diego Leaders Vote to Oppose Trump's Border Wall," *San Diego Union-Tribune*, September 19, 2017, http://www.sandiegouniontribune.com/news/politics/sd-me-wall-council-20170919-story.html.

THIRTEEN: CUBA—AN OBSESSION WHOSE TIME HAS PASSED

1. M. Ward and J. Devereux, "The Road Not Taken: Pre-Revolutionary Cuban Living Standards in Comparative Perspective," *The Journal of Economic History* 72:1 (2012): 104–32.

2. Vladimir Ilyich Lenin, "The Three Sources and Three Component Parts of Marxism," in *Lenin's Collected Works*, Lenin Internet Archive, 1996.

3. See Michael J. Bustamante, "Trump's Rollback on Cuba: The Consequences of Undoing the Rapprochement," *Foreign Affairs*, June 19, 2017.

4. Christopher C. Muth and Steven L. Lewis, "Neurological Symptoms among U.S. Diplomats in Cuba," *Journal of the American Medical Association*, February 15, 2018, https://jamanetwork.com/journals/jama/fullarticle/2673164.

5. Evan Dyer, "At Least 5 Canadian Diplomats and Families Hit by Mysterious 'Sound Attacks' in Cuba, Source Says," CBC News, September 15, 2017, http://www.cbc.ca/news/politics/cuba-sonic-sound-attacks-canadian-diplomats-1.4289996.

6. *Annuario Estadistico de Cuba 2016*, "Turismo," Edicion 2017, Oficina Nacional de Estadistica e Informacion, 9.

FOURTEEN: THE REST OF LATIN AMERICA AND THE CARIBBEAN—THE GOOD NEIGHBOR POLICY

1. Public Law 113–278, U.S. Department of the Treasury, December 18, 2014, https://www.treasury.gov/resource-center/sanctions/Programs/Documents/venezuela_publ_113_278.pdf.
2. Executive Order 13808, U.S. Department of the Treasury, August 24, 2017, https://www.treasury.gov/resource-center/sanctions/Programs/Documents/13808.pdf.
3. Francisco Rodriguez, "Why More Sanctions Won't Help Venezuela," *Foreign Policy*, January 12, 2018.
4. Alex Gray, "The World's 10 Biggest Economies in 2017," *World Economic Forum*, March 9, 2017.
5. "Haiti," Office of the United States Trade Representative, https://ustr.gov/countries-regions/americas/haiti.

FIFTEEN: WALK SOFTLY AND CARRY A BIG STICK

1. Jessica Durando, "Donald Trump's Big 10 Foreign Policy Pledges—Will He Stick to Them?," *USA Today*, November 17, 2016, https://www.usatoday.com/story/news/world/2016/11/17/trump-foreign-policy-campaign-promises/93802880/.
2. David Jackson, "Trump Announces Steel and Aluminum Tariffs, but with 'Flexible' Exceptions," *USA Today*, March 8, 2018, https://www.usatoday.com/story/news/politics/2018/03/08/trump-planning-make-formal-tariff-announcement/406065002/.
3. "U.S. Department of Commerce Announces Steel and Aluminum Tariff Exclusion Process," U.S. Department of Commerce, March 18, 2018, https://www.commerce.gov/news/press-releases/2018/03/us-department-commerce-announces-steel-and-aluminum-tariff-exclusion.
4. For example, "Crimea was TAKEN by Russia during the Obama Administration. Was Obama too soft on Russia?" @

realDonaldTrump, Twitter, February 15, 2017, https://twitter. com/realDonaldTrump/status/965943827931549696?ref_ src=twsrc%5Etfw&ref_url=http%3A%2F%2Ftime. com%2F5166652%2Ftrump-tweets-russia-obama%2F.

5.   Jonathan Lemire and Vladimir Isanchenkov, "Slamming Putin Call, McCain Goes After Trump for 'Congratulating Dictators on Winning Sham Elections,'" *USA Today*, March 21, 2018, https://www.usatoday.com/story/news/politics/2018/03/21/ slamming-putin-call-mccain-goes-after-trump-congratulating- dictators-winning-sham-elections/444726002/.

CHAPTER 16: MORE WINNING

1.   Adam Taylor, "North Korea Has Threatened a U.S. Attack for Years. Why Aren't You Scared?," *Washington Post*, August 17, 2015, https://www.washingtonpost.com/news/worldviews/ wp/2015/08/17/north-korea-has-threatened-a-u-s-attack-for- years-why-arent-you-scared/?utm_term=.fae12a058767.

2.   Evans Revere, "Kim Jong Un Will Not Give Up North Korea's Nuclear Weapons," *Newsweek*, April 4, 2018, http://www. newsweek.com/kim-jong-un-has-no-intention-giving-north- koreas-nuclear-weapons-870042.

3.   Emily Cochrane, "President Trump a Nobel Laureate? It's a Possibility," *New York Times*, May 9, 2018, https://www. nytimes.com/2018/05/09/us/politics/trump-korea-nobel-peace- prize.html.

4.   Mark Landler, "Trump Abandons Iran Deal He Long Scorned," *New York Times*, May 8, 2010,] https://www.nytimes. com/2018/05/08/world/middleeast/trump-iran-nuclear-deal. html.

5.   Colum Lynch, "Trump Boycotts UN Migration Talks: The White House's 'America First' Policymakers See Little Gain in Setting the Global Rules for Migration," *Foreign Policy*,

December 2, 2017, http://foreignpolicy.com/2017/12/02/trump-boycotts-u-n-migration-talks/.

6.   James Robbins, "So Far, US Intervention in Syria Looks Like It Accomplished the Objective," *The Hill*, April 18, 2018, http://thehill.com/opinion/national-security/383762-so-far-us-intervention-in-syria-looks-like-it-accomplished-the.

7.   Benaoudi Abdelillah, "After the 'Almost 100 Percent' Defeat of ISIS, What about Its Ideology?," Al Jazeera Center for Studies, May 8, 2018, http://studies.aljazeera.net/en/reports/2018/05/100-percent-defeat-isis-ideology-180508042421376.html.

8.   Patricia Zengerle and Lesley Wroughton, "Trump Nominee Pompeo Promises to Be Tough on Russia, 'Fix' Iran Deal," Reuters, April 12, 2018, https://www.reuters.com/article/us-usa-trump-pompeo/trump-nominee-pompeo-pledges-to-be-tough-on-russia-fix-iran-deal-idUSKBN1HJ0HO.

9.   Amir Tibon, "Saudi Crown Prince: We Share Common Interests with Israel, but There Must Be Peace with the Palestinians," *Haaretz*, April 3, 2018, https://www.haaretz.com/middle-east-news/saudi-prince-israelis-have-the-right-to-have-their-own-land-1.5974278.bv

INDEX